TUNED IN
MEMOIRS OF A PIANO MAN

Jim Wilson

**BEHIND THE SCENES WITH MUSIC LEGENDS
AND FINDING THE ARTIST WITHIN**

©2024 Jim Wilson
All rights reserved

Copyright © 2024 Jim Wilson

All rights reserved. No part of this book may be reproduced or transmitted in any form or by any means, electronic or mechanical, including photocopying, recording or by any information storage and retrieval system without permission in writing from the publisher.

Willow Bay Media—Sherman Oaks, CA
Paperback ISBN: 979-8-9895384-1-6
Hardcover ISBN: 979-8-9895384-0-9
eBook ISBN: 979-8-9895384-2-3
Library of Congress Control Number: 2023923540
Title: *Tuned In: Memoirs of a Piano Man*
Behind the Scenes with Music Legends and Finding the Artist Within
Author: Jim Wilson
Digital distribution | 2024
Paperback | 2024

TUNED IN

Emerging from a troubled childhood in a broken West Texas home, a young man moves to Los Angeles to pursue fame and fortune as a singer-songwriter. He soon strays from his mission when his piano tuning sideline blossoms into a career as piano technician to the entertainment industry's biggest names. His help in the development of the world's first MIDI-adapter for acoustic piano leads to him sharing adventures, sessions, meals, and laughs with dozens of his childhood heroes. His front row seat provides him with a rare and fascinating view into their creative processes.

But when his world is shattered by his dearest friend's sudden and untimely death, he is forced to question the true meaning of success. He returns to his heart's purpose, takes a leap into the unknown, and sets out on a solo career, recording and performing his signature style of piano-featured instrumentals. Along the way he battles countless obstacles, including crippling panic attacks.

After four Billboard Top-20 albums, two PBS specials, and over 75 million worldwide streams of his compositions, Jim reflects on his life in music. He offers us a candid, humorous, insider's account of the raucous LA scene and shares engaging tales of his time spent with music legends.

Tuned In is an inspiring story of one man's relentless pursuit of a dream, and a revealing testimony to the power of music in all our lives.

Endorsements

"*Tuned In* is a fantastic read! Fascinating insider stories. World traveler, gifted artist, and his knowledge of all things piano is incredible. Great job with all you've accomplished!"
- **David Foster**, *16-time Grammy-winning producer*

"I adore this memoir so. *Tuned In* is a truly fascinating tale by a fascinating man. I can't wait to re-read it with the television off."
- **Martin Short**, *actor, comedian, singer, writer*

"... a wonderful story that will encourage the reader to follow their dreams."
- **Alan Bergman**, *lyricist with 3 Oscars, 4 Emmys & 2 Grammy awards*

"I don't trust just anyone to care for my pianos. Jim has been the man to do that for me for over 35 years! His story's enlightening and inspiring, especially for anyone trying to make it in music."
- **Diane Warren**, *Grammy, Emmy, & Oscar-winning songwriter*

"Not only has Jim Wilson made my life more harmonious for the past 30 years, but he used his amazing gift to enhance the work of many a musical legend. He shares this long and amazing career with us in *Tuned In*. I could not put it down! Brilliant, funny and touching."
- **Ed Begley Jr.**, *author, actor, environmentalist*

"Jim Wilson can do anything with or to a piano, writes music beautifully, out-skis me and now this; a most interesting life recalled with the clarity and flow that a good memoir requires."
- **J.D. Souther**, *multi-platinum, Hall of Fame songwriter*

"Brother Jim, thank you from the bottom of my heart for your profound professionalism in restoring and caring for my piano over the decades."
- **Quincy Jones**, *28-time Grammy-winning producer*

"Over the decades I've known Jim Wilson, I've found him to be a meticulous craftsman, a wonderful artist, and honest to the core."
- **Herb Alpert**, *Grammy-winning artist, co-founder of A&M Records*

"Jim is a genius technician, musician, and a dynamite piano tuner! *Tuned In* is fascinating. Who knew? Congratulations, Jim!"
- **Barry Manilow**, *Grammy, Emmy & Tony-winning Hall of Fame artist with 85 million albums sold*

"…Jim's book is filled with wonderful stories and anecdotes of his adventures in our musical world. I recommend it highly."
- **Carole Bayer Sager**, *Grammy & Academy Award-winning songwriter*

"Who'd have thought the story of a piano tuner could be so enthralling? *Tuned In*, Jim Wilson's beautifully-woven tale, gives an emotional, creative, and revealing insight to the world of music from bar bands to superstars. Deeply honest and personal, occasionally heart-rending, often hilarious and enlightening about what makes music and musicians tick. Little wonder so many musical heroes took him to their hearts."

- **Neville Farmer**, *author, music journalist, filmmaker*

"*Tuned In* is so much more than I expected. Jim shares his adventures and experiences with some of the world's greatest music icons, filling every page with humor and insight. But more than that, his story is both inspiring and relatable, and will resonate with anyone who has ever faced adversity in pursuit of their goals. Highly recommended."

- **Ray Romano**, *Emmy-winning actor*

"Your love of music and the heart and soul that you put into tuning is captured here. Thank you."

- **Herbie Hancock**, *15-time Grammy-winning artist*

"Your musical sensibility is wonderful. …You captured a part of my heart."

- **Arlo Guthrie**, *multi- platinum Americana folk icon*

"My friend Jim is an articulate and succinct storyteller; a literary artisan. I enjoyed every page of *Tuned In* - I couldn't put it down!"

- **Walter Afanasieff**, *Grammy-winning music producer, songwriter*

"Your gorgeous music inspires me to play again!"

- **Olivia Newton John**, *Grammy-winning singer, actor, activist*

"I so enjoyed reading *Tuned In*. Jim's traveled life's unsteady road with an open heart while seeing the world through hope-filled eyes."

- **Melissa Manchester**, *Grammy-winning artist*

"I loved *Tuned In*. It's a great, fun read. It's an inspiring story of perseverance and a window into the LA music scene."

- **Steve Porcaro**, *Grammy-winning songwriter, founding Toto member*

"Besides being a piano master, my old friend Jim Wilson is a great cat. His book *Tuned In* is a fantastic read – check it out!"

- **Steve Lukather**, *Grammy-winning songwriter, founding Toto member*

"Congrats on your well-written memoir, *Tuned In*, Jim. What a fun read! So many fantastic stories and your journey from piano tuner to recording artist is relatable and uplifting!"

- **Stanley Clarke**, *Grammy-winning artist*

"Your writing is keen, quick-witted, entertaining and informative."

- **Richard Carpenter**, *multi- platinum recording artist*

"To have our pianos tuned over the decades by a master like Jim Wilson is totally satisfying. But hearing him play his own music is sheer joy."
- **Mike Stoller**, *Hall of Fame songwriter of over 70 classic hits*

"Jim's experience as a musician offers him special insights in service of his own music, as well as the musicians he works with. Congrats, Jim, and happy reading everyone!"
- **Patrice Rushen**, *Grammy-nominated artist*

"Jim Wilson's entertaining memoir reads like a musician's version of 'Forrest Gump,' offering rare insights into the offstage lives of some of the music industry's most famous and fascinating characters. Two thumbs up!"
- **Michael Neill**, *international bestselling author of* The Inside-Out Revolution *and* Creating the Impossible

"Northern Seascape is a delicately-woven romantic classic, a magical musical carpet ride of melodic beauty."
- **Carole King**, *Grammy-winning artist & songwriter*

"Beautifully written and told, *Tuned In* is a heartfelt and deeply moving memoir of one of the unsung greats who's had a 'front-row piano bench' to some of the greatest moments in modern music history."
- **Dave Koz**, *Grammy-winning artist*

"... a fabulous book! What a life, what a career, what a storyteller."
- **Loren Gold**, *keyboard player for The Who and Chicago*

"... full of fascinating stories and adventures. *Tuned In* is brilliant — a beautifully written memoir!"
- **Nathan East**, *Grammy-nominated bassist, producer, songwriter*

"I've known Jim for years and I trust him beyond. He can make a toy piano sound good!"
- **Courteney Cox**, *Emmy, Golden Globe & SAG-nominated actress*

"I recommend *Tuned In* to anyone ... it's not just about music, pianos and the biz, it's about life and how to deal with it when the shit gets thrown hard early on. A wonderful story by a great dude."
- **Richard Page**, *hit songwriter, Mr. Mister founding member*

"*Northern Seascape* is a beautiful, inspiring work. I highly recommend it."
- **Dan Fogelberg**, *multi-platinum recording artist*

"What a surprising read! ...a deeply personal story about how seemingly random events led Jim out of darkness and created a life of purpose and inspiration. Jim is a dear friend, a master craftsman, and a great storyteller."
- **Paul Mirkovich**, *musical director for* The Voice

"Yours is beautiful, melodic, emotional, delicious music."
- **David Crosby**, *multi-platinum Hall of Fame recording artist*

"Without guys like you, guys like me would surely be lost. Thanks for all the excellent piano care over the decades, Jim."
- **Stephen Stills**, *multi-platinum Hall of Fame recording artist*

"I admire Jim's musicianship and creativity."
- **Burt Bacharach**, *Grammy and Oscar-winning songwriter*

"Congrats on your heartwarming and inspiring memoir, Jim! A beautiful tribute to the power of friendship, music, and the human spirit!"
- **Steve Tyrell**, *Grammy-winning Producer & artist*

"Jim Wilson is one of the best piano tuners I've come across."
- **Chick Corea**, *27-time Grammy-winning artist*

"I shouldn't have been so surprised that Jim's rascal gift as a storyteller would produce such a great read…but wow! With an extraordinary eye for detail, *Tuned In* captures not only the bygone era of the 80's LA Studio scene and the dawn of MIDI, but also reveals through his own vulnerability the heart of every artist drawn into our city of dreams."
- **Eric Persing**, *Spectrasonics founder*

"Your music is mystical and calming. I use it to lose myself."
- **Lionel Richie**, *Grammy-winning artist*

"Jim rebuilt and tunes the piano handed down from my grandmother, he's played me beautiful songs, and now he's taken me on his life's journey so far. He's a skilled writer and *Tuned In* is a wonderful read!"
- **Lisa Loeb**, *Grammy-winning Recording Artist*

"*Tuned In* is a captivating window into the brilliant and inspiring mind of Jim Wilson, whose natural elegance, playfulness, exuberance, and talent has allowed him to seamlessly grace the worlds of some of the greatest legends on the planet! His own music has opened hearts and captured imaginations, and his story is a treasure!"
- **Lili Haydn**, *Grammy-winning artist*

"*Tuned In* has heart, humor, and humility. Lovely storytelling from a lovely guy!"
- **Larry Klein**, *Grammy-winning producer*

"… I'm blown away by not just the stories but what an incredible raconteur Jim is. Such a great read."
- **Denny Tedesco**, *Award-winning director,* The Wrecking Crew

"Jim Wilson's wonderful memoir is a heartfelt tale of the ways the ordinary and extraordinary worlds of the music business intersect that few outsiders will ever experience."
- **Zac Rae**, *music producer, member of* Death Cab for Cutie

"With Jim's usual affability and good humor, *Tuned In* gives us an intimate look behind the scenes of his famous, and infamous - clients and friends, a group I'm proud to be a part of."
- **Marc Shaiman**, *Oscar-nominated, Grammy, Emmy & Tony-winning film composer*

"From the moment I started reading *Tuned In*, I became totally engrossed. Jim's style of writing is compelling, extremely easy to read and triggered wonderful memories of my own life."
- **Peter Collins**, *rock producer (Rush, Alice Cooper, Queensrÿche)*

"*Tuned In* is a wonderful ride! Thank you, Jim for letting me play a small part in your adventures."
- **Matthew Wilder**, *Grammy-winning producer*

"Jim Wilson was 'the man behind the curtain' for decades, tending the pianos of some of our greatest artists before stepping out on to the stage with his own gorgeous and timeless music. Bravo, Jim!"
- **Jean Fogelberg**, *Artist, Photographer, wife of Dan Fogelberg*

"*Tuned In* is a story of redemption and reinvention. Jim played in the personal sandbox of the most creative and innovative musicians of our era and in an oily rags to artistic riches story, he found his own inner artist and became a composer of the highest order."
- **Daniel J. Levitin**, *4-times New York Times bestselling author*

"For decades, Jim has taken care, time and consideration with our pianos, as well as filling our house with his beautiful playing, and recollections. And now, his insightful, humorous stories are passed on to the reader. *Tuned In* does not disappoint. *Enjoy!*"
- **Katey Sagal**, *Golden Globe-winning actress*

"*Tuned In* is absolutely tremendous. It's a gripping story of perseverance told with warmth, humor and unfailing honesty. I couldn't put it down!"
- **Adam Belanoff**, *TV producer, writer*

"Jim Wilson: great technician, talented musician, lovely man."
- **James Newton Howard**, *Oscar-nominated, Grammy & Emmy winning film composer*

"*Tuned In* is an incredible, inspiring story. A real page-turner."
- **Chris Standring**, *recording artist with ten #1 Billboard hits*

"Jim, you're the one that connected Yamaha with Elton. Thank you for steering him to us all those years ago. You're truly a man of many talents: an amazing piano technician, a great piano player, an excellent writer. Congrats on your amazing book, *Tuned In!*"
- **Bill Brandom**, *former National Piano Service Mgr, Yamaha Corp.*

The events in this book are portrayed to the best of my memory. In some cases, names and identifying details have been changed to protect the identities of people depicted.

Dedication

For Ethan, Jace, Serena and Bella;
Henry, Katelyn and Aaron;
Dylan, Ryan, Archer, and Sarah;
Bowie and Bradley.

"Children are the living messages we send
to a time we will not see."
- Neil Postman

Table of Contents

PART ONE: Gearing Up
Prologue: Meet the Beatle 2
Chapter 1: The Guitar 7
Chapter 2: Music and Mischief 13
Chapter 3: Things Fall Apart 17
Chapter 4: High School 24
Chapter 5: Capers and Close Calls 29
Chapter 6: Hit the Road, Jim 35
Chapter 7: Easy Does It 43
Chapter 8: The Abyss 49
Chapter 9: Tuning School 53
Chapter 10: Loose Change 58

PART TWO: Tuning Up
Chapter 11: Emerald City 64
Chapter 12: On the Eve of the 80s 69
Chapter 13: City of Dreams 72
Chapter 14: Biz Takes Off 77
Chapter 15: The Buffet 84
Chapter 16: Forte 93
Chapter 17: London Calling 100
Chapter 18: London Calling, Again 113
Chapter 19: London Still Calling 124
Chapter 20: Go For It, Jimmy 129
Chapter 21: Paul 132
Chapter 22: You've Got a Road Trip 136
Chapter 23: Part of the Plan 142

PART THREE: Tuning In
Chapter 24: Claude 156
Chapter 25: Malls and Halls 166
Chapter 26: Green Hill 179
Chapter 27: Jason 188
Chapter 28: Touring Tales 192
Chapter 29: A Place in My Heart 200
Chapter 30: The Genie Grants Me Three Wishes 211
Chapter 31: Slaying the Dragon 219
Chapter 32: Dénouement 227

CREDITS 242
ABOUT THE AUTHOR 246

PART I
Gearing Up

"A journey is a person in itself; no two are alike. All plans, safeguards, policing, and coercion are fruitless. We find that after years of struggle that we do not take a trip; a trip takes us."
— John Steinbeck

PROLOGUE
Meet The Beatle

August 30, 1985

"You must be Jim!"

He calls me by my name. And just like that, I'm once again the 8-year-old boy who obsessed over this icon's hit songs; the pudgy kid who yearned to enrapture fans with music; the dreamer whose life direction was shaped by the trail this legend blazed. It feels like I have cotton in my mouth. Amazingly, my lips move, words come out.

"And I'm guessing you must be ... I wanna say... *Paul?*"

He laughs and extends his hand.

My anxiety begins to ease. Just. I've met and worked for quite a number of celebrities by now, but this is Paul McCartney, a frigging Beatle. His music has underscored my whole life, made me cry, laugh, sing at the top of my lungs, worked its way deep into my musical DNA.

This is like meeting Mozart, Gandhi, and Obi-Wan Kenobi, rolled into one. I mean, here's a guy who's literally changed the world with his music.

But I don't have the luxury of succumbing to nervousness. I'm here on a limited mission: to install an adapter in Paul McCartney's piano and show him how to work it.

Thankfully, I can speak with assuredness about the adapter installation. I even suggest ways I could improve the touch and tone of his Hamburg Steinway B grand piano.

Have I overstepped my bounds?

But he smiles.

"Have at it!" he says. We agree to meet the following morning and I ask what time.

"Tennish, anyone?" He gives a grin and his iconic raised eyebrow. That a figure from the musical version of Mt. Rushmore enjoys a corny "dad joke" puts me further at ease.

Alone in his studio, I hit pause for a second to take in where I am: Hog Hill Mill, an eighteenth-century windmill overlooking the English Channel that Paul's converted into his personal recording studio. Scanning the room, I see the usual trappings: amps, guitars, microphones, an "iso booth" where vocals are recorded, rows of console tape with mixer markings stuck on the wall.

But this isn't just any studio. It's the Santa's Workshop where one of the most extraordinary musical geniuses of our time transforms the ideas in his head into reality. I sneak a closer look at the dozen drawings taped to the wall. Puzzled by these peculiar pictographs, I squint my eyes and try to decipher the first one. I slowly realize this is Paul's clever way to represent his vision of each song's mix. Each graphic is a road map of sorts, using different shapes drawn with felt pens to depict the positioning of each element in the mix — a red circle in the middle represents the vocal, two green ovals to either side represent the stereo guitars, a black rectangle at the bottom symbolizes the bass.

I take in the row of guitars. Ten instruments in a stand is not unusual — I've seen as many in countless LA studios. But *these* guitars?

One in particular has a distinctive shape that stops me in my tracks. I hold my breath as I ponder the history of Paul's left-handed Hofner bass, one of the most iconic instruments in all of modern music.

What would it have been like to stand on stage, enthralling screaming fans with this Hofner, at Liverpool's smoky Cavern Club, on the Ed Sullivan show, in Shea Stadium, or atop the Apple building at that legendary rooftop concert?

Drawing closer, the bass line to "Come Together" starts playing in my head. Followed by "Taxman", then "Day Tripper" — this instrument has anchored countless Beatle classics.

At the Louvre, 15 feet is as close as you can get to the Mona Lisa. Glancing left and right as if there were a docent standing guard, I reach toward the strings and lightly pluck the low E.

Man, if this thing could speak.

Late into the night, I work to regulate, voice, tune, and install the "Forte MIDI-Mod" — the world's first MIDI-adapter for acoustic piano. Just a couple of years earlier, I had the good fortune of having a hand in its development. Bartolomeo Cristofori's "PianoForte" was fashioned from its meek predecessor the clavichord 300 years ago. Now for the first time, it could connect to the new world of electronics via our adapter.

Looking back, it's humbling to think that I — a diffident kid from a small West Texas town — would become part of a bridge from 17th century northern Italy to a recording studio on the south coast of England belonging to one of the world's most influential recording artists.

For many years I was about the only guy on the planet you could get the MIDI-Mod from. I had the honor of serving the royalty of rock: Elton John, Phil Collins, Keith Emerson, Pete Townshend, Lionel Richie, Bruce Springsteen. But Paul McCartney had been my first musical hero. I wanted to deliver above and beyond his expectations.

It's the wee hours of the night and I finally wrap up my work. Paul's driver and personal manager, John Hammel, gives me a lift to The Mermaid Inn, in the town of Rye. A sign on the building says "Rebuilt in 1400 A.D." The inn dates back to 900 A.D. and had been home to pirates after raiding ships at sea. Blackbeard himself might have roamed these halls. Exhausted, I drift off with visions of merciless marauders dancing in my head.

Saturday morning. The skies are a canvas of vibrant blue as my taxi winds its way through the picturesque English countryside. But I'm too preoccupied to appreciate the beauty. Prone to panic attacks, I measure my breath. Somehow, I managed to keep it together yesterday with Paul. But that meeting had been quick and relatively predictable. Today, I need to teach him the features of the adapter. I've developed a slick, LA veneer I can hide my insecurities behind but as soon as Paul walks in, I drop my guard. He's in a light, playful mood, not an ounce of pretension.

I jump into tutorial mode. I point out that his grand now has a MIDI output, which I've connected to a synthesizer, that he can trigger from the piano. I show him how to turn on the unit, how to transpose. He sits down beside me on the bench and begins to check out the unique blend of his piano doubled by an electric piano sound. He plunks around, plays a few chords. I switch the synth to a string pad sound and he varies his chord choices, playing longer-held notes. He looks at me and smiles. "Lovely!"

He launches into a chord progression. "I've been working on this piece, but I'm stuck for a middle-8 section." He plays and sings the verse and chorus he has so far. His voice is competing with the one in my head telling me *this is really happening, so just chill the fuck out and be here.*

Like a cheeky bastard, I step well beyond my boundaries with a suggestion. "Fantastic! For the bridge, what about going from C, to B7, to E7, to A minor?" He tries the chords on for size and stops. "Hey! That's me "Yesterday" change!"

Oops. Embarrassed that I'd unwittingly proposed that Paul McCartney plagiarize himself, I laugh and quip, "All my chords come back to me in shades of mediocrity." He gets the reference. "Paul Simon, right? Great lyric."

The morning goes on, I ease into the moment. He's Paul McCartney, but also a great dude, a musician, a kindred spirit with a razor-sharp wit and a limitless reserve of amazing stories. Bouncing around from one topic to another, we talk about his friendship with Jimmy Page, my brother's bout with substances, Paul's recent work with David Foster, whose glowing introduction landed me here.

We talk about our mutual friend Steve "Luthaker" ("no, trust me Paul, it's *Lukather*"), and how hanging with Luke was "like being a high school kid all over again." We chat about his old Northern England rivals Gerry and the Pacemakers, an aunt in Liverpool whom I "must visit one day if you're ever up north," and his early rock influences.

Paul starts playing a Beatle song and I join in on harmony. Looking back, I recall it being "Can't Buy Me Love", but if I'm honest, it's all a bit of a surreal blur.

Four hours fly by. When he walks me to the studio door, he smiles and says, "Any time you're in the UK, give us a bell."

As the lush, green fields of Sussex fly by the limo, a ray of sun lights my face. I catch my smiling reflection in the window. Part of the trick I played on myself to keep from getting overwhelmed was to convince myself, "This ain't no big deal. This happens all the time." But that mental Novocaine is wearing off and I'm shaking my head, laughing, wondering how the hell I got here.

I picture my chubby, insecure 7-year-old self. I wish I could embrace him and reassure him that everything's going to work out. I'd tell that music-obsessed miscreant from a broken home to just hang tough.

There'll be plenty of challenges to come, but one day you'll blast off in a rocket ship built for one. You'll share adventures, sessions, meals, and laughs with your heroes, including Paul McCartney, Elton John, Carole King, and Dan Fogelberg. But more important than rubbing shoulders with them, your front row seat will provide you with a rare view of their creative processes that will inspire you on your own musical mission.

Dark nights of the soul will push you to your limits, but they'll be the necessary fire that will forge you, helping you tune in to your deepest purpose. You'll perform to audiences around the world, have chart-topping albums, PBS specials, and your music will be streamed by millions of fans around the globe.

CHAPTER 1
The Guitar

I'm seven years old. A rerun of a *My Three Sons* episode is just wrapping up on our tiny black and white Zenith TV.

Mom comes in and asks me to join her on an errand. I enjoy going for rides with her and it beats cracking open schoolbooks. Why not?

We jump in her car – a funky old Peugeot coupe, that like Mom, had French origins and was a one-of-a-kind in the Texas Panhandle. We're going to return some paint brushes to a friend from her art class named "Toy." *Funny name for a man*, I thought.

Toy, an affable, lanky figure with an ever-present Marlboro between his fingers, looks happy to see Mom. He gives me a pat on the head. "Well look what the cat dragged in!"

Mom gives me a stern look. "Don't touch anything."

As they're sipping their white wine and talking boring grownup talk, I scan the smoky room: life-sized, black & white pencil etchings of posed, nude women, piles of dirty laundry, a brass statue he's made in the art class he and my mom attend.

And then in the corner, I see something else. A dusty relic, a guitar leaning against the wall in the corner. I've seen Roy Rogers playing one on TV, but this is the first one I've seen in real life.

I look back at Mom who is paying no attention and creep closer to the guitar. When I touch it, I feel the grit of dust and a shiver of anticipation. I've never held a guitar before, but when I sit down and balance it across my right knee, it feels right.

My fingers barely reach around the neck. I quietly pluck the open strings and realize when you play the lowest string twice, then the second string, then the first, second and third strings in order, you have the first few notes of "Taps!" ... Well, almost. I sit up a little taller, fascinated by the sounds I've just created, enthralled by the vibration that's resonating against my body.

I don't think anyone's noticed, but when it's finally time to leave, Toy motions his Marlboro to where I'd been sitting. "Hey, I saw you plucking around on that guitar. Did you like it?"

I look up at Mom, then at Toy. I light up. "Yeah... it's really cool!"

Toy smiles, pats me on the shoulder. "Take it, it's yours."

Those four words, and that lovely, impulsive gesture, will alter the course of the rest of my life. I can now discover music on my own terms. Just a couple of months before, I'd taken a few piano lessons at my mother's insistence and decided that if music was about those stupid dots and sticks and rules to memorize, I wanted nothing to do with it. Every Good Boy does not necessarily Do Fine. Being more of a right-brain-oriented kid, I had more ease with listening to a song and figuring out how to pick it apart by ear.

From Toy's four words going forward, music becomes the driving force of my life. My new guitar would be my constant companion, a lifeline to a kid struggling to fit in.

—

Red rover, red rover, send Carol on over!

It's a beautiful spring day on the Olsen Park Elementary School playground. The smell of fresh cut grass fills the air, as does the relentless quarter-note monotone of the sprinklers, occasionally breaking into double time. We're now halfway through the group of fellow second graders and I still haven't been called.

Peter, the guy calling the names, is not just one of the popular kids, he's head of an elite club of which I could never dream of becoming a member. He wears a constant smirk of superiority. Recently, he'd pranked me into playing a game of "52 Pickup" and enjoyed snickering at me when I was on my hands and knees picking up the cards. But that didn't stop me from wanting to be accepted by him. He held the keys to the kingdom.

We're now getting closer to the bottom-of-the-barrel-pickin's for this popular childhood playground game. Peter's looked right through me several times. I finally catch his eye. He sneers and says, "Not you, Chubs." I glance at Carol, the girl I have a mad crush on. She sees me and quickly looks down. I feel like a pudgy nobody with *LOSER* tattooed across my forehead.

Among my peers — whose dads are doctors and lawyers — I feel like an outsider. A vagrant looking into a department store window at stuff intended for people of privilege. People who are worthy.

But when I went home and picked up my guitar, I felt cool. And the better I became, the taller I stood. I'd been completely invisible to David Mitchell, the coolest dude in our class. But in years to come, he'd be reaching out to me, wanting me to teach him fingerpicking patterns on guitar. I'd go from being a nonexistent blob to somebody who mattered.

Though feelings of inadequacy would continue to lurk in the shadows, music gave me a way to process my feelings of self-doubt and morph them into something I took pride in. It gave me an identity, a sense of belonging. Music became my salvation.

I often think about the "Power of One" — one thought, one decision, one chance encounter, or in the case of Toy, one gesture that can literally change destiny.

I wish I could talk to Toy now. Whatever musical successes I've had, he sparked with his "take it, it's yours" act of kindness. And I'll come to realize a deeper meaning to his four words — the biggest obstacles between me and all I seek are the ones in my mind. I'm the author of whatever life narrative I choose to write; the brass ring is mine for the taking.

"I'm forever grateful to you, Toy," I want to say.

But unfortunately, I can't. My mother's art-making, Marlboro-smoking, impulsively generous friend passed years before I realized the power of his gift. Each album I make is my best attempt to pay it forward.

Music sounded different to me after that guitar entered my life. Though I didn't know it at the time, that old guitar was not only a skeleton key to unlocking the mysteries of music, but gave purpose and direction for the rest of my life. I'd sit with my guitar and pick out the melodies of songs on the records my mom and dad would play — everything from *My Fair Lady* to Harry Belafonte to Joan Baez. Among my cherished musical memories, one would prove particularly seminal.

TUNED IN: MEMOIRS OF A PIANO MAN

Oh Shenandoah, I long to see you
Away you rolling river
Oh Shenandoah, I long to see you
Way, we're bound away
Across the wide Missouri

Mom is standing beside the record player, singing this song, swaying gently. Her face is transfixed with a wistful, nostalgic look. I'm right beside her, but she's transported miles away, on a raft floating down the Missouri river. She has a special place in her heart for folk songs, but this one's different. On some instinctive level, I feel this song is expressing some undefined yearning deep within her.

This moment — that melody, those lyrics, Mom's poignant sense of longing — burrowed deep into my musical DNA. I still hear echoes of it in compositions I write to this day.

Both my parents loved music, but neither had the chance to pursue that love professionally. Children of the Great Depression, they were both raised in poverty — Mom in rural Vermont, Dad in rural Texas. Both had absentee fathers. Mom's father was in a Canadian mental institution, which was how they treated alcoholism at the time. My paternal grandfather, yet another Jim Wilson, split the scene when my dad was just a baby. Years later, Dad drove for hours to meet him, and all he remembers from this one-time rural encounter is grandad's Native American wife applying a manure poultice to her leg. This image has curiously become part of my image memory bank, my mythology.

So, by necessity, both my parents were raised by single mothers. By horrible coincidence, they both lost their childhood homes to fires and had to rely on the charity of the community to survive. These losses seared into them a sense of frugality; a determination born of desperation. The latter being a characteristic I'd recognize as a driving motivation in myself.

While neither Mom nor Dad played instruments, music was a formative force in their lives and helped to bond the family together.

Holidays were especially meaningful to my mom because it was the only time of year her whole family — separated after the fire — was reunited. The smell of holiday dinner filled the air, as did the sound of their singing seasonal songs. I could feel the gravity of that history when she sang — there was always a tinge of bittersweet melancholy in her voice.

My dad's love of singing also dated back to his childhood when he sang in church. I remember an occasion when he sang for me. "I've always prided myself at having a good voice," he said launching into "Blue Moon." It was a slightly awkward moment with him singing as if it were an audition. Looking back, I see that music was expressing what words could not. I could feel there was an artist buried deep inside him, also driven to express his deeper feelings through music. Though we never discussed it, I felt a kinship with him on this level.

My parents met when my dad was a pilot in the Air Force. He had flown cargo planes in the Second World War (and had even been part of the Berlin Airlift.) Mom was in the Women's Army Corps. She was an Honor Society student at the University of Vermont (and would go on to teach five languages and speak seven — unlike yours truly, who'd become a B and C student, and who could only claim to speak a second language if you counted Pig Latin.) She was working her way through school as a waitress at Howard Johnson's when she heard about an opportunity to supplement her income as a WAC recruiter.

After leaving the service, my dad became a salesman. And how. Over the course of his life, he'd sell everything from freezers, concrete roofing tile, wigs, and cars, to success motivation tapes and mobile homes. He'd get bored with one job, then move on to the next: landscaping, house painting, you name it. But it was hairdressing that brought both Mom and Dad to the Texas Panhandle in 1960.

Dad's sister Billie Jo had moved to Amarillo, put herself through hairdressing school and started her own salon. Business was taking off. She could use a hand and reached out to her little brother, living in Uvalde, Texas. By then, Mom and Dad had two kids, both born near air force bases: my sister Jenny in Greenland, and me in Greenville, South Carolina.

With the Plymouth station wagon loaded to the gills, Mom, Dad, seven-year-old Jenny and five-year-old me began the eight-hour trek to Amarillo. But the soundtrack to this trip was far from pleasant. A prolonged, bitter argument between my parents — largely about Mom's exasperation with Dad's inability to stick with a job — foreshadowed clouds on the horizon of their marriage.

Having grown up in progressive Vermont, my mom's first impressions of Amarillo were less than favorable. If the winds came from the west, it bathed the town with the glorious fragrance of pig shit. The old Volvo station wagons with "I'm Just Wild About Harry!" bumper stickers she was accustomed to seeing on the streets of Burlington were replaced with ranchers in 10-gallon Stetson hats, driving pickups with gun racks and trailer hitches. The lush green hills she'd known as a child were replaced with dry, dusty plains. The wide-open prairies were flat as a cow patty and featureless — apart from the occasional windmill or the 47-foot-tall cowboy statue in front of the Big Texan restaurant, where your 72-ounce steak was free if you could eat it and all the fixin's in an hour.

But she soon came to love the towering cumulonimbus clouds and sunsets that stretched as far as the eye could see. She'd even adapt to the friendly, warm hugs from strangers — a stark contrast to the cold, keep-your-distance customs of New England.

We settled into Panhandle life in our home on Albert Street in a new division called Olsen Park. Less than a block to the west of us — where there's now an endless sprawl of homes and streets — were maize fields as far as a kid's eye could see.

My intrepid sidekick during that time was Tippy — half Chihuahua, half Dachshund, 100% pure love. She followed me into the maize fields, to school, rummaging around new houses being built across the street. Sometimes, she'd even come with Jenny and me to my Aunt Billie's and Uncle Moon's home where we ate Eskimo Pie ice cream bars and watched *Gilligan's Island* – on their color TV, no less. The same TV that would soon transmit a thunderous sonic boom that would change my life and the lives of countless kids my age.

CHAPTER 2
Music and Mischief

Sunday evening February 9, 1964

Some events are remembered more for their aftermath than the event itself. For me at least, that was the case with the Beatles first performance on *The Ed Sullivan Show*. I was eight. Though I was among the 73 million viewers watching, I now remember less about their performance and more about the fallout. The craze that followed was insane. Every radio was playing Beatles songs non-stop — they held the top five slots on the *Billboard* pop charts. Beatle merch was sold everywhere: Beatle wigs, Beatle boots, Beatle dolls, and Beatle songbooks were flying off the shelves.

It was an era when artists who conformed to a very square persona sang songs written by "professional" songwriters — saccharine songs like "How Much Is That Doggie in The Window." When John, Paul, George, and Ringo exploded on the scene — with their shaggy hair and with songs they wrote themselves — they shattered the status quo. Swept up in the mania, I devoured their music and obsessed over their pictures.

All the kids on my Albert Street block were into the Beatles — Blair and Mark Camp, Randy Oates, and Steve Dunnagan, who'd soon have a profound musical impact on me. My first public gig would be with Steve just a few years later.

The ultimate Albert Street Beatle-fan was David Alsobrook. The two of us were thick as thieves. In three years, he'll part his long hair down the middle and wear grannie glasses just like his hero, John Lennon. Our jaws will drop as we obsess over every note of the Beatles groundbreaking album, *Sgt. Pepper's Lonely Hearts Club Band*. Eventually, David will do a 180, follow in his dad's footsteps and become a well-known evangelical preacher. David will go on to write over 40 Christian-themed books, distributed in 50 countries around the world. More than a million copies of his books will be printed in Africa alone.

But now, it's a chilly March afternoon in 1964. David and I are sequestered in his messy bedroom, carving out our plans to become the next Lennon & McCartney. "A great writer has to have a pseudonym and so should we," David declares, offering no evidence to back up his claim. He chooses the name "Al Fresca" and I come up with "Jimbo Sperra." Stardom is surely around the next corner. That neither of us knows shit about writing songs is of no consequence.

For the next few years, when we aren't listening to music or trying to write songs, we're dedicated juvenile delinquents. We sneak out of our respective houses after our families have gone to sleep. Cloaked by darkness, we do stuff like breaking into Crockett Jr. High and taping Playboy centerfolds to the roll-down maps in the front of the classroom, then rolling them back up for a nice geography lesson surprise on Monday morning. South America never looked so enticing.

A dinky portable transistor radio provides the soundtrack to our late-night prowls. We listen incessantly to Morgan Midnight, the famous local DJ on the Top-40 AM radio station, KFDA, *"Playing all the Hits, All the Time!"* Music is the through-line of our lives, so one night we decide to find out where all those cool songs are coming from.

"Let's see if he's in there!" It's the witching hours of a Friday night and I'm fixated on meeting Morgan, a bona fide rock star in our eyes. We bang on the station's glass doors until an unshaven dude, in a T-shirt two sizes too small, his exposed, white belly hanging over his belt — presumably the janitor — finally comes to see what all the commotion is about. He flips on a light in the lobby, cracks open the door a few inches. "Yeah? What is it?"

"Is Morgan here? Can we meet him!"

"Yeah. You got him. Whadda ya want?"

Turns out Morgan is hardly the Adonis we've envisioned. And he's the sole occupant of this postage-stamp-sized facility. We hide our disillusionment and somehow coax him into letting us hang out with him as he spins the records. He leads us into the control room, clears some empty Chinese food cartons from a table, rolls up a couple of chairs.

"You're not supposed to be in here, so not a peep." He gives a stern look, we nod eagerly.

We watch with fascination as Morgan — the biggest celebrity we could ever hope to meet — pulls out a 45 vinyl, cues it up and waits until the current single is fading out.

He dabs out his Camel cigarette and clears his throat. He flips a switch and a red "ON AIR" sign illuminates over the door. Leaning into the microphone, he breaks out his hyped-up, heavily modulated DJ voice.

"*That was 'She Loves You' by the Beatles! Got a favorite song you wanna hear? Give us a call on the request hotline! ... Now here's 'Carrie Ann' by the Hollies, comin' at ya!*"

Between songs, Morgan chats with us two knuckleheads in his normal, low-key voice. Record fades out, then... boom! Here's that amped-up, *life-is-a-party* voice again. The disparity between the two personas is jarring and I'll never forget how much smoke and mirrors gets pumped over those airwaves. It's my first lesson in image versus reality. While we'd been conjuring up visions of a DJ bopping around to music, the reality was some lonely dude cueing up records in the midnight to 6 a.m. shift in a run-down office in a crappy strip mall. Pay no attention to the man behind the curtain.

Not far from KFDA is Sunset Center, a shopping mall that David and I often carouse the halls of late at night. I have the keys to Aunt Billie's beauty salon, Lady Faire, where I have my first job. After everyone's gone, I sweep up hair, mop the floor and clean the mirrors for five bucks. My after-hours access to Lady Faire — and therefore the rest of the mall, via an inner alleyway — leads to more than a few hijinks over the next decade.

Just a mile south of Sunset Center is a different setting where many childhood memories would be made. A setting that's now buried under tons of concrete.

It's unlikely that Eisenhower had me specifically in mind when he envisioned a system of superhighways that would crisscross the United States. But if you took a ruler and drew a straight line from the house I grew up in to the house I'm living in now, you'd have basically drawn the western half of Interstate 40. That direct route would one day become the yellow brick road I'd follow to the Land of Oz where I'd fulfill my dreams. But as a child it was my playground.

TUNED IN: MEMOIRS OF A PIANO MAN

The freeway-constructing juggernaut that rolled through cities, devouring homes, buildings, and anything in its way, missed my Aunt Billie Jo's house by 20 feet, and my mom's by two blocks. If you lived directly in its path, tough shit. The government claimed eminent domain, gave you "fair market price" for your domicile and sent you on your way.

It's the summer of '64. They've just demolished the houses where I-40 will be constructed a mere stone's throw from home. The open ditches and scattered piles of broken concrete resemble the aftermath of a war zone. Once the workers have gone for the day, our battleground beckons. David Alsobrook and I return to the fortress we've constructed out of rebar, crushed asphalt, and chunks of cement. From this stronghold, we launch our rock missiles, fire our stick rifles at incoming Viet Cong and just generally be bad asses. Then, from atop one of the massive earthmovers, I scan the horizon for approaching enemy combatants and hurry back down the ladder.

"COVER ME!" I yell and David opens fire with his invisible Howitzer as I sprint from one dirt pile to another. There's a little cubby hole in the fort / clubhouse to stash our contraband. Between skirmishes, we ogle girly mags while puffing on cigarettes from the packs I've swiped from my mom's carton of Kents.

A newly-constructed drainage system runs right down the middle of the future freeway, 10 feet underground. It's *just* big enough to accommodate a young boy — which we interpret as an open invitation to go spelunking. We begin crawling westward and soon realize there's no room to turn around. We have no choice but to continue on our hands and knees in the claustrophobic darkness until surfacing an hour later over a mile west of home, coming up around where the Bell Street exit is now.

I was terrified but committed — a theme I'd become well familiar with later in life. Fourteen years later, I'll continue that westward journey, only this time behind the wheel, driving the remaining 1,074 miles to Los Angeles.

CHAPTER 3
Things Fall Apart

It's a lazy summer afternoon. I'm watching cartoons on our black-and-white TV in the living room. What begins as overheard strains of a heated discussion between my mom and dad behind their closed bedroom door starts drowning out the sound from the TV. Shouts. Screams. Something thrown across the room.

World War III had broken out just 20 feet away from me. I couldn't make out the actual words being said but I still remember the terror I felt in my gut. The hatred and scathing vitriol detonated behind those doors carved a Mariana Trench-deep scar in my psyche. For my parents, divorce was the merciful option.

Buried deep somewhere among the crevassed vault of my brain, a lasting decision was locked away: if this is what marriage is about, I don't want any fucking part of it.

It was into this napalm warfare that my brother Paul David Wilson was born just months before. Could it have been a more tumultuous time? Our family unit crashing and burning, my baby brother entering stage right, Dad exiting stage left, Kennedy's assassination, the Beatles exploding onto the American scene. It was a chaotic cauldron — the world was in turbulent transition and so was I.

I'm nine. Rose, my blind, French-speaking maternal grandmother, has come from Montreal to help Mom with the new baby. There's now a bedroom shortage and I'm the odd man out. Tucked up against a wall in the kitchen is my new sleeping arrangement: a little single bed that doubles as a sofa during the day. Zero privacy. Just as I'd be drifting off to sleep, a light would flick on, and water would run. In the morning, I'd be startled out of slumber by the sound of clanging pots and pans. But these shitty accommodations will lead to my first major act of self-determinism. An act that continues to inform who I am to this day.

TUNED IN: MEMOIRS OF A PIANO MAN

Just off the kitchen is a huge walk-in storage closet. My dad dabbled in photography and had used that space as a dark room before he moved out. Now a HAZMAT dumping ground, it's crammed to the gills with dozens of gallon jars of photo-development chemicals, tables, trays and tongs, a negative enlarger, and a gazillion boxes of who knows what.

I pitch the idea of me claiming that space as my bedroom to Mom who says that once Dad comes by and empties out the closet (i.e., never), we can "have a conversation about it."

Weeks go by and it's clear that my proposition is dead in the water. I hatch a plan to claim the room in the dead of night. I wait until the family is fast asleep. Only the faint sound of my grandmother snoring down the hall breaks the silence. It's *go time.* Slowly and methodically, I stealthily disassemble my bed, set it on its side against a wall. I begin moving all of dad's stuff out of the closet — bottle by bottle, box by box — putting everything where my bed had just been. Throughout the night, I slowly empty the contents of that closet and quietly reassemble my bed in there, step by step. Finally, it's the wee hours of the morning, and my first man cave is now complete.

Exhausted, I take a deep breath and survey my new kingdom. The stark light from the sole, incandescent bulb overhead offers the room no flattery. There are no windows, the floor is barren plywood, the walls are unpainted sheetrock. But man, does this unadorned place feel like paradise. Most importantly, it's one of my own making. My sanctuary. My head hits the pillow and I drift off to sleep with a self-satisfied grin on my face.

"Oh... my... God..."

It's the following morning, and Mom is standing in disbelief upon first witnessing the mountain of boxes and bottles that now reside where my bed had been just hours earlier. I'm anticipating that she'll be furious with me, but the clarity and decisiveness of my action leaves her no option but to accept that I have made my move and that's that.

Many lessons got baked into my DNA from that act of self-determinism:

1. If it's to be, it's up to me. In this new fractured family reality, I'll

need to fend for myself.

2. Sometimes it's better to apologize later than to ask permission first. (The only person I really needed permission from was myself.)

3. All it takes is all you've got. If your intention is clear and strong enough, you can move mountains.

4. Most importantly: even the most seemingly insurmountable obstacles can be overcome if you break them down to individual bits.

In years to come, I'd apply those lessons to countless things in my life and my music career. Many of my major successes trace back to this "break it down, bit by bit" principle I learned that night.

In another year, I'd have a different man cave — one with an actual window.

—

In early 1965, just after the divorce, my dad — a country boy at heart — moved to a place out in the sticks, 15 miles north of town. He bought a 17-acre property, barren but for a Quonset hut that he envisioned using for training and boarding horses. He dreamed of, and would ultimately create, 440 English Riding Academy, where he'd teach dressage and show jumping. With its English saddles and fancy uniforms, it was an idea way ahead of its time for a part of the world deeply entrenched in cowboys, rodeos, and calf roping. He purchased a mobile home to live in while he made plans for building his dream home on the property.

Years later, Dad would come up with a clever idea to fast-track his plan. He caught wind of a home that had been slated for demolition on the south side of town. He was told if he wanted it, just come get it. He took all the measurements from the perimeter of that house and poured the corresponding foundation on his property.

On D-Day, I rode inside the house for several miles as it was being moved across town. I still recall the unsettling feeling of looking through the grate of the floor furnace as the earth began moving beneath the house; the surreal nature of the world slowly passing by the windows. People watched jaw-agape as this home came creeping down the street at 5 miles per hour. Telephone wires had to be lifted for the house to roll under, care had to be taken as the monstrosity rounded corners and clipped a stop sign or two. It was an all-day affair ending with his free home being lowered onto its new foundation, which was miraculously only off by an inch or two in a couple of places.

But his dream home was years from becoming a reality. For now, while Paul and my big sister Jenny stayed in town with Mom, I moved in with Dad in the mobile home. With bedrooms just barely bigger than the bed, and the cheap faux-wood paneling, the Ritz-Carlton it wasn't. But I had my own bedroom. And unlike the commandeered dark room, I finally had a window — a portal that provided me with a scintillating view of an endless sea of tumbleweeds and mesquite bushes.

The area we lived in was sparsely populated, with only a handful of neighbors within a mile radius. Most memorably, my new friend Carlos Vasquez and his family just to the east of us provided a different kind of window into a world I knew nothing about.

"Time to come in for supper!" It's getting dark and Mrs. Vasquez is rallying the troops from the back door of their home — a makeshift dwelling of hastily constructed additions. They've invited me over for a proper Mexican dinner, which is served at the same time every day and it's expected that every family member be there. Inside, illumination in several of the rooms is provided by a light bulb hanging from an extension cord. The carpet is worn, the furniture is tattered. The faint smell of propane lingers in the air, competing with the aroma of the feast Mrs. Vasquez is preparing.

Mr. Vasquez is singing gloriously off-pitch, reveling in his festive, accordion-driven ranchero music, which emanates from a transistor radio with a tiny, distorted speaker. It's not my kind of music, but I can see how deeply it speaks to him; what kind of joy music can bring to people of other cultures. He dances up behind his wife, now standing at the stove, and gives her a hug and peck on the cheek.

After the meal, I thank Mrs. Vasquez and head back to my tiny room in our mobile home. It would be years before I appreciated the irony that of the two families, mine may have been slightly better off financially, but theirs was the one that was rich in what truly matters — family love.

Some months later, on an ordinary summer night, Dad's taken me to see the movie *Winning* at the drive-in. I guess he's thinking a film starring Paul Newman as a race car driver is a safe bet for a father-son outing.

Turns out the movie is about a painful marital split with a young boy becoming a casualty. Dad's just as surprised as I am when I burst into tears at the end. The on-screen drama, masterfully underscored by composer Dave Grusin, has spoken to emotions deep inside me. It's unearthed feelings about our fractured family that I've yet to process. Reality finally hits me: things are never going back to the way they were. After a moment of awkward silence, Dad puts his hand on my shoulder. No words are spoken, but I sense that I'm being received, my feelings are being understood. Everything's going to be alright.

The film's moving combination of music and drama makes an indelible impression on me. I can't put it into words, but I sense what a powerful storyteller music can be, and I feel art's ability to serve as a transformative, healing balm. Today, I realize as a composer I've strived for my music to serve this objective ever since.

Throughout this time of confined country life, I pour my feelings into my guitar. I try to pick out melodies of pop songs that permeate the airwaves by artists who provide the soundtrack of my life, everything from the Beatles and the Byrds, to the Monkees and Herman's Hermits.

On special occasions we jump in my dad's Nash Rambler and head to the drive-in for burgers, fries, and a shake. The lights from the AM radio illuminate his face as he smiles and nods his head in time to the pop music filling the car. If the chorus is strong enough, he just might sing along:

Downtown, things will be great when you're
Downtown ... Everything's waiting for you.

Sometimes I'd chime in as well. Guy time. I now know that music added to the bond I had with my father. It provided hope for a lonely, insecure 10-year-old boy and gave me an identity. I fantasized that one day I could make music that just might move my dad like the music we enjoyed together.

But the limits of our bond would soon be tested. It's a miracle our connection endured the financial setback I was about to cause my father. It's a brisk, breezy country morning, the skies are deep blue — a perfect day for roaming around my dad's ranch. My friend Tommy has come from town to hang out. I'm showing him the 10-horse boarding stable my dad has recently finished building by hand. We're having a blast taking flying leaps into a pile of sawdust in one of the stalls.

We've pilfered a pack of Marlboros and are now puffing away on our cigarettes while sitting on the sawdust mound. How badass are we? We put our cigarettes out on the ground. At least I think we have.

It's 30 minutes later when Tommy and I, now inside the mobile home, hear the approaching sirens. We wonder where the fire trucks are going. Even when they turn down my dad's driveway, we still don't connect the dots. It's not until we go outside that we see the raging inferno the trucks are rushing toward. Four of Dad's 10 new stalls are engulfed in flames, which are shooting 15 feet in the air. I feel a grip of terror in my stomach. *Have we caused this?* We run to the scene. The firemen work with trained precision, putting out the fire in minutes.

In years to come, few memories will hurt as much as the look on my dad's face seeing the stables he'd worked so hard to create, now a pile of smoldering ashes.

"Did you two see what happened?" Dad turns to us with tears in his eyes.

"No Dad, we have no clue." I can't bring myself to confess the truth: I had to have been the cause of this unforgivable calamity.

It's Tommy who later that evening fesses up to his parents, who then call Dad.

"Were you two smoking cigarettes on a pile of sawdust?" Dad has come into my room and can barely contain his anger.

"Yes, but we put the cigarettes out. That couldn't have been the cause."

"*Of course it was!*" His face is red, he's glaring right through me. I can't look him in the eyes. I sink deeper into my chair, suffocating in remorse.

Realizing it was pointless to continue the lie, I finally took responsibility for the crushing blow I'd dealt my dad. He vented his rage and hurt over the next half hour. He was devastated about the loss, but equally angry that I'd lied to him. He didn't lay a hand on me, but whatever beating he could have given me paled in comparison to the guilt I felt having added to his already difficult financial hardships. I hadn't just let my father down, I'd dug a pit he was going to have to climb out of.

We came to an agreement that I'd work off my debt by helping with the reconstruction. In time, the stables got rebuilt and amazingly, Dad forgave me. But forgiving myself was another matter — true redemption wouldn't come until decades later.

After a period of farm life, it became clear I was more of a city mouse than a country mouse. As much as I loved my dad, I missed my friends and realized the slow tempo of isolated rural life wasn't for me. I moved back into town and lived with Mom, Jenny, my grandmother Rose, and two-year-old little bro Paul.

While I didn't fully grasp it at the time, I've come to have nothing but immense respect for how Mom pulled herself through that stage of her life: a 38-year-old single woman, attending night classes at West Texas State University to get her Master's degree so she could teach English, while cutting hair in our converted garage to provide food for her three kids and her mom. Thinking back on what she endured for our benefit, I feel a swell of emotion in my chest. Things were falling apart, but Mom was doing everything she could to hold us together.

CHAPTER 4
High. School.

Robert Ray flipped the record over, dropped the needle, and began playing side two. I wasn't yet sure what to make of this music, but my cousin was insistent on playing it for me. He was turning me on to Bob Dylan's *Highway 61 Revisited*, pointing out his favorite riffs and the stellar, poetic lyrics. I was too young to understand Dylan's references to inequality and cultural corruption but the more I listened, the more I became hypnotized by his image on the album cover. I was intrigued by his tussled hair and self-assured, yet mildly confrontational gaze into the camera. I got that this artist really had something to say.

It was the summer just before my first year of high school and Robert Ray was breezing through Amarillo. He was probably only 19 but had been hitchhiking and taking buses across the states. With his long hair and guitar slung across his back, he was the epitome of laid-back, California cool. He even had a similar nasal-twang to Dylan's when he sang: *"Like a rolleeeng stohhhnne... no derrekshin hooooome!"*

He enthralled me with stories of entertaining fellow passengers on the Greyhound bus. Breaking out his guitar, he'd launch fearlessly into a song, and rouse his bus mates into a sing-along. The infatuated girl beside him later nodded off with her head on his shoulder. Man, that's the life for me. I was in awe of his self-assuredness and the way his music seemed to be a magnet for others.

Enter the 70s. Boys' hair got longer; girls' skirts got shorter. The world around us pulsated with newfound freedom. I discovered pot. But more significantly, I discovered James Taylor, whose *Sweet Baby James* album I played on heavy rotation. His songs felt like they *needed* to be written, like music was his crucible; his means of turning pain into purpose. His unique, mellow blend of folk, blues, and even country rock influences spoke to me on every level. I worked up "Fire and Rain" and "Country

Road" on guitar. It felt as comfortable as slipping into well-worn denim jeans. I wanted nothing more than to connect with people through my music like Robert Ray and James Taylor could.

My friend Steve Dunnagan also played guitar and when he discovered I did as well, we started jamming together. He taught me the Travis picking style — a fingerpicking pattern developed by Merle Travis. We worked up a few songs by artists like Cat Stevens and Crosby, Stills & Nash and soon got our very first gig at The Hole in the Mall in Western Plaza. We were scared shitless, but we brought the house down. And by that, I mean the crowd was up and happy, and then we began playing. To a scattering of late-afternoon day-drinkers, we muddled through our songs and received a solitary applaud. We got five bucks. Each. In cash. We'd hit the big time.

As we were packing up, the next act began his set. Guitarist, entertainer-extraordinaire Scott Nelson schooled us on how it's done.

"You guys ready to party?!"

Scott — a large dude with a personality to match — had a strong, clear voice and performed with authority and charisma. In no time, he had the crowd singing along, applauding wildly. We were humbled but inspired. I didn't know it at the time, but Scott would become an important part of my musical legacy down the road.

One of my favorite hangouts at that time was a store called TMI (Texas Musical Instruments) at Sunset Center, where I'd go and drool over the guitars. The owner, John Souther, was really cool and I'd often go there just to talk music with him. He sold me my first 12-string guitar. His son, J.D., was "out in LA" writing with a "hot new band that just got signed called The Eagles." That someone from our little hometown was actually "making it" in the music business seemed completely surreal, but it gave me hope that my dreams might actually be possible.

But dreaming is one thing, and following through on making dreams happen is another. In reality, I was an irresponsible, 16-year-old, long-haired hippie escaping into my room, my haven. I'd painted the walls a deep royal blue, one of which was bedecked with a five-foot-tall white peace sign. On another, I had a poster of a seagull silhouetted against a sunset — its caption would prove to be a vital directive for my life: *The important thing is this: to be willing to let go of what you are for who you could become.*

I also had the famous poster of Farrah Fawcett in a red bathing suit, but that's another conversation.

In the sanctity of my room, I'd put on my headphones and rock out to Black Sabbath, Led Zeppelin, and Grand Funk Railroad, then lose myself in the introspective melancholy of albums like *Harvest* by Neil Young, *Simple Man* by Graham Nash, and *Tapestry* by Carole King. If you'd have told me that one day I'd go skinny-dipping with Carole at her ranch in Idaho, I'd have said you were crazy.

But escape into my own space wasn't always an option. My mother had remarried. My new stepdad, Lou, was very pragmatic and responsible — everything my father wasn't. Lou was less than warm and fuzzy with me. To say that he resented having to share his household with a reprobate is an understatement. I'd retreat into my music in my bedroom, and he'd retreat into his tall glass of Smirnoff vodka.

Lou felt I needed to learn accountability, so he assigned me housecleaning chores every Saturday morning. If I focused, I could knock out his checklist of sweeping and mopping the kitchen floor, cleaning the countertops, and emptying the trash in 30 minutes max.

But I'd procrastinate and drag my duties out for hours. To my adolescent psyche, it felt like I'd been sentenced to hard time. "You aren't my dad," I'd mutter under my breath as I slammed the door to my bedroom. Looking back, I see he had my best interests at heart and was just trying to provide the discipline that was missing in my life. And as much as I resented him treating me like an irresponsible kid, I was about to discover he may have had a point.

"The following four people are being fired for incompetence…"

Ken — the pompous, ginger-haired manager known for making wildly inappropriate comments about female employees' anatomies — grabbed his belt, adjusted his pants, and looked up from the list on his clipboard. The smug expression on his face made it obvious he enjoys dropping the axe. He peered over the top of his wire-rimmed glasses at the group of us gathered for a special, "attendance-mandatory" staff meeting at the McDonald's on I-40 and Western. Just a few months ago, as a 15-year-old, I'd lied about my age, saying I was 16, the minimum hiring age. I'd worked my way up from cleaning tables in the "Metro" to

"French Fry Chef", an esteemed position that pulled down the handsome wage of $1.85 an hour. Sure, I'd sneak bites of fries whenever I could, but I'd always make certain no one saw. And Ken not only knew about our secret "babe alert" code — "Nine on three!" meant there was a girl who was a 9 at cash register number 3 — he participated.

But I'd been reliably late from day one, so when my name was among those being fired for "incompetence" — whatever that fancy word meant — it wasn't a complete shock.

The McDonald's gig was just one of many I'd have during the nomadic blur of my first couple of years at Tascosa High School, bouncing from home to home, job to job. I'd live with my mom in town for a while, then by myself in a bunkhouse at Lake Tanglewood — a man-made lake 20 minutes south of town — where I was the garbageman for a summer. I lived with Dad in the country again, then back with Mom, then later with Aunt Billie Jo. I was a janitor at Sunset Center, made concrete roofing tile with my dad, and was an apprentice house painter for my Uncle Moon. The only connective tissue through those years was my obsession with music — my guitar followed me everywhere I went. It once even helped bridge a culture gap between West Texas and Europe.

"Ich bin ... gehen ... Rot Fluss."

My face turned cherry red as Heidi and DeeDee looked completely baffled. I'd worked hard to memorize these five words (*"I am going to Red River"*), but I'd mangled them so badly, they didn't even recognize I was trying to speak their language.

As luck would have it, the two foreign exchange students for our high school, Heidi Gabriel from Vienna, and DeeDee Hoffinger from Paris were assigned to my homeroom. Each gorgeous and exotic, I couldn't believe they were seated right next to me. I had mad crushes on both.

They'd sit across from me whispering back and forth to each other in the language they mutually spoke most fluently — German. We laughed about my miserable attempt to impress them. We soon became friends and spent time hanging out.

"You really should visit one day." Heidi takes a sip of Boone's Farm apple wine out of a Dixie cup. I'd somehow managed to get both her and DeeDee alone at the bunkhouse in Lake Tanglewood. I played guitar for them. I even scooted next to Heidi to teach her a few chords, but my powers of seduction were wasted on these worldly Europeans. While my infatuation with them would remain unrequited, they had a lasting impact on me.

They shared stories with me about growing up in their respective cultures, where there were multiple political parties and diverse religious beliefs. Everyone seemed to speak several languages and had their finger on the pulse of what was happening in the rest of the world. It felt like a stark contrast to the conservative environment at their new West Texas high school, where our Rebel mascot was a rifle-and-bayonet-wielding cartoon soldier, complete with his Confederate cap and walrus mustache.

Heidi — who I'd visit in Vienna years later — and DeeDee provided my first window into the idea that, hey, maybe America isn't the center of the universe after all. Perhaps there are other people from other cultures who take as much pride in their countries as we do ours. A fish doesn't necessarily know it's in water until it leaves its fishbowl.

Meanwhile, I was doing all I could to prepare myself for a life of making music. I was active in the school and church choirs, took guitar lessons, wrote songs, and even started a little band with my friends Rick Faucett and Steve Dunnagan, performing "Dreamtime Lovin'" — a song Steve, his brother and I wrote — in a talent show for the student body.

At the same time I was taking steps toward my goals, I was derailing myself by getting too high to function, waking up too hungover to follow through on my intentions, and worse yet, doing stupid shit that easily could have landed me behind bars. The biggest threat to fulfilling my dreams was me.

CHAPTER 5
Capers and Close Calls

I know something doesn't look quite right but I can't put my finger on it. I've just left Lady Faire Beauty Salon and, having recently gotten my driver's license, I'm now driving my blue Opal Kadett down Western Avenue. Not helping with my inability to discern just what's off with this picture is the fact that I'm stoned as fuck. My relationship to the law of gravity is tenuous at best. It's not until I see the red lights flashing in my rear view, hear the siren wail and the cop telling me over his loudspeaker to *PULL OVER!* that I put it together that I've been driving without headlights.

I take the first right into the McDonald's parking lot at Western and I-40. The same McDonald's from which I'd recently been fired. The same McDonald's on which I'd helped Dad install concrete roofing tile when I was 15. The same McDonald's where I took a hammer and nails and immortalized my and Janet Larsen's initials in a corner of the parking lot.

I park, get out and lumber towards the cop car. I open his passenger door and slide into the front seat next to him.

I squint as the officer turns on his harsh overhead light, which reveals to him the vision sitting to his right: a baked, 17-year-old hippie, with hair down to his chest, funky-ass, bushy sideburns, glassy red eyes, and — as I would later discover — a baggie of pot sticking out of my front shirt pocket.

"Man! I'm such a knucklehead for driving without my lights. So sorry!" I smile and pat him on the knee, as if I'm laughing at myself with a buddy.

He's so caught off-guard by this unconventional move he doesn't quite know what to say. I remember feeling that if you're vulnerable with people, if you display a sincere gesture of trust, the universe provides you with a magical shield of protection.

But maybe that was just the pot talking.

"Uh ... *yeah*... you definitely didn't have your lights on." He fidgets with his citation tablet. "I need to see your driver's license, please."

I get him talking and somehow even muster a laugh out of him. He either doesn't notice the ounce of pot sticking out from my shirt or he's choosing to overlook it.

"I'm going to let you off with a warning this time but be careful out there."

"I sure will, Officer. Thank you so much."

As his car drives away, the glowing golden arches beckon to me. What better place to discover you have the munchies than in the parking lot of a McDonald's? I go inside and there at the counter waiting to order is my friend, Richard Hazelwood.

"Man! You won't believe what just happened!" I tell him about my saga. We laugh about it and take our food to go. We're sitting in my car and before we eat our Big Mac and fries, decide to smoke another joint. Richard rolls a massive stogie and fires it up. In no time, the car is dense enough with smoke you need a machete to cut through it. Richard is just about to take another hit when out of the corner of my eye I see a cop car pull into the parking lot.

"Fuck! The cops! Put it down!" My heart is going a million miles an hour.

The car stops directly behind mine. Panic sets in. Richard takes the remainder of the still-lit joint, tosses it in his mouth and swallows it. The cop gets out of his vehicle, walks up to my side of the car, and taps on my window. Pulse racing, I roll down the window and watch as the cumulonimbus cloud of smoke billows forth, enveloping his face. He pauses for a second.

"You forgot your license," he says, handing it back to me. I thank him profusely and he walks away.

There's zero chance he didn't notice the smoke emanating from my car. Maybe he pitied me. Or maybe he had a kid my age. But I chose to think he saw a measure of good in me and knew that had he busted me, my life would have taken a ruinous turn, all because of a lapse in judgment. Under the draconian Texas laws at the time, possession of even a small amount of pot was a felony regarded somewhere between murdering your mother and blowing up a federal building. What a debt of gratitude I owe this guy.

—

There are countless instances in my feral youth that could've sent my life in a dark direction had the cards fallen another way. By the time I was 12, I'd been picked up by the cops a half dozen times for petty theft, curfew violations, vandalism, and trashing someone's houseboat dry-docked in their backyard. In my teens, we pushed the envelope even further, breaking into clothing stores and streaking on Polk Street. Maybe I thought thumbing my nose at authority was cool, maybe I liked the thrill of a narrow escape. Or maybe some shrink might say I wanted to fit in with friends who filled the empty void of family, that I was acting out and my behavior was a cry for help. In truth, it was probably a little bit of all of the above. Regardless, it's a miracle I didn't end up in prison.

Thankfully, I reached a turning point one Saturday. After sleeping in until 3pm, I staggered out of bed, still high from the previous night. I got pissed off at the dazed stoner looking back at me in the bathroom mirror. So much for my plans to work up new songs on guitar. A few beers with friends didn't derail my ambition, but I was fed up with dissipating my focus overindulging in cannabis. I'd had enough of sabotaging myself with my lack of discipline and wasted weekends of zero accomplishment.

I'd eventually learn the word "moderation", but for now I knew if I wanted to make anything of myself, I had to clean up my act. Though I did a fair job of correcting course, there was still one more caper to come that would have guaranteed time behind bars if not for some incredibly good fortune.

As the headlights approach us on this desolate Texas panhandle road, we wonder if that could be Greg headed to our soirée. My little campfire party out at Dad's house in the country way north of town was winding down. The few of us who remained were nowhere near ready to throw in the towel, but we were running low on party fuel. Back into civilization we go, barreling down the road on a mission to fetch beer, chips, and dip. The approaching car — the only lights visible for miles — indeed turns out to be Greg's tricked-out black VW bug. Both cars slow down and come to a stop, side by side, in the middle of the road beneath a clear, starlit night.

"Fancy meeting you here!" Greg rolls down the window to his old VW bug. "Where ya headin'?"

"We're going back into town for supplies," says one of the guys inside our car. That same guy — whose voice sounds suspiciously like mine — then points to a building 15 feet away and flippantly adds, "…and to break into that beer shack!"

In Amarillo at that time, they had a "blue law" that prohibited selling alcohol within the city limits on Sundays. I guess the idea was that the good Lord frowned on folks imbibing libations when they should be attending church. This law paved the way for some resourceful folks setting up extemporaneous businesses just outside the city limits. As fate had it, our two cars' trajectories intersected precisely in front of one such roadside shack.

Seconds after those off-the-cuff words are uttered, the tire tool in Greg's trunk comes out and the padlock is pried off. The beer inside doesn't stand a chance. Over the bottom half of the Dutch door we go. In no time, we're heading back to the party with our treasure in stow: 11 cases of beer. Score.

The party has dwindled down to just Greg, Rob, Ken, Sam, and me. We sit around the campfire laughing at our good fortune. Pirates returning from the open seas with our stolen booty.

Then it dawns on us — the shack's still open and there's plenty more booty to be had. We scramble into two cars and make a beeline to the source of all goodness in the world to any delinquent boy: unlimited beer.

We have our shit together this time. Down the assembly line comes case after case of Coors, Budweiser, Heineken, Schlitz Malt Liquor, and Michelob. We're in and out in just a few minutes. Dirt and gravel spray behind us as we peel out. We race back to my dad's ranch five minutes away. We sit around the fire and clink toasts to our pilfered pilsners.

Then reality starts setting in: (1) that shack is gonna be crawling with cops soon, (2) they are gonna be searching the area for the banditos and (3) where the hell are we going to put all this beer? We're all still living with our parents in town, except I have a crash pad that we can use, thanks to a girlfriend who'd moved out of a house and let me use the last few weeks remaining on the rent. It was the first of several party pads.

Clock is ticking, gotta get a move on. Into two cars we start disbursing the 42 cases of beer — that precise quantity we'd soon know because the newspaper article a couple of days later would say "Parched Prowlers Make Off With 42 Cases of Beer."

Rob has a 1951 Chevy sedan panel wagon. In its former life, it was used to deliver milk. Tonight, it'll deliver a different kind of nectar. Three of us will ride in that car with the majority of the beer, then another of us will ride with Greg in his VW with the remainder of the haul. Locked and loaded, we pile into our cars.

Turning the key, Rob discovers that his battery has died. Ugh. No worries. My dad's house is on a hill. We push the car, get it rolling down the incline, then "pop the clutch." "BOOM!" ... The drive shaft breaks in two.

Fuck.

OK. Think fast. We get Greg's VW in position facing downhill so we'll have a rolling start. We remove the spare tire from the "trunk" — located in the front of a VW — and carefully position six cases in there. We can *barely* close the hood. We then remove the back seat and neatly stack several rows of cases there. Rob is the smallest of us and can just fit into the tiny space above them. On the floor in front of each front seat, we place two cases of beer. On the driver's seat are two cases of beer, then atop those sits driver Greg, on whose lap sits Ken. On the passenger seat are two more cases of beer, atop which is me, and in my lap sits Sam. Whatever the weight limit of a VW is, we are several hundred pounds over it.

Key turns, engine starts. Greg *slowly* eases out on the clutch. We inch forward. So far so good. We slowly begin rolling down the hill, knowing we have to gain as much momentum as possible. The road descends a few hundred feet, bottoms out in a gully, then goes back up the other side. We're beginning our ascent up the opposite hill and quickly start losing momentum. Sam jumps out and helps push the car to the top of the hill, then hops back in. Rolling through the stop sign, we just make it.

Every tiny bump in the road we hit bottoms out the car, scraping the underside against the pavement. But we're on our way. Just 15 more minutes and we'll be in the clear, unloading our stolen treasure.

We're slowly rolling down the desolate road when the now-illuminated scene of the crime begins coming into view: two Texas Highway Patrol cars, doors flung open, parked in front of the beer shack. Both cars have their spotlights fixed on the building, both officers are leaning into the shack surveying the carnage. Pulse is racing, prison is now a certainty. As we get closer, we tell Rob — cramped in the back with no way to see out — what's coming up and to not make a sound. He's certain we're winding him up and begins yelling, "Here we are coppers, come get us! *Suckers!*" We punch him in the arm and whisper-yell, "SHUT THE FUCK UP! We're serious!" Thankfully, he zips it.

As the two patrolmen are peering into the scene of the crime, just behind them, a *"putt putt putt putt"* sound breaks the silence of an otherwise dead-still Texas night. Had they turned around, they would have seen a seriously overloaded VW bug riding just inches above the pavement with five guys and 42 cases of beer.

To the cop in the McDonald's parking lot who chose to turn a blind eye – or in his case, nose – and these two Texas Highway Patrolmen who unknowingly turned a deaf ear, I owe my prison-free youth.

The last day of high school finally rolls around. It's a chaotic day of bittersweet goodbyes to favorite teachers and everyone signing yearbooks with disposable platitudes (*Don't ever change! ... Let's hang out this summer!*) The final bell comes, and the last tether of high school is severed. I'm standing by my car and turn to take one last look at the school. I feel a mixture of excitement and the dread of uncertainty. My future in music is calling me, but I'm unclear on what my next move is. School may be over, but I'm still a Rebel without a clue.

CHAPTER 6
Hit The Road, Jim

I can hear someone thrashing on the drums in the band room from all the way down the hall. The cacophony and chaotic tempo lead me to safely assume this particular someone isn't Ringo Starr.

I poke my head inside the musty-smelling room. Behind the rows of chairs and music stands, to the left of the timpani, sits a drum kit and the room's lone occupant. He's lost in the music and doesn't notice that I've walked in. Either that or his long, stringy blonde hair is blocking his view of me. It's when he turns toward the cymbal for his big finish that he spots me. He looks like he's just gotten busted for trespassing, which in fact, he has.

"I was just trying to figure out how to play in 5/4." He smiles and laughs. "I guess it's probably obvious I'm not a drummer."

Bob Denton was a well-known singer-songwriter in the Panhandle and, on that day, he'd sneaked onto the campus of Amarillo Jr. College. I was two weeks into my first semester of my sophomore year there, having enrolled in music theory, ear-training, and music history classes. Bob was not a student. He had no business being there and was clearly thumbing his nose at the rules. He was, in other words, a man after my own heart.

I tell him I've heard great things about him. He sets the drumsticks down on the snare and brushes his hair out of his eyes. "Thanks man. Are you a musician too?"

I tell him I play acoustic guitar, sing, and write songs and that I've been doing some gigs around town as a solo artist.

He turns to face me. "What kind of stuff do you play?"

"The usual." I shrug, a little self-conscious. "You know, Loggins and Messina, Crosby, Stills & Nash, Neil Young." He nods. The more we chat, the more it becomes clear we share the same musical DNA.

Back in my little apartment on Washington Street near Ellwood Park, I play him a few tunes. "You're great, man!" he says and launches into a pitch.

"I'm about to head to Colorado to perform at the ski resorts. It's a blast. You ski for free, perform from 4:00 to 7:00 for Happy Hour, then let groupies have their way with you at night. You should bail on college and join me."

Bob possesses an intense charisma and powers of persuasion. After an hour of arm-twisting, he presents logic that topples the final pilar of my resistance: my main reason for going to college is to become a professional musician. This fork in the road is a short-cut to my destination. His seductive offer hits the trifecta: skiing, performing, adoring groupies. I'm in.

And I have just the vehicle to make all this possible: an ancient Metrobus that in its former life had been a Bookmobile. As sleek and trim as a hippopotamus, as speedy as a snail on Valium. Someone had painted the top half white and the bottom half fire engine red. They'd converted the interior into a camper.

Stepping into the bus, you walk past a little storage closet just behind the driver's seat. Next to that is a propane stove, above which are cabinets. At the back of the bus is the seating area with a cool dining table. At night, the whole affair converts easily into a double-decker bed situation. From the front, the dual windshield panels, and grille just below them kind of resembles the spectacles and mustache of Theodore Roosevelt. I'd tricked out "Teddy" with a tape player that could accommodate either 8-Track tapes or cassettes — talk about your cutting-edge technology.

The next couple of weeks fly by. Bob and I work up songs for our repertoire: "Sundown" by Gordon Lightfoot, "Peaceful Easy Feeling" by the Eagles, "The City of New Orleans" by Arlo Guthrie. We need a name. Bob had toured under the pseudonym, "Zigfield Weaver." He suggests that we go by "Zigfield and Weaver" to cash in on whatever brand capital he's earned so far. I have no better plan. Why not? He becomes Bob Zigfield, and I'm Jim Weaver. We get head shots, have 8x10s and flyers printed, stock up on food and supplies, and tie up loose ends before we hit the road.

D-Day arrives. On our way out of town, we decide to stop at Billy's Band-Aid to get some guitar strings. Over in the corner sits a lonely upright acoustic bass for sale. 150 bucks and she's ours. A hell of a bargain, but it's still a hefty chunk out of the $382 in my brown vinyl banker's bag — my life savings that's supposed to fund us until we get paying gigs. We both look at each other and shrug. Why not? Neither of us know how to play it but we can learn. How hard can it be? It barely fits in the 7-foot-tall storage closet behind the driver seat.

We point our wheels in the direction of the Rockies and with Joni Mitchell's *Court and Spark* blasting through the speakers on a continuous loop, Teddy devours the white stripes on the highway like a Pac-Man game. To this day, when I hear just a few bars of Joni's song 'Free Man in Paris', I feel that exhilaration of embarking on my new life as a professional musician.

A few hours later, I awake to the sound of grinding gears. Bob is furiously downshifting. Teddy — an ancient Metrobus designed for light city driving — is now headed up a dark, steep mountain dirt road. The engine overheating, Bob pulls to the side of the road. Deciding this is indeed a good hill to die on, Teddy is putting his foot down, threatening to leave us stranded here in the middle of nowhere.

The ever-dimming headlights reveal a gate in the barbed-wire fence just to our right. I get out and open it. Teddy has just enough juice to start up and drive us onto whoever's property this is.

When we wake, we step out into the morning sun and the glorious vistas of what will be our home for the next while. We're parked alongside a dirt road, on what is presumably someone's private property, beside a winding mountain stream, running through a lovely meadow, against a backdrop of snow-capped peaks. Breathtaking.

For the next two weeks, we rehearse outside in the brisk November air. We trade off playing "Frieda", which, for some unknown reason, is what we've named our six-and-a-half-foot tall upright bass. Both of us learning as we go, on the job training at its best. Bob's a bit of a taskmaster, but I respect that his being a stickler for perfection is part of what's made him so good. He's older and more experienced than I am, and I'm OK with following his authoritative lead. For eight hours a day, we polish our repertoire until our fingers give out. When brain fatigue begins setting in, a dip in the cold stream wakes us up. A quick PB&J sandwich with a side of baked beans and it's back to rehearsing.

Soon our set is ready. We're running low on supplies. We need a shower and a laundromat. The nights are getting cold. Time to head out. Fortunately, Bob had parked Teddy facing slightly downhill for easy push starting. We pop the clutch, the motor cranks, and we're off. Destination: Durango, Colorado.

Bob has performed for student union audiences on college campuses before. He has the bright idea of doing our first gig at Fort Lewis College in Durango. He cold calls them, asks to speak to the person in charge of booking entertainment. He breaks out his hyped-up, uber-slick radio announcer voice and impersonates our manager, Walt.

"Walt Myrick here. I represent the duo, Zigfield and Weaver. There's an opening in their upcoming tour and they could be available to perform a concert in your Student Union later this week."

By the time he's done, the booker can't believe his luck. One of the hottest duos since Loggins and Messina, since Batman and Robin, since Bert and Ernie, *just so happens* to be rolling through town and is willing to humble themselves and perform at their little college? What astonishingly good fortune! Sight unseen, music unheard, Bob, aka "Walt," books a Friday night concert in the Fort Lewis College Student Union building.

With five days to go before the big event, we set up camp in the college parking lot. We make friends with students, play songs in their dorm rooms. We're sounding pretty tight; the buzz starts spreading. We plaster the halls with 8x10 flyers promoting the big concert. Our new student friends wrangle meal passes for us, and we join them for free dinners each night in the cafeteria.

The big day comes. A line of eager fans is already forming before we finish our sound check an hour before showtime. I'm no stranger to pre-show jitters, but all my gigs before this have been low-pressure, quasi-background-music shows. This has been billed as the Second Coming of Christ and I'm shaking in my boots. I'm bordering on a full-blown panic attack. I've mentioned nothing to Bob about this ongoing predilection – – dating back to when I was in 6th grade having to read in front of the class, so I discreetly step outside for a few minutes to jump up and down, shake my hands in the air, take a few deep breaths. Back inside, I get another shot of adrenaline when I peek from behind the curtain.

The capacity of the room is 150 people, but they've squeezed in an extra 50 against the back wall. Another 75 people are gathering around the entrance in the hall. Palms sweating, breath shallow and rapid, my nervous system is responding as if a vicious dragon is about to devour me.

"Ladies and gentlemen, please give it up for *Zigfield and Weaver!*" bellows the student MC.

We hit the stage, launch into "Mr. Bojangles." Fingers trembling, voice quivering, I somehow make it through the first song. The applause feels like a warm salve. My shoulders ease, I exhale. The dragon moves a couple of steps back. A few songs in and I muster the nerve to crack a joke, incorporating the name of a popular teacher. Huge laugh. This is beginning to resemble something like fun. Almost. A few more songs and we have them singing along and clapping. The set flies by and in a nano-second, it's over. Standing ovations, encores, heaven.

There's little substitute for the self-confidence boost you can only get from slaying a dragon. And performing has always been of the 50-foot tall, fire-breathing kind for me. I gained ten feet in stature that night.

Over the next six months, Bob used his slick manager schtick to land us gigs across New Mexico, Colorado, and Texas, performing at happy hours at Purgatory Ski Resort, dinner clubs in Aspen, bars in Amarillo.

Unfortunately, Bob was threatened by anyone with talent and needed to feel like he was top dog. A few months into our time together, our gifted singer-songwriter friend Jerry Johnstone joined us in Durango for a weekend visit. The three of us were on our way to lunch when an argument broke out between Bob and Jerry. It escalated into screaming fits of rage. *"I'M GOING TO MAKE IT FIRST!"* Bob spewed at Jerry, strangling the steering wheel. *"FUCK YOU, ASSHOLE! I'LL MAKE IT LONG BEFORE YOU DO!"* yelled Jerry in response.

As their caustic words filled the air, I sat calmly in the back seat, gazing out the window at the gorgeous mountain scenery. I smiled to myself, mildly amused that I wasn't even a dark horse entry in their imaginary race. Fine by me.

But it did make me wonder what "making it" might look like, what my specific dream was. To be the next Jackson Browne? The next big behind-the-scenes hit songwriter? I wasn't entirely sure, but I figured I'd have a better shot of defining and achieving my goals through quiet resolve rather than arguing about them.

Over time, Bob's substantial talent became overshadowed by his substantial ego, turning our fairy tale adventure into a living nightmare. He was constantly judging everything about me: what I ate, how I dressed, how I played. He seemed to take pleasure in putting me down. Living 24/7 in such close quarters with him ultimately proved more than I could handle. And after this stint of performing professionally, I'd gained deeper appreciation for how music theory and ear training could figure into real-world application. I wanted to go back to school.

When I broke the news to Bob that I was quitting our duo to return to college, he was furious. At our last gig at Guffy's Bar in Amarillo, while performing "Peaceful Easy Feeling," Bob glared at me and sang "I know you *WILL* let me down." It was a rough ending to our six-month ride.

Nonetheless, I'm grateful to him for teaching me how to rehearse songs until they're bullet-proof, for his example of how to jump fearlessly into the void, and for providing me a jumpstart to my performing career.

JIM WILSON

$1 cover charge, first drink free. See you there?

TUNED IN: MEMOIRS OF A PIANO MAN

"Pick out any piano you want," said Lou, after leading me into the room where they kept the old clunkers.

My stepfather had taken me to Tolzien's Music Store to buy me a piano. Maybe my tour with Bob convinced him I was serious about music. Or perhaps he wanted to reward my decision to return to Amarillo College (though as it would turn out, the return would only last a semester.) Most likely, he realized that I was finally out of his house for good and this was the consolation prize.

Regardless, this was his sole magnanimous gesture towards me and I was grateful. I tried out a few pianos and landed on an old Everett upright. A bargain at $175. It got moved into my apartment, where I worked on my ear-training exercises, laboriously picked out the chords to "Clouds" by David Gates and Bread and transferred my James Taylor "hammer-on" guitar riffs to piano. It was the last year of my teens, but I was lit up like a child to be finally discovering piano on my own terms.

One of the ear-training assignments my professor had given us required buying Beethoven's 9th Symphony. I went to Hastings Record Store and asked the girl behind the counter to direct me to their classical music section.

She said, "You mean like Mo Zark and those guys?"

Close enough.

CHAPTER 7
Easy Does It

"You can play electric bass, right?" Walt sets down his iced-tea and looks up at me, awaiting my reassurance.

It's a Friday in the spring of '76 and I've set up a lunch meeting with my manager, Walt Myrick — the genuine article this time. He'd previously booked me as a solo artist at the Tascosa Country Club, Gardsky's Loft, and a few other little gigs around town. I'm hoping to twist his arm and get him to line up some more gigs for me.

"Well, there's nothing on the table for solo acts right now, but there's an opportunity that just opened up with Easy that could be amazing for you," Walt says, referring to a show band he manages — the most popular one in the tri-state area. They're a big deal. Booked solid, they play to packed audiences wherever they go.

This could be good. I cock my head and nod.

"They're looking for a new bass player. Auditions are on Monday." Walt asks if I play electric bass.

"Absolutely." I lie through my teeth; my Pinocchio nose grows an inch. Truth is I've never touched one in my life. "Tell me the time and place on Monday and I'm there."

It's now Friday around 2 p.m. I go directly to Billy's Band-Aid and Billy Stull, being a mensch, lets me have a new Sunburst Fender Jazz bass on consignment. I go home and in the absence of a real bass amp, plug it into my P.A. system. I begin transferring the elementary chops I'd recently learned on acoustic bass over to electric bass. It's the same layout but a totally different feel.

For the rest of the night and for 14 hours a day on Saturday and Sunday, I work straight through. I practice scales, work up pop songs, refine my technique. I pick apart bass lines on James Brown records, study Willie Weeks bass solos from Donny Hathaway's *Live at the Bitter End*. I'm going to do whatever it takes. I fucking want that gig.

TUNED IN: MEMOIRS OF A PIANO MAN

It's Monday afternoon, I roll up to the Ramada Inn at I-40 and Ross. I stride up the stairs to the Red Lion Lounge, I'm loaded for bear.

At least that's the posture I'm taking. Inside, I feel like the impostor that I am. The three band members are sitting at a table in front of the stage. As I approach them, I feel the sticky brown carpet beneath my feet. The smell of stale cigarette smoke and a thousand spilled Budweisers hang heavy in the air. The sexy, dim lighting of a nightclub has been chased away by the overhead work lights and unflattering afternoon sun coming through the windows. It has all the charm and ambience of a police interrogation room.

"How's it goin', guys?" I half-smile and nod with as much cool as I can muster, in defiance of the gnarly knot of tension in my gut.

Walt introduces me. "Jim, meet Jackie Haney." Jackie is the front man, playing lead guitar and vocals. Standing to greet me, he's a little shorter than I am, but big in stature. He flashes a smile that beams charm and self-confidence. For years to come, I will unwittingly emulate his smooth performing style and audience patter (*Keep on drinkin' what you're drinkin' and thinkin' what you're thinkin' — We'll be right back!*) before connecting with my own voice.

Next up is Frank Romero, the drummer with the perfectly-styled, Eric Estrada hair and Fu Manchu mustache. He's a solid, no-bullshit dude. I instantly get that if I want his respect, I'm going to have to earn it. He makes direct eye contact, smiles, gives me a firm handshake.

Finally, there's Charlie Clinton, with the oversized wire-framed glasses and ready smile. His affable, teddy-bear demeanor gives no indication of what a brilliant keyboard player he is.

The three of them couldn't be more welcoming. But I'm still wrestling with a gnawing anxiety, certain their cordial hospitality will instantly vaporize when they discover I'm a complete fraud. After some small talk, Jackie says, "Well, shall we?"

I walk on stage, plug my Fender Jazz into the amp. Jackie says, "How about we just jam on 'Feelin' Alright'?" Sweet. Basically, just two chords: C and F. I got this.

Frank counts us off, we jump in. I throw in some nice walkups, a couple of pseudo-flashy riffs. I break out a couple of *how-badass-is-this?* guitar faces. I try to look like I know what the fuck I'm doing. We land the plane.

A couple of songs later, Jackie smiles and shakes my hand. "Thanks for coming in, Jim. We're looking at a couple of other players, but we'll be making a decision in the next week or so."

I haven't cinched the deal, but I haven't blown it either. I want to let them know how serious I am about getting the gig, that I want another shot.

I collect my bass. Heading toward the exit, I get a bright idea. I turn back to face them. "Would you be up for letting me come to your gig tomorrow night and record your sets?" Jackie says sure thing. I return the next afternoon and set up my Teac 2340 4-track reel-to-reel tape recorder to capture the separate tracks: the bass part, the bass player's harmony parts and the band mix.

For the next 10 days, I spend every waking moment mastering all 40 songs, including "I Love You More Today Than Yesterday" by Spiral Staircase, "Wake up Sunshine," "Only the Beginning," and "Saturday in the Park" by Chicago, "My Girl" by the Temptations, and "This Boy" by the Beatles. One of Easy's trademarks is that all four band members are lead singers and this song is a good four-part harmony showcase.

Jackie puts all the set lists together and typically opens the show with up-tempo songs like "Walking in Rhythm" by the Blackbyrds, "Long Train Runnin'" by the Doobie Brothers, or "How Long" by Ace. I double-down on drilling these songs, knowing the adrenaline is going to be pumping harder when the lights first come up. The last thing I need is one of my panic attacks right out of the gate. The band's song choices are a bit more sophisticated than the average Top-40 cover band and I feel like a fish out of water.

Have I bitten off more than I can chew? I push through self-doubt as I work my ass off, getting all these songs down cold in under a couple of weeks, on an instrument I've never played. All with no guarantee that I'll get the gig.

I pester — I mean, hang out with — Charlie the keyboard player at every opportunity and I'm relentless in the job of selling myself. "You guys will never find a more motivated bass player." I come to their gigs every night. I'm a pit-bull on a pant leg.

A couple of weeks later, I audition again and get the gig. Truth be told, I think I've just worn them down with my persistence and they've come to realize there's no getting rid of me.

What a blast the next few months were. New group pictures, getting fitted for suits for our floor shows, daily rehearsals. The songs were great, we were sounding tight. Among other songs, I sang lead vocals on "The Way We Were," "Sister Golden Hair," "The Look of Love," "Lowdown" by Boz Skaggs, and "One of These Nights" by the Eagles. The band even backed me on one of my originals that I played on my acoustic guitar.

Each show had four sets, the third of which was our Vegas-style "floor show," complete with costumes and choreography. Our 50s show was nostalgic; our Disney tribute was a crowd-pleaser. Then there was our "Easy to Love America" — a patriotic salute to our country's bicentennial anniversary. A show that even your great-grandmother might have found a bit too cheesy. Despite my efforts to destroy them, pictures still exist of the four of us in matching red and white striped pants, white frilly shirts, adorable plastic derby hats, and a bowtie fashioned out of blue pipe-cleaners.

Our first road gig together was in Scott's Bluff, Nebraska. The band owned a huge cargo truck that had a sleeper section behind the seats in the cabin. We loaded up the equipment and with "Dance with Me" by Orleans blasting through the speakers, we were off. There's nothing like the feeling of heading off to make music with your buddies with just the open road ahead of you. Our manager had us booked solid: Clayton, New Mexico; Arcola, Illinois; a dozen cities in six months.

Then there's the girls.

Ask any musician who played in a popular band in the 20-year "free-love" era that was after the birth control pill but before a virus that could kill you: there was no shortage of adoring fans wanting to have their way with you. Not gonna lie, it was a fun period. No pretenses, no promises, no consequences — or so I thought. Shallow, party of one ... your table is ready.

JIM WILSON

When we weren't on the road, we lived at the Ramada Inn, where we performed to full houses six nights a week in the Red Lion lounge upstairs. My folks couldn't have been prouder. Dad said we were "as good as, if not better than the Beatles." I gently tried making the distinction that, for starters, they wrote their own material; we were just a cover band. He was having none of it. We were just weeks away from getting discovered, so prepare for the big time.

TUNED IN: MEMOIRS OF A PIANO MAN

Our band Easy (and no, the irony of the name wasn't lost on me) became a magnet for some colorful characters. One particular Amarillo fan, Perry, was a frequent guest and made friends with each member of the band. Night after night, he came in and stayed for all four sets. Quite the jetsetter, Perry had his own Lear Jet that he kept at Tradewinds, a private airport east of town. In spoon-fed increments, he made hints about his famous sibling.

It's a Wednesday night. The house is packed, we're just about to start our set. Perry comes in and sits at his usual booth just beside the stage. He's sporting a jersey that says "MANILOW" across the back. During the first break, we sit with him and he shares with us that he recently reunited with his long-lost brother. "I spent the weekend with Barry in LA and told him all about you guys. He'd love to hear you sometime." He's even brought us all autographed Barry Manilow albums from the man himself. Across the front of the album cover, mine says, *"TO JIM, LOVE, BARRY"*

Wow. We're now on Barry Manilow's radar. What's more, Perry is part owner of the Frontier Hotel in Vegas. "I can't get you on the stage in the main showroom, but we have a wonderful little club that we could start you out in. You'll do great there." The pay is going to be double our current rate. Things are really about to explode for us.

Each time he comes in, the deal in Vegas is getting closer to being locked in. He just has to clear it with his partners. We're ready to jump in the van and head to Vegas at a moment's notice.

Then Perry vanishes.

Later, we discovered that "Perry" had fabricated the whole thing. Well, not entirely. His actual sibling was indeed a celebrity of sorts. His real-life brother, Len, was a popular local weatherman. "Perry" suffered from schizophrenia and had been institutionalized, suffering from delusions of grandeur. Decades later, the real Barry would become a client, with whom I'd share this wild story.

Meanwhile, it turns out that Perry wasn't the only one with inner demons to wrestle with.

CHAPTER 8
The Abyss

It was an otherwise ordinary afternoon when I got the unexpected call. On the other end of the phone was the pretty redhead I'd been seeing since shortly after joining the band. She drew a slow breath before breaking her news. The test results had come back. She was going to become a mother, and I a father. I struggled for a response as I took on the weight of her words.

This would be a welcomed announcement in the right circumstances, but it was the last thing a free-wheeling, 19-year-old kid with dreams of moving to LA wanted to hear. Despite her reassurances that I needn't worry, that raising this child was something she wanted to do on her own, that she'd never vilify me (and true to her word, she never did, though she had every right to), it did little to un-freak me out. Though part of me accepted this new reality, a bigger part would remain in denial for years.

Sunset is descending on the snow-capped Sangre de Christo mountains in the distance. We've just rolled into the parking lot of the Desert Inn in Sante Fe, New Mexico, where our manager, Walt, has booked us for a week-long stint. We brace ourselves against the cold December air as we get out of the van.

After a five-hour drive from Amarillo, unloading the van, setting up our equipment, doing a quick soundcheck, I'm more than exhausted. I'm starting to develop a mild fever, but it's still manageable. I have just enough time to go to my room, change, and head to the stage. Showtime.

My implosion happens slowly at first. Like gradually increasing gusts of winds that steadily evolve into a tornado. One that ultimately rips through a midwestern town, leveling everything in its path. All the components for an impending disaster are in place: a head full of worries, a body succumbing to illness, the crappy nightclub with a stage hastily thrown into the corner of the room as an afterthought.

The enthusiastic audiences we're used to playing for are replaced by a sparse smattering of people who seem annoyed by our intrusion on their conversations. Our floor show is out of place. Wrong room, wrong crowd. What gets huge laughs with our adoring fans is greeted by the sound of crickets here.

My going to "bad fantasyland" over my impending fatherhood status — news I'm desperately struggling for a way to process — is compounded by the stress of now being saddled with a monthly mortgage payment for a house I've just purchased, further exacerbated by an increasingly brutal virus. My state of denial is like driving with the parking brake on. It's all leading to one of the worst nights of my life. With each passing song, the flu and my state of mind are getting worse. The room starts slowly rotating off axis.

We take a break. I go into another room and sit by myself, looking out a window, trying to get a grip. Next set comes; my downward spiral only gets worse. Feverish and light-headed, I begin hallucinating that everyone is looking at me with scorn and disdain. I can't even look my bandmates in the eyes. Bad tapes start playing in my head — *I'm a loser, I'm a fraud.*

The tapes play louder, the imagined judgmental sneers from the people in the audience become more disdainful. I'm certain there's no escape from this ever-increasing delirium. *The centre cannot hold.* It's more than a panic attack, it's some kind of mental breakdown. It's like a bad acid trip.

On stage, mid-song, in a cold sweat, I make a desperate decision. Lost in a labyrinth of all-consuming fears I conclude that the only way out of this is to end my life. As soon as this set is over, I'll return to my hotel room, I'll take a bunch of sleeping pills, run a bath, and somehow drown myself. I'll ram my head on the bottom of the tub, inhale deeply, filling my lungs with water. It will just be a short moment of discomfort, then I'll be free from this torment.

The set finally ends. I make a beeline back to my room. I set out the pills on the counter and fill the bathtub with water. I lie there on the bed, writhing in agony from the flu, imploding from the demons to whom I've handed over complete control of my mind — allowing them to grow into larger-than-life monsters.

I can't go forward, I can't go back, I can't stop coughing. Minutes pass by like hours as I lay immobilized in indecision.

Suddenly, the Living Love Center in Berkley, California comes to mind. A year earlier, I'd had a profound transformation after immersing myself in a month-long spiritual retreat/self-betterment resident program there, studying under author/teacher, Ken Keyes. It's the middle of the night but thankfully, someone answers. Better still, they're willing to take the time to talk to a stranger and know the right things to say.

"What's the worst that could happen?" this Good Samaritan keeps asking me, gently helping me unpeel the onion, layer by layer, demon by demon. Little by little, they walk me through each "horrible" scenario, helping me to realize that these menacing beasts are of my own making. The problem isn't reality, it's my unwillingness to simply be with it. The mind can be the most savage weapon of all.

In years to come, I'll understand the matter isn't my circumstances, it's how I choose to frame them. Just stop long enough to breathe, face each issue, and allow it to be whatever it is. What you can't confront has power over you.

After a sleepless night, dawn begins peeking through the window. A ray of light, a glimmer of hope. I'm drained from the interminable hell I'm emerging from, but I sense that I just might be alright. As I take my first proper breath in what seems like forever, I feel my shoulders drop and my insides begin to untangle.

The guys come and check on me. I hint at what kind of hell I've been through but let them believe the only issue is the flu. Charlie's great — he finds a doctor, sets up an appointment, takes me across town to get antibiotic shots. The other guys are also supportive, bringing me food. They play that night without me. I mend.

My enduring gift from that night was getting a better understanding of how easy it is to surrender all my power to monsters whipped up entirely by my imagination. As Mark Twain once said, "I have known a great many troubles in my life. Some of which actually happened."

While I was fortunate enough to walk back from the edge, I know not everyone is. I've known people who were not so lucky and got pulled into the vortex, choosing a permanent solution to a temporary problem — an unbearable loss for those left behind. I now have nothing but empathy for anyone fighting those demons, as well as a profound appreciation for the "bonus decades" I've been granted since I was able to avoid falling into the abyss.

In time, our band ran its course, and we parted ways amicably. I came away from that six-month run with great performing experience, but more importantly, a life-changing idea. Charlie had a sideline of tuning pianos, and one day I accompanied him on one of his jobs. He'd been doing it for years and made it look effortless.

As I watched him work, I got hit with a lightning bolt realization. He's a seasoned pro now, but he had to have started somewhere. Why couldn't I learn it as well? The more I thought about it, the more I saw how perfectly this path aligned with my goal of making music in Los Angeles. As much as anything, my last couple of years of traveling taught me I needed a fallback position. Life on the road is great, but you're never sure when the next bookings will come. What better "day gig" than tuning pianos? Most everyone in the music biz in LA was sure to have a piano, so this would put me in the right circles. I could be my own boss, make my own schedule. Whatever it took, I was going to learn this new skill.

Lit up with this new life direction, I found a listing of all the piano tuning schools in the U.S. Of the 17 letters I hand-wrote to each school on the list, all but three came back marked "Return to Sender." Was piano tuning becoming a dying art? It would ultimately come down to a little family-owned school back east.

CHAPTER 9
Tuning School

Cleveland, city of lights, city of magic.
"Burn On Big River" — Randy Newman's sardonic dig at this industrial town — may have seemed a bit harsh to some, but considering that the Cuyahoga River once got so polluted with petroleum chemicals that it actually caught fire, he may have had a point.

Turns out the piano tuning school most suited for my needs — and still in business — was in a gritty neighborhood, in this not-so-fair city on the shores of Lake Erie.

"What a drive you just had!" Bob Perkins is most welcoming as I walk into his "Perkins School of Piano Tuning and Technology" after my two-day drive from Amarillo. He's a wiry fellow with a handlebar mustache who looks right at home in this sea of old pianos. Pianos that his students learn their craft on, which Bob then offers for sale — a win-win arrangement.

A shrewd businessman, Bob had gotten a great deal on this three-story building at 99th and Lorraine. He has the tuning school in the basement, a piano store at ground level, and rooms on the second floor that he rents to students.

Bob leads me up the stairs to the room that will be my home for the next six months. Very little has changed from when this floor had been a dentist's office. The door to my room – a time warp portal into the 1930s – has a wobbly old doorknob and a frosted glass panel in the middle. Though someone's scratched off the letters, you can still make out where the dentist's name had been. Setting down my suitcase, I wonder how many root canals have been performed in the approximate area where I'll be resting my head. A dingy, small affair but at least it has a window, which offers a scenic view of the Kroger grocery store parking lot.

"Had an uncle from Texas. Died of cancer last month. Good

riddance." Charlie, the fellow student who'll live across the hall from me for the next six months, is making small talk the best he knows how. He's a tall, scraggly dude with long hair parted down the middle. He's a bit of an eccentric, but then again most of the 20 or so students in my class are paint-outside-the-lines characters – myself included.

There's Gary, the beer-drinkin' good ol' boy from Philly; Jim, the erudite professor-type from Spotsylvania, West Virginia (with whom I'd walk 20 miles of the Appalachian Trail one weekend); Stella, the brainiac piano player with nerdy glasses; Bruce, the lanky French-Canadian from Toronto; Fred, the guy with a crew cut and a plastic protector in the pocket of his short sleeve shirt who says stuff like "What can I do ya for?"; and Bob, the sweet but naïve blind kid from Idaho. All of us are drawn to a service gig that is on the periphery of the music world — a career where you're not tethered to a timeclock, nor chained to a desk.

There are countless millions of pianos in the U.S. – from the ancient uprights that've seen better days, to the magnificent $200k instruments on stages and studios. There's room in this profession for the guys doing a few tunings a week as a sideline, to the musicians who want to tune their own piano, to the highly-skilled piano techs catering to the most discriminating music makers. To me, it just seemed like a cool means of supporting myself while I was trying to make my mark in the music biz in LA.

I'd only signed up for the course that focused on piano tuning basics. But Bob also offered an auxiliary "Grand Piano Restoration" course where he would teach you to completely disassemble a piano, destring it, repair and refinish the soundboard, paint the gold plate, restring it, install new dampers and action parts. Though I'd come here with the sole intent of just learning basic piano tuning, I decided that I'm here anyway — why not take the extra course? Even if I never used these skills again, I'd at least have a better appreciation for the piano.

Bob spent one-on-one time with each of us, teaching the basics of tuning, starting with how to "set a temperament" — tuning each note within an octave in the middle of the piano, counting the beats that occur when two notes of an interval are played. This octave becomes the foundation for the rest of the tuning.

He went on to teach us every other aspect of maintaining and rebuilding this incredibly complex instrument. We learned that the actual playing mechanism of any piano is called an "action," which has several thousand moving parts that work in an ordered sequence.

He showed us how the action translates finger movement into sound: the player pushes down on the key — essentially a lever, which then pushes up on a second lever called a "wippen." This motion pushes up a third lever: a "shank", at the end of which is a felt mallet called a "hammer." The hammer strikes the string, causing it to vibrate at a specified frequency. Bob taught us the painstaking procedure of how to "regulate" an action, making over 30 adjustments for each 88 keys. The goal is to optimize an action's performance, making it feel more responsive to the player.

He then taught us the incredibly involved art of "voicing" which refers to the meticulous craft of improving the piano's tone, using a variety of tools. The technician "needles," reshapes and works with the hammers to make the tone brighter or warmer according to an artist's preference. This aspect of piano care – more than any other – is where the artistry comes in. It takes years, if not decades to excel in this field, learning how to make an instrument not just speak, but sing with a warm, rich tone and a wide dynamic range.

Bob encouraged us to further our piano tech skills through seminars offered by the Piano Technician's Guild – of which I'd soon become one of their youngest "Craftsmen" members.

I used this six-month period as a time of self-improvement. In addition to practicing tuning three to five hours daily, I took piano lessons with a teacher across town. I spent several hours a day working on becoming a better musician — practicing piano scales, doing vocal exercises. Free time on the weekends was usually spent dating Bob's beautiful Italian daughter, Jody, who remains a friend to this day.

I left Cleveland armed with the skills that would not only support me in Los Angeles but lead me to opportunities I never imagined — ultimately connecting me to some of the most significant artists of our time.

It's the fall of 1977. Still intimidated by the idea of moving to LA, I return to Amarillo, deciding it's a safe place to hone my piano technician skills.

TUNED IN: MEMOIRS OF A PIANO MAN

Art Nizzi, whose Nizzi's Music Store is the regional center for music teachers and students, is incredibly supportive of my new venture. He gives me a list of piano teachers in the area and in no time, I'm inundated with tunings for teachers and their students in small towns around the Panhandle: Borger, Fritch, Pampa, Dumas, Claude, Clarendon. At 25 bucks a pop, I'm rolling in dough.

I catch wind that Van Cliburn is coming to town and go to the Amarillo Symphony office to purchase tickets. Everyone has gone to lunch except for the manager, who apologizes for not knowing where anything is. "You're in luck. We have a few tickets left for Mr. Cliburn's concert," he says. I tell him I'm a fan of Van's work, especially so because my life revolves around the piano — not just as a budding pianist, but also as a piano technician.

"You're a piano tuner? Our tuner just moved and we're looking for one. I know it's incredibly short notice, but might you be available tomorrow?"

We make arrangements for me to tune the symphony's 9-foot Steinway for a rehearsal the following day. The conductor likes my work, and they hire me to tune for the remainder of their season's upcoming concerts. I've graduated from tuning school just two weeks before and I'm now the official piano technician for the Amarillo Symphony. Crazy.

In the months ahead, I would avail myself of the free tickets and *carte blanche* I'm given and am enthralled by the Symphony's performances of Debussy, Liszt, Mozart, Brahms, and Vivaldi. I experience concerts from every possible vantage point: the balcony, the front row, the wings, backstage, even beneath the stage.

Van Cliburn's concert is now just a few days away. He asks to meet with me to discuss the voicing of the piano. His manager introduces me, I shake Van's hand — apparently, a bit too vigorously. His manager's eyes grow wide, he takes a sharp breath. "Careful! *Please!*"

Van tells me he likes the piano but finds the tone "a bit too dark. Can you please make it a bit brighter for me?"

"Absolutely." I pray I can deliver on my promise with this $80,000 instrument. Once they leave, I remove the action, do a light filing of the hammers which is fortunately just enough to satisfy Van's desire to make the piano "speak" a bit more clearly. In years to come, I would develop the mastery and confidence to deliver any type of requested tone, but for now I was lucky that I could solve the problem with just low-hanging fruit.

The day of the concert comes. Piano's tuned, crowd's in place. Van is about to perform Beethoven's famous Piano Concerto No. 5: "The Emperor." He walks on stage and the fans shower him with applause. He stands beside the piano, smiling, bowing. He assumes his seat on the bench and the crowd quickly falls silent. He takes a slow breath, nods to the conductor, who raises his baton. My heart races as I anticipate hearing his first few notes — this is my first time working for a piano master and the work I've done is an integral part of the sonic delights we're all in for.

Van performs the epic concerto flawlessly. The evening flies by. We give him an enthusiastic standing ovation. He treats us to several encores. Magic.

Afterwards, he's very appreciative of my efforts and writes an incredible endorsement for me:

To Jim Wilson — with my sincere appreciation for your work on the piano and for your faithful attention to the details of the voicing. Many thanks — all the best of wishes. Sincerely, Van Cliburn.

I wasted no time in having his words turned into a printed promotional piece. I knew it was those kinds of endorsements I'd need when I headed to LA. But another road trip was in my more immediate future.

CHAPTER 10
Loose Change

"Hey, I think you missed the exit!" My little brother Paul cranes his head as the sign speeds by.

It's the late autumn of '78. I've decided to pay a long overdue visit to my son Jason, now almost three, living with his mom, Jeneanne, in Oklahoma City. I'm more than a little distracted. My palms are a bit sweaty as I grip the steering wheel, taking the next offramp.

In the cupholder sits a jar of coins I've been collecting for Jason since the year of his birth — 1976. Outside the maternity ward at Northwest Texas Hospital in Amarillo, I'd made a pest of myself taking up a collection of Bicentennial quarters, figuring they'd be worth something one day. This will be the first time to see Jason since he was just a few months old. I'm still trying to wrap my head around the fact that I'm a father.

When I invited Paul to join me on a four-hour road trip, he jumped at the chance. I'm relieved he's here — I'm not sure when we'll get to spend this kind of hang time together again. LA is calling and my days in Amarillo are numbered. But if I'm honest, as much as anything, I want his emotional support.

In our broken home setting, I often felt more like mentor to him than big brother. He'd always looked up to me — watching films I watched, listening to music I liked. We were always close, but when he took up drums it felt like we had a secret language in common. We were buddies and knew how to make each other laugh. I felt the responsibility of being his role model, but I enjoyed it.

"We should be just a few blocks away now." Paul glances up from the map, then at me. He takes a beat, picking up that I'm a little on edge. "You okay?"

I look at Paul. Now 14, he even kind of resembles me with similar brown eyes and hair. I see so much of myself in him, but the nine years in age difference between us sometimes feels cavernous.

"Yeah. All good, man." I can't even drop my façade with my brother — the one person who knows me better than anyone.

Paul clocks a Dairy Queen coming up on our right. "Hey… if you want, you can just drop me off there and meet with him by yourself."

"Are you sure?"

"Totally. I have my Walkman, got my tunes. I'm all set."

I give Paul some money for lunch and head out. I feel shitty leaving him alone, but no less shitty than how I feel about the ambivalence buried in my gut. I have no reason to doubt Jeneanne's word, but the bullshit head game I let myself play — hanging on to a sliver of doubt about my paternity — allows me to kick the *be-a-responsible-adult* can down the road a bit further.

I find the street, park the van, take a deep breath. Stepping onto the sidewalk, I scan the suburbia around me. I second-guess what a normal walking pace should be, all the way up to the house — the house with a lime green plastic bat, a canary yellow Super Soaker, and three red wiffle balls strewn in the grass.

A little boy with sandy brown hair sits on the curb. He's dragging a broken piece of pale blue sidewalk chalk in a slow wide loop, until he sees me. I stop walking. And breathing.

He looks up and squints, chalk still poised on the sidewalk. "Are you my dad?"

A cannonball to my gut, all the air gone from my body. *I am.*

Jason stands, I lean down, I give him a hug. I turn, not quite in time to hide the tears forming in my eyes.

It's funny the things you remember and the things you don't.

I don't remember how it went.

I remember Church's chicken for lunch.

I remember Jeneanne and Jason across the table.

I don't remember the conversation I assume was amicable while I tried to cover up how awkward I felt.

I remember saying goodbyes. I don't remember the goodbyes we said.

I remember picking up Paul for the return trip to Amarillo.

TUNED IN: MEMOIRS OF A PIANO MAN

Paul hops in, fastens his seat belt. "So how'd it go?"

I remember giving him the headlines. I don't remember the headlines. I don't tell him about the heaviness inside.

I notice Paul tapping his foot to the song on the radio while staring out the window. I've been so wrapped up in my anxiety that I've hardly asked him a thing about his world. "So... tell me what's up with you. What's the latest?"

He tells me his headlines – new school, new friends, books he's reading. He doesn't tell me about any deeper feelings he might be wrestling with. Guess he had a good role model for that.

I sense he's changing. I changed too when I was his age, but his change feels ... heavier. He's always been a sweet, innocent kid. Now he seems a little more emotionally awkward, introspective. He fidgets and avoids eye contact. I chalk it up to adolescence.

With the Oklahoma City skyline receding in my rearview mirror, and the flat, endless landscape of open plains before us, I hit the gas. I look down to find the root of the jangling coming from my coffee cup holder.

Dammit.

The quarters. Close to a couple hundred of those fuckers. Each one from 1976, clanking against each other in competition with the song on the radio as we barrel west on I-40.

I reflect on all I've missed. First words, first steps, first laughs. I resolve then and there to play a bigger part in Jason's life. I resolve to make up for lost time.

It will be years before I live up to that resolution.

—

Later that evening, I decided to go check out this duo I'd been hearing about. It was an otherwise normal Amarillo weeknight, but it was a night that would lead to a life-changing opportunity. I was blown away by Woody Key and Mark Hinton – both exceptional musicians, and their vocal harmonies were spot-on. Between their reputation and incredible talent, I was a little intimidated. During a break, I worked up the nerve to introduce myself to Mark. "Killer harmonies, man!" He was appreciative, we struck up a conversation.

Turned out Mark, another Amarillo boy, was just home for the holidays. He'd been living in Los Angeles, pitching songs for Glen Campbell's publishing company. I told him I was a songwriter, hoping to move to LA soon. The following week, we got together and shared some songs. He was impressed with my writing. "I think you're just a few months away from being a hit-songwriter." It was a carrot he dangled in front of me for years – one that never seemed to get any closer.

A couple of months later, he called from LA. He was getting divorced and was going to get an apartment in North Hollywood. Did I want to come out and split the rent with him?

This was my chance. Opportunity wasn't just calling, it had kicked down the door and was grabbing me by the collar. I'd been dreaming about moving to Los Angeles for years. I'd scraped together *just* enough savings to pull this off and I was now fresh out of excuses.

I wrapped up loose ends, said my goodbyes. I loaded my Ford Econoline van floor-to-ceiling with everything I owned: boxes of clothes, several pieces of furniture, a P.A. system, my acoustic bass "Frieda", my tuning tools, and stereo speakers stacked on the passenger seat. Every square inch was filled except for a space on top of my spinet piano, where I'd put a foam pad for sleeping.

I jumped on a westbound entrance of I-40 — the very freeway I'd played under as a kid. I pointed my wheels in the direction of LA, the Land of Oz, and never looked back.

Not that I didn't want to, I just couldn't see out the damn windows.

PART II
Tuning Up

"Tip the world over on its side and everything loose will land in Los Angeles."
— Frank Lloyd Wright

CHAPTER 11
Emerald City

After a two-day drive from Texas, I'm stiff, weary and in need of a shower. But as my van pops over a hill on the west-bound 210 freeway in Pasadena this Monday night in January 1979, my first impression of Los Angeles makes my jaw drop.

Before me lies an endless, rolling carpet of twinkling lights that stretches out towards the mirage of the LA downtown skyline in the distance. I roll down my window and the air is a thick, intoxicating blend of Southern California fragrances: night blooming jasmine, citrus blossoms, pittosporum trees in full bloom. Jackson Browne's *Running on Empty* is blasting through the car speakers.

I feel a rush of excitement as reality hits me — this is your new home, among the millions of people in that sprawling, glimmering horizon. Small town boy, meet big city. I'm eager to put my heart and soul into fulfilling my dreams.

It's about 6 p.m. when I roll into the dirt parking place of the humble North Hollywood apartment at 11865 Magnolia Boulevard that my new friend has chosen for us. Mark — whose long hair, mustache, and skinny frame gives him an uncanny resemblance to magician Doug Henning -- greets me and helps me bring in the most valuable items.

It's a one-bedroom apartment, so we flip a coin to see who'll get the bedroom. I come up on the wrong side of the coin toss and am relegated to sleeping in a bed roll on a foam pad on the floor of the living room. All good. I'm so happy to be here, I'll sleep on a bed of nails for all I care.

"There's this great band you gotta hear." Mark sets down his gin and tonic. "They're a bunch of top studio musicians who play just for the fun of it called Just for Grins. They're performing tonight at a bar called Jason's in Burbank. You wanna go?"

Here's that Power of One thing again: one person, one event, one moment in time that has the power to shape your destiny. This night will prove to be one of those turning points. Much of the success I'll come to enjoy in LA will come from seeds planted within hours of my arriving in LA.

I laugh to myself as we walk towards the bar. Here I am in January without a coat while the town I just left was covered in snow. We stroll into the bar, the band is doing a killer rendition of "What You Won't Do for Love," by Bobby Caldwell. Mark is right. These guys are phenomenal. Tony McShear on vocals, Don Heffington on drums, Chris Boardman on keyboards, Dan Sawyer on guitars, Doug Livingston on steel guitar and keyboards, Scott Page on sax. Every one of these guys is a heavy hitter, recording or touring with the top acts of the day: Seals and Crofts, Supertramp, Lone Justice.

Mark introduces them to me all one by one. Each of them has a piano they want me to tune, each will become my friend and champion, raving about the quality of my work. A few weeks later, I come to another of their performances and Tony announces, *"Ladies and gentlemen, visiting us tonight is the best piano tuner this side of the Mississippi. Give it up for... Jim Wilson!"*

In months to come, recommendations from these guys will lead to a steadily-growing clientele, including several LA recording studios — all tracing back to that first night that we met.

They also made an impression on me with just their way of being. They were all ridiculously talented but didn't feel a gnawing need to prove it to anyone. Their laid-back, self-assured demeanor proved that talent speaks for itself. If there was an LA attitude, they exemplified it.

As it happened, Tony lived just a few doors down from Mark and me. "Peruvian dancing powder" turbocharged many a late evening — I'd thankfully learned "moderation" by now — with the three of us discussing music, picking apart songs, shooting the shit. On more than one occasion, as we were winding down, the sun was coming up.

I played Tony a few songs and he did me the favor of providing useful, truthful feedback. "The chorus is strong, but your verses need work." Then he'd give examples of how something could be better. His tough love wasn't always easy to hear, but he was always right. He set the bar high for me.

Tony made distinctions between a good idea and a great idea. "It's like holding up a diamond to the light and you keep turning it slowly, trying to find just the right angle. When you do, the light makes the diamond sparkle gloriously." I came to learn that the difference between average and stunning can be just the slightest twist.

One day Tony says, "If you're around tomorrow afternoon, swing by. My friend Cyndi Wood is coming over to hear some songs and if you want, I'll introduce you." Cyndi had been a Playmate of the Year and appeared on the cover of Playboy six times: more than any Playmate at the time. I'd also heard she was in the movie *Shampoo* and had a scene in a new film soon to be released, *Apocalypse Now*. I was well familiar with her world-class beauty. Would I like to meet her? Uh, yeah.

I knock on the door at the appointed time. Tony lets me in, I feign surprise when I see her. "Oh, I'm sorry. I didn't know you had company."

Tony plays along. "No problem. Jim, this is Cyndi. Cyndi, this is Jim." She has a petite figure, Natalie Wood eyes, and perfect skin. She's dressed down, but she's still stunning.

"Nice to meet you," I manage to spit out, despite my jittery nerves. We all chitchat for a bit. She's very sweet, asks what I do. I tell her I'm a songwriter and she lights up. "Cool! I'd love to hear your songs sometime." She smiles. I feel my face flush as she gives me her number.

In a couple of days, I finally muster the nerve to call her. "You wanna come over and hear some tunes?"

The next day, there's a knock on my door. My heart races as I let her in. She's one of the prettiest, sexiest women I've ever seen and she's coming to visit me in this modest little apartment with a cottage cheese ceiling and green shag carpet. We make small talk and soon find our way to the piano. She sits down beside me on the bench, I sing some songs for her. She scoots a little closer but I'm too nervous to make the first move. I begin another song, my voice cracks and we both laugh. It's just the crack in the ice I need. I take a breath, go in for the kiss.

Our romance underway, I soon hang a rope across the living room and drape sheets over it to make our own little hideout. The more I get to know her, the more I'm drawn in by her resourcefulness and creativity. She has a combination of worldliness and a childlike innocence that I find alluring. What were the odds of me — a Texas boy straight off the turnip truck — moving to a town of 8 million people and within three weeks start dating the girl of my dreams? I felt like I'd won the lottery. Looking back, maybe my unjaded naïveté was the very thing that drew her to me.

"Well done! Wanna come in and have a listen?"

I release the talk-back button and give Cyndi a thumbs up through the window. We're in the studio and I'm producing a few demos for her. Besides being a talented actress, I discover she's an accomplished singer. She's just done a vocal on a track on which I've played piano and guitar and she nails it on the very first take.

Later, during a break, Cyndi makes a phone call and returns to the control room with some fun news.

"My dear friend Jeane is in town recording at Wally Heider Studios. She said she'd love to meet you and just invited us to come sit in on her session."

We finish up and head to Hollywood. On the way, Cyndi fills me in on Jeane Manson – just one of the many interesting, artistic friends Cyndi seems to be a magnet for.

"Jeane's also from LA and has been a Playmate. In France, she's a *huge* recording artist with a ton of gold records."

Apparently, Jeane had been on vacation in Paris as a teen when she accompanied a friend to a talent contest. Jeane entered the competition as a lark, but it became a steppingstone that ultimately led to her getting a record deal. In the years that followed, Jeane would become a household name in France.

Wally Heider Studios on Sunset Boulevard is legendary. As we're walking down the hallowed halls, I think of all the epic artists who've walked these same steps: Jefferson Airplane, The Eagles, Crosby, Stills & Nash. I'm in awe.

"Right this way." The studio receptionist opens the door to the control room for Cyndi and me. Renowned producer Milt Okun is at the helm behind the recording console and Jeane's old boyfriend, actor and bon vivant, Bill Jordan is to Milt's left. Through the glass window, we see Jeane behind the microphone, in the throes of singing a passionate take. A classic blonde-haired California beauty, I'm struck by her hazel blue eyes. We sneak in the control room and stand at the back, trying to not draw attention. Nonetheless, Jeane spots us and stops her take.

TUNED IN: MEMOIRS OF A PIANO MAN

"Cyndi! Is that you!" She removes her headphones, runs into the control room, and throws her arms around Cyndi.

"Jeane, this is my boyfriend Jim I told you about."

Jeane has a warm, radiant smile that lights up the room. She introduces me to Milt, then Bill, who looks familiar to me. It takes a second to put it together that I'd seen him starring as Buddy's manager in *The Buddy Holly Story*. I even remember his face from when I was a kid, watching my favorite TV show, *Flipper*, on which he was a series regular.

Bill has dashing, movie-star good looks and a larger-than-life presence. He has a charming smile and huge, deep laugh — he's the embodiment of charisma. He's a well-known actor but has no ego and treats me like an equal. With his massive paw, he shakes my hand, looks directly into me and I feel *received*. I've never met anyone like him.

We all chat for a bit before Jeane heads back to the studio to go for another pass at the song. Milt gives her a suggestion on phrasing and says, "OK… we're rolling." Jeane is a pro and I'm fascinated with how effortlessly she delivers a flawless take. Before we part, Jeane insists that we all get together again before she returns to France.

A few nights later, Cyndi and I join Bill and Jeane and a couple of Jeane's friends for dinner at a swank restaurant in Beverly Hills. As the wine flows, the conversations turns more lively. They all have an ease about them that draws me in. They're all making a living in the arts — accomplished people who seem to effortlessly manifest their dreams. I'm enamored, though a bit envious.

But there's no affectation about them and they're genuinely interested in me, asking about my aspirations. I measure my words, trying not to put on airs. "I'm a songwriter," I tell them, though I don't yet feel I've earned the right to own that proclamation. Part of me feels like an unsophisticated hick from the dusty plains who has bluffed his way into this hip scene of fascinating people, but they all seem to like me anyway. The tab for this casual outing burns through my meal budget for a month. But it was a small price to pay for friendships that began with Bill's firm handshake and Jeane's warm hug that afternoon in a Hollywood recording studio — friendships that influenced me profoundly and have weathered the test of time.

CHAPTER 12
On the Eve of the 80s

There's a long line of cars ahead of us on Charing Cross Road, all waiting to get into the Holmby Hills party. It's New Year's Eve and Cyndi and I are wearing the required attire: me in my pajamas, silk bathrobe, and slippers, she in her skimpy nightie. We finally make it to the entrance gate. There's a security guard holding a clipboard, checking off names. Cyndi rolls down the window, he looks inside. He doesn't bother checking the list and waves her through.

We round a corner and before me is the massive, gothic Tudor stone castle I've fantasized about since I was a kid. It's the iconic Playboy Mansion and it's lit up like a palace in a fairy tale.

We park and walk down the flagstone-lined drive, past the colorfully illuminated fountain surrounded by fragrant flowers. Entering through the massive, wooden arched door, I catch my breath as I take in the scene: twenty-foot beamed ceilings, marble floors, sweeping imperial staircases – we've stepped into King Arthur's castle. Loud dance music fills the air, everyone's in pajamas and sheer negligees. Many women are just in bras and panties. The place is jumpin', as is my pulse. This is the famous, end-of-the-year exclusive extravaganza to which Hugh Hefner has invited Cyndi, along with dozens of other Playmates and A-list celebrities.

Around the corner comes a famous face. Damn if it isn't the man himself — Hef. "Hi Cyndi! Welcome!" Cyndi introduces me, I shake his hand.

"Quite the shindig! Thanks for having us," I say, as if he'd invited "us."

A server walks by with a tray full of champagne glasses, followed by someone with a tray of hors d'oeuvres. We help ourselves to both. We follow the music to the dance floor to an undulating sea of people lost in rapture. Cyndi and I join them for a couple of dances, then she says,

"I'll go get us a table, enjoy yourself!"

The song ends. A couple near us stops dancing, and the guy walks away. The girl left standing there is Hef's former girlfriend, Playmate Barbi Benton. As the music starts up again, she looks at me and smiles. Maybe it's the champagne talking, but I smile back, shrug and say, "Shall we?"

"Sure!" She's in a festive, carefree mood as we dance to an up-tempo party song. I take her hand and spin her around. I'm trying not to think too much about the surreal nature of it all. Song ends, I thank Barbi for the dance and head off looking for Cyndi.

Wandering through the festive revelers, I recognize a dozen famous faces, all exuding an alluring air of nonchalance. I overhear folks deep in conversations about movies, cigar-smoking big wigs making deals, an ingenue laughing over someone's risqué joke. I feel like I'm on a movie set. This exclusive party is the hottest ticket in town — the place where people go to see and be seen. But I'm a bit awestruck and all I want to do is hide and watch.

"Over here!" Cyndi signals to me from across the room. I join her in the buffet line, we load up our plates with gourmet delicacies, and head to our table. There's a huge outdoor carnival tent they've set up on the back lawn, inside which are a dozen or so big, round tables. Cyndi's reserved a couple of places at one of them for us. We set down our plates, take our seats. I turn to the guy sitting to my left. It's Alice Cooper. Woah. He introduces himself, we make small talk. I tell him I've been a big fan since day one and played *Killer* until the vinyl wore out. I'm a little intimidated but avoid making a complete fool out of myself — though perhaps he might have told you differently.

As Cyndi and I are wrapping up dessert, I ask her to tell me about the "grotto." She finishes her last bite of chocolate mousse and playfully points her spoon in my direction. "Better yet, how 'bout I just show you?" She smiles, takes my hand, and leads me on a tour of the grounds. Familiar turf for her, but it's my first time here and I'm captivated by it all. Walking down the tiki torch-lined path that winds through the manicured grounds, we pass the koi pond on the right and monkey cages on the left. Ahead are flamingos and peacocks roaming around the estate.

Following the sounds of splashing and laughter, we come upon the stone-lined pool. A woman takes a running cannonball leap, drenching her three girlfriends. There's not a single bathing suit among them.

Then, just behind the waterfall, there it is — the famous grotto. Illuminated by dozens of candles, this shallow pool in a secluded cave looks like something out of a mountain paradise. Through the flowing water we see a couple that are getting acquainted, very. Chuckling to ourselves, Cyndi and I raise our glasses to them. We continue our amble, making our way back inside the mansion.

As she begins chatting with an old friend, I venture off in search of a bathroom, helping myself to a private tour while I'm at it. I wander into the kitchen, grab an eclair, and take a bite. The staff spots me. I smile and give a thumbs up, nodding as if I'm the Chief Eclair Inspector. I make my way through the screening room, trying not to gawk at still more celebrities and Playmates: Monique St. Pierre in a spirited conversation with Candy Loving, Warren Beatty clinking a toast with Jack Nicholson, and damn, is that Dorothy Stratten talking with James Caan over there? Crazy.

I rejoin Cyndi just in time for the big countdown.

Three! ... Two! ... One! ... HAPPY NEW YEAR! Fireworks illuminate the sky, everyone's kissing everyone to the strains of "Auld Lang Syne."

1980 has arrived. The champagne-buzz; a new decade on the horizon, in a town where dreams come true daily — it's a heady mix and I'm feeling like anything's possible. On the threshold of the 80s, I have a heart full of hope.

But looking back, I may have also had a head in the clouds. I was becoming dazzled by the glitz and glamour of a show-biz town. The smoke and mirrors of Hollywood can be an addictive drug.

CHAPTER 13
City of Dreams

"I love Los Angeles. It's a city that's held together by dreams."
— Ben Kingsley

Ben really nailed it with this summation of our town, bound together in suspended animation by our collective aspirations. I am one of the hundreds of thousands of people who came here driven by a dream to succeed in music or film. Many find a nice place in the sun, a smaller number punch through to the very top.

Most never quite find a footing and return home to Des Moines, Paducah, Buffalo, or any of the hundreds of cities or countries they came from. On their way out of town, they'll pass a dozen more people arriving to take their place in their pursuit of fame and fortune. The constant ebb and flow of dreamers creates a dynamic tapestry of humanity.

Some end up as a vital part of the infrastructure that "stokes the star-maker machinery" — the influx of people pursuing their acting ambitions creates the endless need for drama schools, costume houses, production companies, and food trucks, just to name a few of the hundreds of support businesses.

Shoring up those who are aspiring to make it in the music world are countless businesses and occupations including recording studios, voice teachers, music schools, guitar stores, and well, piano tuners.

A true melting pot, all nationalities, races, and religions are represented here in LA. In my high school class of 700 people, there was one African American guy. Within a few short months of arriving in California, I interacted with people who'd come from all corners of the globe — Iran, Korea, Ecuador, Spain, the Philippines and France, to name a few. I'd ultimately exchange ideas with Hindus, atheists, and people of Jewish, Muslim and Buddhist faiths. As part of my everyday life, I now interacted with people from many different cultures, and started seeing that other people had arrived at their points of view with the same level of conviction as I had. Looking back, I understand now that it's harder to "otherize" people when you've had personal experience with them.

Running atop the Santa Monica Mountains is Mulholland Drive, a winding road with sweeping views of hundreds of square miles of LA and the Pacific Ocean to the south and the San Fernando Valley to the north. I had a favorite spot that overlooked the countless twinkling lights below, lit up like a sparkling jewelry box. Whenever I got discouraged, I'd head there to revisit my dreams. There are thousands of people down there with aspirations just like me. Many are making them come true. Why couldn't I be one of them?

By a twist of fate, I connected with a piano tuner who was leaving LA. We worked out a deal for me to take over his major accounts: the Bonaventure Hotel downtown, Monkees producer Michael Lloyd, the famous Roxy nightclub on Sunset, the infamous Sunset Marquis (the hotel of choice for visiting rock stars), a few recording studios, and Tony Roma's — a popular rib joint with three LA-area locations, all of which offered live entertainment.

After a few months, I became friendly with the manager of the Tony Roma's Beverly Hills location. I told him I was an entertainer and he was amenable to giving me a shot at performing there. It seemed like a perfect low-pressure gig where I wouldn't be the center of attention.

Nonetheless, nerves got the better of me leading up to my first gig. The entertainers that did best there were showy performers who did Broadway-type songs. In other words, not me. But I was determined to fit a square peg into a round hole and worked up some "up-tempo" songs on piano — which for me at the time, meant anything faster than a funeral dirge. And though they only employed piano players, I supplemented my song list with a few upbeat guitar songs.

It's a balmy Tuesday night. I park my car and walk the two blocks to Tony Roma's. I pause outside, take a deep breath, push open the front door. With guitar in hand, eyes squinting to adjust to the dimly lit room,

TUNED IN: MEMOIRS OF A PIANO MAN

I make my way toward the piano. I fumble through dozens of people engaged in conversation while devouring ribs and onion rings.

"Pardon me! ... Sorry! ... Comin' through!" I already feel like an intruder.

I finish setting up, do a quick mic check, nervously fiddle with some knobs on the PA. I know that to grab their attention — or even be heard at all above the din of yakking and laughter — I'll have to pull out the sharpest arrow from my quiver. I steady myself and launch into "Never Be the Same" by Christopher Cross. I muster every bit of passion I possess. I play the final note with gusto. I anticipate the roaring ovation that is sure to follow.

Instead, I hear the continued cacophony of the crowd. Then after couple of seconds, I finally hear one appreciative person in the corner:

Clap... clap ... clap...

"Thank you!" I muster a grateful but humble smile.

Turning to acknowledge them, I see that the sound I'm hearing is someone slapping the bottom of a ketchup bottle.

Ouch.

In their defense, Tony Roma's ribs and onion rings are very, *very* tasty.

The gig is from 9 p.m. to 1 a.m. Just a mere 3 hours and 55 minutes to go. Sweet. I do eventually end up earning some appreciative fans, but it's brutal. I perform a few more nights there before surrendering to the obvious: that type of gig is for an entertainer with a command of party songs — not the first words you'd use to describe me.

Not having properly learned my lesson, I soon do a similar gig at the swank Hotel Bel-Air. This time, I'm performing even more pensive original compositions than before. I finally get the memo that I'm a fish out of water when a lady in a fur coat walks up, put a $20 bill in the tip jar and says, "Can you play something from *Cats*?"

I am, however, a bit better prepared when Cyndi recommends me for an interesting gig. A new nightclub named Chippendales is all the rage. The first of its kind, the club features male strippers catering to their all-female audience. Hundreds of women crowd into the standing-room only frenzy. Before the strippers come out, an entertainer warms up the audience, playing guitar and singing songs. Their regular entertainer needs a couple of nights off and Cyndi insists to the manager that she has "just the guy" to fill in.

Right. The dude with the setlist laden with mellow ballads, is *just the guy*. But Cyndi's really stuck her neck out for me, so this time I work up a few raunchy Bad Company and Foreigner songs on guitar. I'm on it.

The day before the gig, Cyndi says, "By the way, you can wear jeans, but you have to perform shirtless, with just a collar and bow tie."

Now she tells me.

I figure *what the hell?* Sometimes sacrifices have to be made for one's art. I take a white dress shirt, cut away everything but the collar and show up to the gig in the required attire. Feeling the air against my bare skin as I approach the stage just feels wrong. I feel at any second, I'm going to get busted for indecent exposure.

I make my way through the crowd of tipsy, amorous women, plug in my guitar, and lay into "Hot Blooded" by Foreigner. The audience goes wild. But in fairness, I could do a somber reading of *War and Peace* and they'd go nuts. It's girls night out, the liquor is flowing and they're ready to see some strippers, dammit!

I rip into another Foreigner song, "Can't Get Enough of Your Love," and a couple of inebriated women dance towards me, waving five-dollar bills over their heads. Stuffing them into my belt, they take the liberty of running their hands up and down my legs, rubbing against me, kissing my arms, and tussling my hair. I'm loving the attention but beginning to wonder just how far this is going to go. My face is turning red and I'm getting flustered, but who am I to stop them? I somehow keep my focus, make it through my 45-minute set. I take a bow and thank the impassioned, appreciative audience. I stick around for a bit to watch the women devour the male strippers.

Though my performing career wasn't exactly taking off — unless you count clothing — my tuning business soon would be.

CHAPTER 14
Biz Takes Off

Even with the new accounts I'd taken over from that tuner and the referrals from the Just for Grins guys, my funds were starting to run thin. My intention when I first came to Los Angeles had been to do the minimum of tuning work so I could focus on songwriting, but I'd underestimated how much I'd need to get by. Living in LA ain't cheap.

It's a hot LA afternoon in the summer of 1980. I've driven across town to take a piano lesson from a new client with whom I'd worked out a deal to trade tunings for lessons. He lives in Eagle Rock, a good 30 minutes from home. I'm on my way back, and I realize a bit too late that I'm really cutting it close on fuel. My van sputters, I'm running out of gas.

A gas station comes into view on my right. I coast to a stop 10 feet from a gas pump. I catch the attention of someone in their car, they look away. I push my van the rest of the way by myself. I check my wallet. Empty. I check the glove box for emergency reserves — nothing. Dammit. I scrounge through the cup holders and between the seat folds and excavate $2.85 in loose coins — just enough to get me home. Pissed at myself for having been so flippant about something so essential, I resolve this will never happen again.

This close call is a turning point. It sears into my brain that the first order of business in LA is survival. This can be an unforgiving town that devours those with no safety net. The "starving artist life" is a romantic idea but living hand to mouth isn't for me. I get out the yellow pages — a historic relic now, make lists of all the studios and churches in LA and launch my assault. I mail them all promotional flyers, follow them up with phone calls.

"James H. Wilson," the flyer reads in big bold letters at the top of the page. I guess I thought using my legal name would make me sound more ... impressive? Just below that it says, *"The word is spreading!"* The flyer — which well exceeds the legal limit of exclamation marks — has grandiose copy and quotes from Van Cliburn and a few other clients. As Mark Twain would have put it, I was born modest, but it wore off.

Between that push and the continued recommendations from my Just for Grins buddies, I'm soon inundated with work. I'm still writing songs but the idea of being able to not just survive, but enjoy a nicer lifestyle entices me to hit the snooze button for a minute on my artistic aspirations.

Mike Garson, the guy with whom I'm trading tunings for lessons, happens to be a renowned pianist, touring the world with David Bowie. Mike becomes my champion. He's good friends with Chick Corea, a jazz-piano icon who in his lifetime will garner a mind-blowing 71 Grammy nominations, winning 27. In Mike's endearing Bronx accent, he raves about me to Chick: "You gotta give this guy Jim Wilson a shot. He's a fantastic *tunah*." My first tuning appointment with Chick is set, and soon, I'm rolling up to the "Love Castle", as I'll soon find he and wife Gayle Moran call it, a stately stone mansion in Los Feliz.

I walk up to his doorstep and pause for a second. I draw a breath to release some of my anxiety. I'm about to meet a legend. I knock on the massive wooden door, which Chick himself answers. He welcomes me inside and leads me to the cavernous music room. It has huge, vaulted ceilings with more than enough real estate for his two concert grands.

"Mike tells me great things about your work." Chick's mild Boston accent and short, curly Chico Marx hair and facial features make for an interesting mix. He's professional and direct but welcoming enough to ease my nerves.

I tell him I appreciate Mike's kind words, it's an honor to meet him, and I appreciate the opportunity to tune for him. He leaves me to my work.

A few hours later, Chick returns to check out my efforts. As he plays, gorgeous music fills the room. I'm in the presence of a master.

He listens intently to the tuning. He looks up at me occasionally and nods. "Nice!" The more he plays, the more enthusiastic he becomes. "Yeah, man!" After 10 minutes or so, he stands up and says, "I'd like you to take care of all my pianos!"

His house is bursting at the seams with pianos of all shapes and sizes: the two 9-foot concert grands in the music room, a Conover "giraffe piano" in the next room, a couple of pianos upstairs, a console piano in the pool room. There's even a couple more concert grands at his new recording studio, Mad Hatter — nine instruments in all. Having a piano legend as a client gives me some serious street cred and shoots my business to the next level. He soon begins raving about me to his friends and colleagues.

Chick and I become friends and have in-depth discussions about philosophy, about our mutually-shared passion for making raw, freshly made vegetable juice, and about music. He comes to respect my musicality and it becomes a ritual that he comes to play the piano after every tuning. At first, it's a ceremony of him checking out the tuning, but it ultimately becomes about his excitement to share a new piece of music he's written. Over the years, I'll be given dozens of private mini-concerts, all with my head sticking inside the piano, savoring the exquisite sounds of a virtuoso at work. On several occasions, I'm the first person to hear a newly-minted composition.

Chick is interested in the craft of piano tuning. In his Bostonian accent, he asks, "Hey Jim, I had this *idear* that maybe we could trade lessons: you could show me a few things about tuning, and I could give you a lesson or two on piano."

Are you kidding? "Absolutely!"

We get him a basic tuning hammer and I show him how best to hold it, make distinctions about how to turn the tuning pin, how to set a unison. He's very attentive. He in turn shows me a finger exercise to improve technique. It's a simple 5-finger pattern, but as I'm about to find out, that's not the point. I sit down and repeat the pattern he's just shown me.

"Great! But now focus on doing it really, *really* slowly, but with perfect consistency from note to note." He puts the metronome on 50 bpm — painfully slow. "This will uncover any time issues you have. If you practice this for 10 minutes a day, for two weeks, I promise your technique will improve enormously. As you're playing, focus on each note having the same volume and duration. No notes overlapping, no gaps between the notes. Try to land the note precisely in time with the metronome." He puts one hand on my shoulder and the other on top of my right wrist. "Keep your body and fingers relaxed and most importantly, make sure that the only finger that's moving is the one that's playing the note. All the other fingertips are resting gently on the keys."

I take his advice, follow his directions to the letter and indeed, I immediately see a major improvement in my technique. This will become exercise number one for me for decades.

In the coming years, Chick and Gayle invited me to their annual Valentine's Day fetes, which were attended by their talented, renowned friends. Chick gave me gracious introductions to Janis Ian, Stanley Clarke, and George Duke — all of whom would become future friends and clients. The highlight of the evening was always the big concert. A constellation of talent would congregate in the music room and one after another, each guest would perform a couple of songs: Chick, Gayle, Janis, Stanley, George, Karen Black, Roger Williams, and Martin Mull, to name a few.

Like the parties at the Playboy Mansion, Chick and Gayle's soirees were star-studded. But theirs were intimate evenings of artists sharing talents with peers. They were magical, one-off variety shows and I was honored to have been invited.

Occasionally, Chick would acknowledge me. "How 'bout a hand for our tuner. Great job, Jim!" I'd smile and wave, feeling a flush of warmth to my face. I'd fantasize what it would be like to play a song for this crowd of respected artists and instantly feel a grip of terror in my gut. This was a far cry from performing for rib-eatin' patrons at Tony Roma's — I was a long way from being ready to embrace this kind of spotlight.

There's a mild breeze in the air on this lovely day in June. I've come to tune the pianos and Chick and Gayle both greet me at the door. "We heard it was your birthday and we wanted to get you a little something." Gayle hands me a wrapped gift. I open it, revealing a treasure from the past — a piece of weathered sheet music of a song called "Jim." Written in 1941, it had been "introduced by Dinah Shore." The two of them have both signed it, *"You are one 'in tune' fellow! Love Gayle and Chick."*

"Thank you so, so much." I feel myself choking up. "How does it go?"

They look at each other and laugh. "No idea!" Gayle says. "Let's find out," says Chick, leading us to the piano. He flips back the cover page, opening a window into a bygone era. He puts it up on the music desk and scans it over. I scramble for my little micro-cassette recorder and hit record. The two of them knock out a quick rendition of Jim for me, Chick sight-reading, Gayle sight-singing:

"Why am I sitting alone tonight?
When I could be out where the lights are bright?
It's all because of JIM
It's all because of JIM
Why am I wasting these precious years,
Why am I crying these bitter tears?
It's all because of JIM
It's all because of JIM"

I'm teary-eyed but grinning ear to ear. They sing a bit, then glance at me, smiling as they continue:

"JIM doesn't ever bring me pretty flowers,
JIM never tries to cheer my lonely hours
Don't know why I'm so crazy for JIM!"

Gayle leans into the last "JIM!" shooting it in my direction with mock scorn.

"OK! I get it! I'm an asshole!" We all have a laugh. It's one of my most cherished birthday gifts.

———

I'd started making some nice coin and decided to take care of a dental issue that had bugged me since childhood: the huge gap between my two front teeth. The proper route would have been braces, but that ship had sailed. I found a dentist in Beverly Hills who promised to fix my teeth with just a special retainer. Fitted with my new dental device, I went straight from his office to a new high-profile client, Dee Murray.

Dee was the bass player for Elton John, which was cool beyond belief to me. I was a little star-struck at first, but Dee was a genuinely lovely person. I'd tuned his piano a couple of weeks before and was now returning with a custom-made bass string I had to install.

Entering his studio, my eyes adjust to the light. I see Dee and several other musicians who all turn to see who's just walked in. All eyes are on me. My breath stops for a second. I'm self-conscious but muster a cool *What's up?* nod.

"Hey Jim, thanks for coming." Dee turns from the mixing console to face me, flicking his long blonde hair out of his face. "We're right in the middle of a session but we'll stop while you put in the bass string. How long do you think it will take?"

I haven't spoken since leaving the dentist's office. I clear my throat.

"About thikthty theh-condth!" Spit flies in every direction from my new mouthpiece.

I couldn't have said, "About a minute"? As if I weren't self-conscious enough already. I turned beet red and made a beeline for the piano.

I went from there to a new weekly tuning account, Studio One, a huge gay nightclub on Santa Monica Boulevard in West Hollywood. I knew so little about the gay reality. In the Midwest at the time, being homosexual wasn't just taboo, it could be downright dangerous. I'd heard more than a few stories of "good ol' boys" beating up on gays to "teach them a thing or two." In the course of doing business with the staff of this popular hangout, I met people who were out and proud, living unapologetically as their authentic selves.

It's a week later, on a lovely Saturday afternoon. I'm doing a tuning for a Stanley Clarke session at Larrabee Studio, also on Santa Monica Boulevard. Stanley's recording engineer, Erik Zobler, an Icelandic dude with handsome features and an easy smile, is setting up for the session. We strike up a conversation. I feel an instant connection with "Zobie," who'll remain one of my closest friends for life.

Erik and I are discussing the perfection of the latest Steely Dan album when Stanley pops his head in the control room door.

"Hey guys, the parade is beginning. I was thinking of going up on the roof to watch for a bit. You wanna join?"

I've heard about the outrageous, annual West Hollywood Gay Pride Parade. Traffic is blocked off on Santa Monica Boulevard and throngs of people — mostly gay men — flock to this epic event. My little Midwest mind is about to be blown.

Erik, Stanley, and I make our way up to the roof. From our vantage point, we see thousands of onlookers lining the street, cheering as dozens of floats stream by. On them are guys in short shorts and Carmen Miranda headdresses waving and smiling. Liza Minelli and Judy Garland impersonators dance and throw flowers into the crowd. Fellows in flamboyant Victorian costumes, guys in nothing but chaps. Women waving rainbow flags openly kissing. Toto, I've a feeling we're not in Texas anymore.

But what really struck me was the volume of people dressed in everyday clothing – jeans and t-shirts, even some in business suits — walking between floats, carrying signs. "I AM OUT, I AM FREE, I AM HUMAN!" Another simply says, "PRIDE!" A mom and dad, whose sign reads "WE'RE PROUD OF OUR GAY SON." All of them taking a stand for their beliefs.

I realized the slightly unsettled feeling in my stomach wasn't about them. It was about me. I was coming face to face with how much I based my self-worth on other's opinions of me, how much I lived in fear of people's judgment. I felt small in comparison.

CHAPTER 15
The Buffet

Through Chick, I met and began caring for the pianos of artists as diverse as Janis Ian, Jeffrey Osbourne, Roger Williams, Wayne Shorter, Herbie Hancock, and George Duke. All gracious, all rolling out the red carpet for me. George was especially welcoming and would greet me with his big trademark teddy bear smile and warm hug.

George treated me like family, inviting me to Thanksgiving dinners, watching Lakers games together on TV. It was a joy to slip into the control room to hear him working on his latest project. "Wilsonian! Come on in!" he'd shout out when he'd see me. A humble man, he preferred to give compliments than to get them. You'd never know what a monster talent / legendary record producer he was. In his lifetime he'd release 32 solo records and win two Grammy Awards.

—

"You know, this is the piano that Gershwin wrote 'Rhapsody in Blue' on." My new client, Englebert Humperdinck, looks at me for a reaction.

I'm at his massive mansion on Sunset Boulevard in Beverly Hills. I've just tuned his 9-foot Steinway concert grand, and he's come into the music room to shake my hand and say hello.

"Wow, that's an impressive lineage." I raise my eyebrows and nod in approval. He asks my opinion of the condition of the instrument. I tell him it's in good shape overall, but it could use new hammers.

"Is that something you do?"

"Absolutely," I hear myself say, though I've only watched it being done once in school. I have a fledgling understanding about how this complex mechanism functions, but I'm still intimidated by it.

"Great. Let's go for it!" He smiles and pats me on the shoulder.

I feel a jolt of terror in my gut realizing my pattern of daring myself to learn something new has once again landed me in the deep end with no life preserver.

I remove the 40-pound piano action and huff and puff as I struggle to load it into my car. I take it to my apartment in North Hollywood and set it up on my glass kitchen table. The flow of work is now steady enough that I can use an assistant. My actor friend David Maples is between gigs and can use the work. I teach him the basics of piano regulation, and he becomes the first of dozens of techs I'll train and employ over the decades.

I buy the necessary jigs and very methodically, we remove the old hammers and install the new ones. Even without someone to watch over me, the job turns out great. The hammers line up beautifully — 88 little soldiers standing perfectly in a row. Gershwin would have been proud, and he wouldn't have to know I'd used his historic piano to teach myself how to install hammers.

Thankfully, my inexperience didn't end in disaster — though it could have. The action had some "sluggish flanges" — translation: think arthritic joints. A popular remedy for this at the time was to apply lighter fluid to the center pin. David had just done that to one section of the action, while I was "traveling shanks" — a process of applying a flame to a wood dowel to correct the angle of the hammer. You don't have to be an Einstein to see where this was heading: flame + lighter fluid + historic piano = potential disaster.

In reality, what followed was a flash flame that lasted a few seconds before I threw a moving blanket over the conflagration. But David — who years later would become a successful TV writer — has regaled people with the tale of "setting George Gershwin's piano on fire" countless times over the decades. David remembers the smoke from the flame was big enough to leave a black soot mark on the ceiling.

In those early LA years, I was writing songs, studying music theory at Dick Grove School of Music, and going to workshops and conferences that touted to teach you the tricks of becoming a "hit songwriter." A big focus of these workshops was finding a clever title and working backwards from there. While certainly a valid approach, it's hardly a prescription for mining the depths of one's soul in search of creating art.

But my commitment to my songwriting goals was beginning to wane. I hadn't yet tuned in to my true musical mission that lit me up on a deeper spiritual level. Also, I was building a name for myself as a technician and enjoying better standard of living. Success came with perks, but it was taking the edge off my ambitions. Comfort kills.

With a successful new business came early starts and long hours. I was getting more and more studio accounts, which usually booked at the last second, so I had to be on call. The pager could go off at 8 a.m. and 45 minutes later I'd be at the Record Plant, Village Recorders, Mad Hatter, Ocean Way, or Sunset Sound, tuning the piano for a 10 a.m. downbeat. This was the heyday of the LA recording boom and sessions were happening daily all over town.

Though my business was on a steady upward rise, my love life was on a rollercoaster. My romance with Cyndi would crash and burn, then months later we'd reconnect, and the flame would be rekindled. Then she'd break up with me saying she didn't want to be in a relationship. Considering that I'd been basing my self-worth on whether or not she loved me, I'd have headed for the exit too.

In time, I began learning the value of giving space in a relationship — the more tightly you hold onto something, the more you push it away. Our on-again, off-again relationship lasted several years, ultimately evolving into an enduring friendship.

Linda Ronstadt once described LA during that era as a "grand buffet." In a megalopolis of 8 million people, one teeming with young, stunning ingenues from around the world, there was never a shortage of candidates for a fling. It was a ceaseless parade of women with beauty sufficient to separate even the most principled man from reason. It was hardly conducive to a monogamous lifestyle. LA was a great town for the young and single, but maybe not so great if you lacked discipline. In a city with seemingly limitless choices of attractive women, my focus was getting diffused.

Not helping with the issue was the faulty "operating system" I was running on. Basing my value as a person on what others thought of me was virtually hardwired into my brain. If women are attracted to me and celebrities respect me, I must be pretty cool, right?

Also factoring into my avoidance of committing to serious relationships was my fear of abandonment — a fear that had gotten baked into my O.S. after my parent's brutal divorce when I was a kid. If you don't let them in too deep, they can't hurt you.

The lazy Susan-style buffet of LA in that era meant that when one relationship ended, the next one magically appeared. I became dizzy from the carousel: the ballet instructor who'd posed for Penthouse; the runner up in the 25th Anniversary Great Playmate Hunt; the assistant acting instructor; the exotic fitness instructor from Africa; the newbie actresses arriving from San Antonio, Madison, or St. Louis. Given the transient nature of most people's stay here, long-term expectations were low.

I was also getting drawn little-by-little into the misplaced values of a show-biz town disproportionately focused on image and status: you are the job you have, the car you drive, the clothes you wear. It is Hollywood, after all. It was an unfulfilling hamster wheel. My artistic drive was dissipating as I was slowly being absorbed into a brand-obsessed town.

But LA is also a major world center — a magnet that draws the best of the best from everywhere. It's a sprawling sea of humanity with countless enclaves of every kind of people. And you never knew who of the people you met just might become the next big thing.

It's an uneventful Sunday night. I've just gone alone to a screening of *Ordinary People* at the Fox Theater on Ventura Boulevard in Studio City. As I'm walking out, I notice a couple of girls sitting in a jeep parked in front. I recognize them as the same girls who'd just been sitting two rows behind me.

I make eye contact with the blonde in the passenger seat. I smile. "So, what'd you think of the film?"

We talk about the heavy subject matter; how compelling Timothy Hutton's performance was.

"So… are you guys hungry? I was just about to grab a bite at Jerry's Deli. Wanna join?" I'm in a nice go-with-the-flow zone and am learning that life rolls much better when I'm able to let go of agendas.

TUNED IN: MEMOIRS OF A PIANO MAN

After a fun hang over pastrami and rye sandwiches, we rally back to my apartment. We sit on the floor and have a blast singing and playing songs on guitar. The blonde has a great voice and cracks us up with her Bruce Springsteen impersonation. She later writes her first name and number on a slip of paper and hands it to me as they're leaving. A girl with a guy's name — interesting.

We chat on the phone a few times, then a couple weeks later go on a date. We hold hands and walk on the beach in Santa Monica. There's something special about this girl and my nerves start getting the better of me. That *it's-ok-if-you-like-me, ok-if-you-don't* cool state of being is giving way to *I'm-punching-way-above-my-weight-class* feelings. The more I try to impress her with a cool image, the worse I'm cratering. The soufflé collapses, the evening ends with a handshake. Ouch. I've rolled a gutter ball. So man, did it ever blow my mind a few years later when Daryl rolled a strike, becoming a national sensation starring as a mermaid in the hit movie *Splash*.

My getting to hang out with creative types was broadening my horizon, introducing me to different points of view. I met people who were vibrating at different wavelengths than I'd known, people with a gift for seeing common things in uncommon ways, people who were up to something in the world. Writers, artists, actors — people who make shit up for a living. Wild. Everyone was working on a new screenplay, a new song, funding a new movie or TV show. It was a whole different mindset, a higher value placed on the intangibles of life.

My work was connecting me with creatives like Jeff Bridges, Charlie Fleischer, Ed Begley, Jr., Don Cheadle, and Keith Carradine. Celebrities who seemed like gods on Mt. Olympus to me were now treating me as a respected artisan. A little starstruck at first, I learned to roll with it and would often share music and meals with them.

Keith had some incredible parties at his home in Topanga, where we had singalongs with his brothers David and Bobby, as well as Scott Glen, Powers Booth, and Dennis Quaid. One night he taught me a fun trick over dinner.

"If you rub your nose with spit, then fog up the spoon, you can get it to hang off the end of your nose." Keith is teaching his 10-year-old daughter Martha Plimpton and me the art of "spoon hanging." I've just housesat for him for a few days, and he's taken us to a nice Topanga restaurant. Soon all three of us have succeeded in gently dangling spoons from our noses. We're unaware that we've been drawing the attention of our fellow diners, and when we get a nice little round of applause, we give them all an exaggerated showbiz bow and a nice, *"Ta-da!"* I've often wondered if Martha remembers that night.

As my reputation spread, my celebrity clientele grew like crazy. Over the coming years it would grow to include everyone from Dr. Dre, Justin Timberlake, Madonna, Queen Latifa, and Pink to Barry Manilow, Neil Diamond, Barbra Streisand, and Cher. Larger-than-life people, but I was now being welcomed graciously into their homes.

I enjoyed numerous in-depth discussions about life with Lionel Richie, traded sick jokes with the Supertramp guys, was treated to freshly-penned songs by Burt Bacharach, was enthralled by Mike Stoller with backstories about iconic Elvis songs he'd written with his partner Jerry Leiber, and had lively discussions about politics with lyric-writing legends Alan and Marilyn Bergman. I shared cigars and wine with Sergio Mendes, got to play poker and jam with the Toto cats, had Harold Rhodes bring Rhodes parts to my shop and refused to let me pay for them, watched Lakers games with Herb Alpert, hung out with then-undiscovered director Stephen Soderberg, and got regularly treated to new song mixes by Eddie Van Halen. I flirted and sneaked a kiss with Connie Stevens on her porch, shared laughs over Corona beers with Princess Stephanie of Monoco — clad in her cut-offs and T-shirt — while sitting on the living room floor of her Beverly Hills home, mingled with stars at Pierce Brosnan's birthday party, and got regaled by Quincy Jones with stories of smoking pot with Ray Charles when they were teens.

I felt like I'd come from the middle of nowhere and worked my way to the middle of everything. It all just seemed so surreal.

All that respect from these famous people was giving me confidence — maybe a bit too much. I was beginning to base my value as a person on how many celebrities I knew. The more I gained in popularity, the more it went to my head. To say I struggled with imposter syndrome was a massive understatement. I felt way out of my depth, but I was learning to hide it well.

And the stark disparity between the amazing mansions of these movers and shakers and my meager one-bedroom apartment only served to remind me I was just a transient in their world. You can visit Disneyland, but you can't live there. I couldn't elude the nagging feeling that I needed to dig deeper to find my true purpose — whatever that was.

But none of those celebrated personalities would have as profound an impact on my life as an LA newbie I was soon to meet.

It's an afternoon in May of '83. I get a call from Claude Gaudette — a guy who's just moved here from Montreal. He's gotten my name from Dick Grove's School of Music where he's a full-time student. He's looking for someone to tune his Fender Rhodes keyboard. A few days later, he's welcoming me into his place at the Oakwood Apartments in Sherman Oaks.

"So... I guess you like records then?" I smile, set my tools down and take in the scene: his tiny apartment is stuffed with recording equipment, musical instruments, bookcases with nothing but music magazines and charts, and an entire wall of shelves crammed with hundreds of LPs. It's clear he's obsessed with the "LA Sound": Toto, George Benson, Earth Wind & Fire, and anything his hero producer David Foster had anything to do with.

Claude's curly hair, small frame and oversized glasses make a striking first impression. I make him out to be in his mid-20s. He has a slightly lazy eye, but his warm, direct presence makes you quickly forget about it. His skin is a paler shade of white, looking like he hasn't seen the light of day in weeks — a "studio tan", as "musos" jokingly call it. I find his heavy French-Canadian accent endearing — "I have some cold drinks in the refriga-*RAY*-ter."

We chat about music, the LA studio scene, his aspirations of becoming a top session player. He strikes me as a sweet, humble, sincere kid, but I can't help but think "good luck with those goals, pal. You and a million other new arrivals are reaching for that same brass ring." I do my work, we shake hands, I head out.

For the next couple of years, our relationship is professional, but friendly. Then one day, I get a call — Claude's moved out of the

Oakwood Apartments and into a rental house. He has a session that evening at his home studio and his piano "sounds gross" — could I please come ASAP? I clear the decks and head over to tune up his Mason & Risch grand. After I finish, Claude comes back in and sits down on the piano bench. He plays for a few minutes, nods approvingly, and we begin our customary post-tuning chat. But this time, our conversation ventures into deeper waters. He wants to know more about the various personal growth workshops I've done, the benefits I've experienced from breath-focused meditation, and the insights I've gained from years of intense Reichian therapy body work.

Then, as I'm turning to leave, I notice a handwritten list on the side table by his piano. At the top, it says "GOALS", then a long list of rows beneath that. The first item says "workout 3x week."

"Sorry. Wasn't spying... but I couldn't help but notice." I point to his list. We get into a discussion about the importance of clarity of intentions. He pulls out a book called *Creative Visualization*, by Shakti Gawain. He says it's become his bible. It happens to be a book I'm also engrossed in at the time.

I tap on the cover of the book. "Dude, my dad turned me on to all this stuff when I was a kid. One of his dozens of occupations was selling success motivational tapes by Earl Nightingale, Dale Carnegie, and Maxwell Maltz. He was always drilling into me about how our thoughts create our reality. He'd lay his favorite Bible quote on me all the time: 'As a man thinketh in his heart, so is he.'"

We start lighting up about our shared beliefs and resolve to do "mastermind" sessions. Claude pulls out a keyring from his pocket. "I still have access to the Oakwood. They have a small gym that's always empty. We should put it to use!"

Our bromance catches fire. It doesn't matter if either of us has worked till three or four in the morning, our commitment to supporting each other in becoming healthier is solid as a rock. Every Monday, Wednesday, and Friday, I show up at his house at 8 a.m. sharp, pick him up, and we head to the "C & J Health Center", as we dub the otherwise vacant Oakwood gym.

We do our mastermind meetings religiously — discussing and setting goals, holding each other accountable to achieving them. In the coming

TUNED IN: MEMOIRS OF A PIANO MAN

years, I'll marvel as one by one, he ticks off his goals with the ease that someone would check off items on a grocery list:
- Become one of the top keyboard players / arrangers in LA — *Check.*
- Buy a beautiful new home — *Check.*
- New car, new pool, scoring films, getting major song cuts by Celine Dion, become David Foster's main arranger, gain recognition as a producer — *Check, Check, Check.*

He's a great champion of my aspirations as well and cheers me on as I too buy my first LA home, a priority topic in our goal-setting sessions.

Claude inspires me on many levels. I'm moved by his deep love for his family, how much he values dinner and wine with dear friends, how much he loves a good laugh. He's a generous giver — to this day, I proudly display the huge Parisian street scene painting on my living room wall he bought me decades ago.

He's a believer in the power of intention but, more importantly, following it up with hard work. He's a perfectionist and I love his example of never stopping until you get the result you want. Claude inspires me to be the best version of myself — the best compliment one can give a friend.

With Claude on one of our M-W-F workouts.

CHAPTER 16
Forte

It's the fall of '84. I'm in a bit of a hurry to get to the next appointment. I'm wrapping up tuning the piano at Sunset Gower studios on the set of the TV show *Name That Tune*. I figure I have just enough time to put away my tools and make it to the next tuning, a recording session at Bill Schnee's.

As I'm finishing, I notice a guy setting up a Fender Rhodes keyboard. I have a hunch it might be Chuck Monte, this guy who's famous for the "Dyno-My-Piano" modification he's created for the Rhodes. It's a must for all the session cats. I really don't have the time, but I follow my instinct. I get up from the bench, walk over and introduce myself.

I had no idea at the time, but this was another of those Power of One moments. My choice to stop what I was doing and introduce myself would ultimately lead to unimaginable experiences.

As I approach him, I see the "Dyno-Rhodes" logo on the keyboard. I ask if he needs help setting up. "Nah. Just finishing up, but thanks," he says. He looks up and smiles. "Chuck Monte." He extends his hand.

I introduce myself, tell him I've heard about the mod he's doing, and that many of my clients rave about it. He says he's heard my name, has a piano at home, and asks if I'll come regulate and voice it for him.

A week or so later I come with my assistant tech, and we spend the day working on his piano. When we're done, I call him in. "Check it out!"

Chuck sits down and begins to play. His eyes light up. "Wow. I can't believe it's the same piano! It's so much easier to play and the tone has so much more depth. Well done!" He pauses and says, "Actually, Jim, if you're free for dinner, I have an idea I want to run by you."

I put away my tools and Chuck and I head to a neighborhood Mexican restaurant. We're seated, we place our orders. Chuck wipes some salt from the rim of his margarita glass, takes a sip.

TUNED IN: MEMOIRS OF A PIANO MAN

He begins his story about a guy he's recently met named Steve Salani, a hardware designer for Sequential Circuits, a San Francisco-based synthesizer manufacturer. Steve's privy to a new protocol in development that is the brainchild of Dave Smith, president of Sequential Circuits and Ikutaro Kakehashi, head of Roland, another synth manufacturer.

The new protocol will be called "MIDI," which stands for Musical Instrument Digital Interface. It's a revolutionary idea that will allow synthesizers manufactured by different companies to "talk" to each other, as well as link them to the world of computers for the first time. It's just on the verge of exploding onto the horizon and will change music production forever.

"Steve and his partner Jeff in San Jose have come up with a prototype of the world's first MIDI-adapter for acoustic piano." Chuck puts his hand over the margarita glass, thanks the server with a nod and a wink. "Steve's a really clever guy and has found a way to adapt the rubber switches that Sequential Circuits uses in their synthesizers to mount them under the keys of a piano."

He explains that Steve's invention is controlled by a small CPU mounted in the piano. This mini-computer receives information from the switches under the keys, then translates those key movements into a MIDI signal that can be sent to synthesizers, doubling what's played on the piano with any variety of sounds. Alternatively, the signal can be sent to a sequencer to be used in music production, or simply to translate the information into music notation.

"I think it's going to revolutionize the world of pianos, but they're better innovators than salesmen. I want to buy them out and have you be the head technician to install it." Chuck takes a beat, waiting for all that data to sink into my overloaded brain. There's a lot to unpack.

"Wow. That's ... heavy. Color me interested." I raise my margarita glass, clink it with his.

Attempts are made for the four of us to get together, but it always seems to get stalled. Soon, I get a call from Steve. He says he's heard great things about me from a few people. He's declined Chuck's offer to buy him out, but wants to meet with me to discuss possibilities. He's coming to LA, and we make a plan to get together for lunch. I feel a flush of excitement. In my gut, I know that something big is going down.

"Just water, no ice. Thanks." Steve's request to the server here at this Four 'N 20 restaurant in North Hollywood begins filling in my first impression. Everything about him speaks to his pragmatic, spendthrift nature: the long, burly beard, the short Supercuts hair, the brown corduroy pants, the utilitarian Hush Puppy shoes. He could pass for Cat Stevens taller, skinny brainiac brother. Though "overly-exuberant" might not be the first phrase that comes to mind describing him, I'll soon find he has a great, dry sense of humor to go with his off-the-charts IQ. His brain can do laps around mine — his never leaving first gear, mine red-lining to keep up.

Steve thinks my piano expertise and high-profile clientele are a good fit for his invention. Over a two-hour lunch, we have a great exchange of ideas regarding how to work together to perfect his creation and get it to the masses. We part with a hearty handshake.

Over the next few months, I'll fly up to San Jose several times, consulting with Steve and his partner Jeff on how to improve his adapter, and how to optimize how it fits into the piano action. The stock switches he's using are way too thick and interfere with the action, making it feel spongy.

"We gotta get a thinner profile, lighter-weight switch or it's not going to fly with the more discriminating pianists," I tell Steve while squishing a rubber switch between my fingers. It will mean him having to design and pay for new custom-made switches. Not a cheap proposition, but to his credit, he steps up.

I know that once we have a few influential players, the rest will take care of itself. Soon, I have artists including Chick Corea, David Foster, and Dave Grusin coming over to my little apartment in North Hollywood to hear this revolutionary adapter I've installed in my Kawai KG2 baby grand piano. They're all flipping out over the new possibilities this opens up for them. They have to have it.

Steve's company is called "Forte", but we need a name for the adapter. I come up with the moniker "MIDI-Mod." Steve likes it and has a logo made. I design and print up promotional flyers with Chick's picture and quotes on front. I mail them to all the studios in town. A&M is one of the first to bite. Once we have them, I now leverage the other studios with that info. It quickly becomes the "must-have" accoutrement. Music Connection, a monthly music-trade magazine, does a two-page feature on me — the only U.S. installer at this point, and the MIDI-Mod. The dominoes start to fall.

—

"That's it! This sound is gonna work perfectly for my new movie!" My new tuning client Carole King has just landed the gig to compose the score for the movie, *Murphy's Romance*, starring Sally Field and James Garner. I've been telling her about the MIDI-Mod, saying we should install it on her Baldwin Acrosonic — the one on which she's written tons of hits. Now here she is in my North Hollywood apartment, checking out the MIDI-adapter in my Kawai grand. She sits down to play, and her eyes grow wide as she listens intently to this new sound. She plays a few more chords and instantly knows this is what she's looking for.

I'm late for an appointment and need to leave but Carole is feeling inspired. "Would you mind terribly if I stay?" she asks. "I need to write the main love song for the closing credits and the ideas are starting to flow."

"Of course! Make yourself at home! Just lock the door behind you when you leave." When I come back a few hours later, she's left me a note that says, *"Jim! I got the song! Thanks so much! Love, Carole."*

A songwriting legend has just written a movie theme ("Love for The Last Time") on my piano in my crappy little apartment. So cool. I think about the guy who lives below me, the one who often sits around in his underwear with his door open for all to see, the one who occasionally pounds on his ceiling with a broom when I play piano too late. He was home when Carole wrote that song and I when I see him next, I nod and chuckle to myself. If he only knew.

The Forte MIDI-Mod is now the hip new thing and is *de rigueur* for every composer and artist. I'm being flown all around the country, installing them for Bruce Springsteen back east, Criterion Studios in Miami, and for Jimmy Jam and Terry Lewis in Minneapolis.

The 1985 NAMM show — the definitive music industry trade show held in Anaheim every year — rolls around and we're the big hit. Everyone is dropping by our booth and checking out the unique sound of a piano connected to synthesizers. Guys in white shirts and ties — who return daily, bringing more guys in white shirts and ties — are particularly interested. They turn out to be execs from Yamaha, who'll come out with their version of a MIDI-adapter for acoustic piano the following year. I barely manage to keep it together when my singer-songwriter role model, Jackson Browne, drops by and soon becomes a client. Pinch me.

Business is expanding rapidly and I need more help. I hire Lorna Guess — a tall, quick-witted girl I met while listening to her husband's cover band — to handle bookings and run my business. I train a couple more techs to help with the three to four installations we're getting every week.

My little brother Paul has finished a couple of years at University of Texas in Austin, but is still unsure about what he wants to do. He returns to Amarillo to live with Mom and stepdad Lou.

"I think Paul's taking drugs." Mom's calling from Texas. She pauses. "He might even be doing heroin." Her voice breaks.

"Mom, Paul isn't on heroin." I glance at the clock, I'm late to an appointment. "If anything, he's smoking pot, but nothing more." I assure her she's overreacting but tell her that I'd love for him to come live and work with me. A plan is set in motion.

"Let's get you unpacked and head out for some Thai food, Little Bro!" Twenty-year-old Paul has just made the same two-day Amarillo-to-LA drive I made five years earlier. Hugging him, I realize how much I've missed having family around me.

We're finishing up our dinner. I clear my throat. "I'm happy you're here, but I just want to lay down some ground rules: clean up after yourself, don't stay out late . . . and no drugs."

I'm addressing my mom's fears as best I know how. It's a far cry from the approach my dad took with me when I was a teen living under his roof, telling me, "I don't *approve* of you smoking pot, but I *accept* that you're going to do whatever you decide to do, and I would rather have you do it under my roof." By doing that, Dad had taken the taboo off the conversation and made it OK to be honest with him.

In stark contrast, by laying down the law with my brother, I think I'm helping him clean up his act. Instead, I've unwittingly made it so he has to go behind my back to get high.

Though nine years younger than me, Paul outpaces me intellectually. With an IQ of 152, he picks up the concepts of piano maintenance quickly and is easy to train. Soon he's assisting me, working on the pianos of clients including Jackson Browne and Quincy Jones.

He has to sleep on the sofa in the living room but doesn't complain. He breaks out his headphones and watches his hero, David Letterman. Paul and I share an irreverent sense of humor and he loves turning me on to comedy bits he's videotaped just for me: Billy Crystal and Christopher Guest on *Saturday Night Live*, and reruns of Martin Short's Ed Grimley sketches on *SCTV*.

The Groundlings Theater is a tuning account of mine and they let me come watch their improv comedy shows for free. I take Paul a few times, and we see Phil Hartman do sketches based on audience suggestions as well as Jon Lovitz unveil his pathological liar, "Yeah, that's the ticket" bit. They call for a volunteer from the audience and I rope Paul into doing it. They sit him in a chair onstage and ask him questions. Painfully shy, he has a look of terror on his face and begins to sweat profusely. I feel awful about nudging him to do it, but he later tells me he enjoyed it.

Paul's learned that his idol David Letterman is coming to California to do a special 2-week stint of *Late Night* in LA. Tickets are in high demand so Paul camps out overnight in line with hundreds of people on a sidewalk outside of NBC studios in Burbank. With luck, he lands two tickets. A few days later, Paul and I go to the taping. After the show, I walk up to Paul Schaefer, introduce myself and start a conversation about pianos. I call my brother over and introduce him.

"Paul, meet Paul…. Paul, meet Paul!" My little bro is starstruck and I'm nervous for him. I feel a pang of empathy as I recognize the same insecurity in Paul that I've managed to gloss over with a slick LA veneer.

"Got a nice little buzz going?"

I've come home one night and in chatting with Paul, it's obvious he's high. His eyes are glassy, he's a little slow with his responses, and he can't look me in the eye. It's time I try to lighten up about the topic. After all, he's only doing exactly what I was doing in my youth.

I smile and playfully nudge him. When I kid him about having a buzz, he acts like he doesn't know what I'm talking about. I take a beat.

"Ah come on… it's OK. You smoked a joint earlier, yeah?"

"No. I swear I haven't smoked any pot."

End of conversation. I can only hope I'll get another chance to reopen a line of communication about the topic. A chance that never comes.

That taboo topic notwithstanding, we still have a great connection when it comes to music, comedy and pretty much everything.

I would later realize I was closer to Paul than anyone. He knew the real me — though apparently, I didn't fully know the real him. Regardless, he was my closest friend.

Still unsure about what career he wanted to pursue in life, his time with me convinced him that piano tuning could at least be a good interim job. I was happy he'd at least pointed his boat in a positive direction. After a year of living with me, we enrolled him in the same piano tuning school I attended in Ohio. He tied up loose ends and was ready to hit the road.

"Have a great time in Cleveland and say hi to Bob Perkins for me, buddy. Love you little bro!" I waved to him as his taillights grew smaller, finally fading into nothing.

CHAPTER 17
London Calling

"Ladies and gentlemen, as we begin our descent, please make sure your seat backs and tray tables are in their full upright position." I'd heard this instruction a million times but never with a British accent.

I'm about to set foot on European soil for the first time. My heart races as I look out the window. Descending through the clouds, the gorgeous English countryside slowly begins coming into view. A patchwork quilt of various shades of green, the muted tones are made even richer by England's trademark overcast skies. Looking closer, I can make out old farmhouses on lush fields lined with hand-crafted stone fences and thick hedgerows. I feel like I'm descending into a Jane Austin novel. The countryside scenes soon give way to endless rows of red rooftops. Finally, the wheels touch down, sending a jolt of adrenaline through me. I'm here!

Bleary eyed from the eight-hour red-eye flight, I lumber out of the plane, and slog through the endless halls of London's Heathrow airport, my carry-on suitcase in tow. I make my way through passport control, collect my bags, then head to customs.

My pulse quickens as the officer asks me what's in the long box. Never mind not wanting to pay the exorbitant VAT tax on the MIDI-adapters, I don't have a work visa. My palms become moist, my smile a little forced. I feel like Brad Davis smuggling Turkish hash in *Midnight Express*. "Just product samples, sir." He gives me a dubious look, holds eye contact. He glances at the line of people behind me, shrugs, and waves me through.

My shoulders drop, I exhale. I head to the exit, rush outside and hail a black cab.

"Where ya headin', Gov?" The driver adjusts his rearview mirror, giving me a nod as I slide into the backseat. Wow. The scruffy beard, the wool newsboy flat cap, the East Ender dialect so thick you can cut it with a knife — this guy is straight off the set of Mary Poppins.

"Cumberland Hotel, Oxford Street, please."

"Right then! What brings you here, mate?"

I contemplate telling Bert the chimney sweep I'm going to install MIDI-adapters for Elton John and Paul McCartney, which will lead to explaining what a MIDI-adapter is, which will lead to explaining what MIDI is. Jet lag is setting in.

"Just for pleasure, mate." I cling to the door handle as he and everyone else drive on the wrong side of the road. Weaving in and out of traffic, the lines on the streets are merely suggestions. The narrow, winding lanes, dating back to when they were meandering cow paths, have all the symmetry of lines drawn by a drunken 3-year-old.

We finally make it to the hotel. I've survived.

"That's 32 quid, mate." He pulls the flag down on the meter.

I fish through my wallet, give him a 50-pound note — a colorful work of art the size of a small British flag. He gives me back change in coins the size of manhole covers.

I tip the driver, exit the cab, and begin to unload my luggage. Before I can touch the suitcase, a porter appears and snaps to attention. "Welcome to the Cumberland Hotel, sir. Let me get those for you."

I'm in a bit of a daze, so I gladly accept his offer. He pushes the luggage cart through the double doors, and I follow behind, entering the palatial lobby of this 5-star hotel. Lovely classical music, courtesy of a live pianist, echoes off the marble floor. The air is heavenly, perfumed by a floral arrangement the size of a Volkswagen. There amidst the Burberry overcoats, silk shirts and immaculately tailored Bond Street suits, I feel more than a little out of place in my schlubby travel sweats.

I get checked in, the porter pushes the luggage cart into the elevator, the door closes behind us. "Room number, sir?"

"509 please."

He hits the five button, and smiles knowingly. "Doing the Jimi tour, are we?"

"Uh… Sorry, I don't follow."

Turns out Jimi Hendrix had stayed in room 507 for the last two weeks of his life in September 1970. Though he actually overdosed in his girlfriend's apartment in a nearby hotel, many tourists come to stay in

TUNED IN: MEMOIRS OF A PIANO MAN

Jimi's last residence — room 507. My room was right next door.

"Oh my god ... that's ... unbelievable." I'm approaching Jimi's room. He walked these exact same steps. I can see him sitting on his bed, practicing a few riffs on his Fender Strat.

With strains of "All Along the Watchtower" playing in my head, I get settled into my room, turn the TV to BBC One's evening news. I'm mesmerized by the music of the dialects of the various newscasters. Turns out, people in Britain speak with British accents — who knew? I'm on the other side of the world, immersed in a culture I'd only read about before. I feel like I'm in a dream.

I get settled into my room, take a quick nap. Afterward, I splash cold water on my face and head out into the commotion and cacophony of Oxford Street, seduced by the sights and sounds of this bustling city.

Easy money! Give it a go! A dapper gent with eyes always discreetly scanning the crowd is luring unwitting victims into a shell game. I watch an American tourist get swindled out of 20 quid, then poof... the conman's cohort signals to him, they fold their makeshift table, and vanish into the mass of people.

Soon, I'm descending the long escalator at Oxford Circus tube station, winding my way down to Baker Street. As the train comes speeding towards the platform, the sound of the sax solo from Gerry Rafferty's iconic hit playing in my head is interrupted by the terse overhead announcement:

MIND THE GAP ... MIND THE GAP.

Before long, I find myself amongst a teeming mass of pedestrians shuffling along the sidewalk on a cool London evening. Across the street, I see the pub my new friend Charlie Morgan has suggested as a place to meet.

A couple of months before, after getting the green light to come MIDI the piano for the *Little Shop of Horrors* soundtrack recording sessions, I called the only British person I knew: a composer named Julian Marshall. Julian was delighted to hear I was heading to his hometown of London.

"You *must* contact my mate, Charlie, who's just gotten the gig as the new drummer for Elton John." Calls were made, arrangements were discussed, a time was set.

I enter the dimly lit, smoky pub. It's a small place, but the mirror behind the bar makes it seem bigger. The bartender wiping down the counter looks up at me and nods. The red digital clock above him says 8:17. I'm late. Over the heads of jovial Brits in spirited conversations with friends, I spot a towering, slender figure with short, dark hair seated at a small table for two. He spots me. We haven't seen pictures of each other but we both break into simultaneous, knowing smiles. He stands to greet me.

"You must be cream-crackered!" Charlie has just introduced me to Cockney rhyming slang.

"Sorry?"

"Cream-crackered, rhymes with knackered. Means 'tired' … I bet you're Hank Marvin as well." He notes the puzzled look on my face. "Means 'starvin'."

"Yes! I'm indeed cream-crackered *and* Hank Marvin! Let's order!"

Charlie's an affable chap, always up for a laugh. We hit it off straight away. Turns out we were born just a few days apart on other sides of the planet. He's as much an Americanophile as I am an Anglophile. Between bites of our meals, he gives me pointers on doing an East Ender dialect, while I coach him on how to do a proper Texas drawl.

"How y'all doin', darlin'?" Charlie's trying out his down-home dialect on our server. He's nailing it but it sounds hilarious coming from a Brit. In the coming years, he'll christen a spare bedroom of his Grove Park home "The James Harold Wilson Suite" and I'll offer the same to him when he comes to LA, labeling my guest bedroom the "Charles E. Morgan Chambers."

Prior to my coming to the UK, I'd had breakfast with film composer James Newton Howard to pick his brain for ideas about my upcoming UK trip. James connected me to Elton, via Elton's road manager Adrian Collee. Elton jumped at the idea of having me MIDI his piano.

The evening flies by. The bartender yells *"Last call!"*

"Well mate, it's been a pleasure," I say, "but I have to get up early. I'll be working on your new boss's piano tomorrow." I stand a bit too quickly, immediately realizing the warm Guinness has kicked my ass. We settle up, Charlie gives me a lift back to the hotel.

Morning rolls around. I stagger down to the dining room for breakfast. Seated, I open *The Sun* newspaper and right there, filling all of page three, is a picture of a smiling, topless girl – apparently a daily feature. I do a double take, shake my head. Man, they do things differently over here.

The overly floral perfume of the woman seated next to me assails my olfactory senses. When my eggs and sausage arrive, I'm too jet-lagged to ask the server if putting grilled tomatoes, baked beans and fried mushrooms on the plate is a mistake. *When in Rome*, I suppose, snarfing down my meal.

Soon, Adrian — a tall bloke with a scruffy beard — and I are packed into his Mini-Cooper, driving west on the M4 to Elton's house, not far from Windsor Castle.

Heading down the long driveway, Elton's massive two-story mansion soon comes into view. I can't tell which covers more square footage though — his house or the garages for all his cars. We pass a half dozen luxury automobiles in the motor court — what I'm guessing are Bentleys and Rolls-Royces. I mean, why not? Elton's reality is so radically different from mine. I can't even begin to imagine what it's like to be one of the most famous people on the planet, with that kind of financial freedom.

Adrian sets me up in the studio behind the house. I work the better part of the day, breaking for lunch. Adrian brings me a pot of tea and a cucumber-and-butter sandwich with all four crusts of the white bread neatly cut off. Adrian tells me this is standard British fare. Where the hell is the rest of the sandwich? It's as if someone began making a proper sandwich only to find the refrigerator was empty.

Elton doesn't emerge until later, in a rush to make it to the airport. He's headed to Los Angeles to record his vocal — along with Dionne Warwick, Stevie Wonder, and Gladys Knight — on a new song called, "That's What Friends Are For." Adrian introduces me. I'm starstruck but manage to not make a complete ass out of myself. A couple of minutes later, Elton's driver nods. It's time.

"Thanks so much for your hard work, Jim. I can't wait to properly try out the piano." Elton shakes my hand.

"My pleasure. So great to meet you. You're a gentleman and a scholar, Elton."

"Yeah, and a great female impersonator too." Elton never misses a beat.

With Sir Elton at his home outside London.

Over the next couple of decades, I'd have the honor of working for him, being flown to a dozen cities including London, Atlanta, New York, and New Orleans. I found him to be extremely intelligent, with a razor-sharp wit and Groucho-like delivery. A few of my favorite memories:

It's somewhere in the late '80's. Elton has come to LA to perform with his pal Rod Stewart at a fundraiser at the Century Plaza Hotel. He's rented my piano for the occasion and I'm backstage chatting with his personal manager Connie Hillman. She mentions that Elton had just played at a private party the night before.

"Wow. I guess that must have cost someone a pretty penny," I say. She tells me the jaw-dropping price for having Elton do such private appearances.

"My birthday's coming up soon. Maybe Elton could perform at my party and we can just trade out his fee in tunings."

She cracks a smile. "A perfectly reasonable offer."

Elton happens to walk up about then, and Connie says, "Elton, Jim was wondering if you could perform at his birthday party in exchange for future piano tunings."

He looks me up and down, gives a wry smile. "He's not gonna live that long."

Another time, Elton is in LA, rehearsing for an upcoming tour. He and the band are at The Complex, a sprawling collection of soundstages and studios on the West Side. I've finished tuning the piano when Elton walks in. I rise, we hug.

"Thanks for coming, Jim." Even after numerous interactions with him, it still strikes my ears funny that this icon knows my name and is greeting me as a friend.

We chat a bit about the piano, exchange a few quips. Elton surprises me with a lovely invitation.

"We're going to hear Bonnie this Sunday night at the Hollywood Bowl. Fancy joining us?"

"Are you kidding? I love her. Count me in!"

Besides being a massive fan of Bonnie Raitt's, I'd been caring for her piano – one with an interesting backstory. Apparently, over lunch one day Bonnie mentioned to Elton how much she wanted to own a piano one day. He excused himself, and made a phone call. Upon returning home, Bonnie found a Yamaha grand waiting for her in her living room. Many people I know in Elton's world speak of his incredible largess.

Now, a few days later, I get a message on my answering machine. "Hi Jim, it's Elton. If you still want to join us this Sunday, give me a call at the Four Seasons. I'm staying under the name 'Binky Poodleclip'."

"Four Seasons, how may I help you?" The receptionist sounds professional and courteous.

"Yes, I'd like to speak to … Binky Poodleclip, please."

"Sorry. Could you repeat that please?"

"Yes, that's Binky Poodleclip. B-I-N-K-Y P-O-O…"

"Got it. I'll put you through now, sir. Have a wonderful day."

Elton answers. We have a laugh about the pseudonym. "I had to retire the ones I used to use: 'Sir Colin Hot Dog' and 'Fred Flintstone'."

I tell him how much I appreciate the invite, that I'm looking forward to the show.

"My pleasure. Concert's at half-7, so perhaps arrive here around 6?"

"Sounds great, Binky. Or do I call you Mr. Poodleclip?" I get a groan and small chuckle out of him.

6 p.m. Sunday rolls around. I make it up to Elton's penthouse suite, knock on the door. His personal assistant Bob greets me and leads me to a sofa by a grand piano. Elton soon emerges, I stand and give him a hug. We talk about how much we love Bonnie's music; we talk about his first LA shows — the famous August 1970 Troubadour concerts that *LA Times* music critic Robert Hilburn reviewed.

"That review was really what broke the whole thing wide open for me." Elton was just 23 years old. Damn.

He steps out onto the balcony, looks down on to the driveway several floors below. He comes back in, sits at the piano. Bob and I gather round, Elton's dresser joins us. Elton plays a new song, "Live Like Horses."

Yeah. You know, just hangin' with Elton John, who's singing us a new song in his penthouse suite before we head to see his friend Bonnie Raitt at the Hollywood Bowl. Nothing special.

Bloody hell.

"Wow. That's fantastic, Elton. I love the chord changes in the chorus. Great song. ... Hey, you really should think about doing this professionally." I get a half smile out of him.

He rises, walks over to the balcony, takes another look over the rail. Turns out the limo has been there since Elton first started looking. He's been waiting on our police escort to arrive. As one does, of course.

With everything now in place, off the four of us race through the streets of LA. Two cops on motorcycles speed ahead into the intersection, our limo proceeds through the light, the other two cops leapfrog ahead, repeating the cycle. I make a mental note to hire cops to help me navigate LA rush hour from now on.

We make it across town to the Bowl in record time. We're escorted backstage, into Bonnie's dressing room, joining her and her other guests, Jackson Browne and Bruce Hornsby.

"Damn. You have more security than President Clinton!" Bonnie hugs her dear pal, Elton. Elton makes introductions. We chat for a bit, then are ushered to our box seats. I'm sitting next to Elton. Lights go down, show begins. Bonnie and band sound amazing. A few songs later, she begins singing my favorite song, "I Can't Make You Love Me."

I look at Elton, I put my hand on my heart, shake my head in awe, and point to the stage. "This song absolutely slays me."

He smiles and nods in agreement.

The evening flies by. Soon we're back in the limo, speeding across town, police escort leading the way.

"I bet you get pestered by a lot of rabid fans," I said. "I guess you need all this extra security for protection?" I nod towards one of our cops whizzing by.

"Nah," he smiles. "I just hate traffic."

—

It's just after lunchtime on a Monday when the phone rings.

"EJ wants to take you up on your offer." Elton's tour manager is calling me from the road.

I'd been having conversations with Elton about how to handle the heavy action on the 9-foot concert grand he toured with. A technician in the UK had recently installed new, heavier hammers on the piano. Through no fault of the piano manufacturer, the end result was that the piano required more effort to play. One day, Elton brought it to my attention.

"The keys feel like they're made of bloody concrete!" Elton looks at me over his shoulder, playing the piano. We discuss sending the piano to my shop in LA so I can address the heavy action. But what to do about a replacement piano for him to tour with while I'm doing the work?

I'd had several engaging conversations with Elton about various piano brands. I told him I was really impressed with the strides in quality Yamaha had made over the decades and thought they'd developed into a world-class piano manufacturer.

"I've been working with the head of their Concert and Artist division. If you ever want to give their latest models a try, I'd be happy to arrange it." I soon filled in Elton's tour manager, Keith, about the offer, not thinking much about it.

A few weeks later I get the call from Keith. Elton wants me to do the work on his touring piano's action. "Meanwhile, could you call your contact at Yamaha to see if they'd be open to providing Elton with a piano to try out?"

I say that's great and I'm sure I could arrange it. "How soon are you thinking?"

"Tomorrow night in New Orleans."

I take a quick breath, look at the clock — it's coming on 1 p.m. in LA, so 4 p.m. on the East Coast. "Wow. Let me jump on this and see if I can pull a rabbit out of my hat."

I hang up and call Eric Johnson with Yamaha in New York. Mostly when I call him, it goes directly to voicemail. This time, he picks right up.

"So, Eric, how would you like to have Elton John as a Yamaha artist?" I tell him about the situation, he jumps into action locating the nearest concert grand to the venue.

I throw some clothes in a suitcase, grab my tools and equipment and race to LAX. Elton's camp flies me on the red-eye first class and I arrive at the venue via limo at 9 a.m. I go straight to work, installing the MIDI-adapter, doing friction reduction, regulation, voicing and tuning. Racing against the clock, I just finish working on the piano when Elton and his entourage walk in for sound check at 2 p.m.

Elton gives me a hug, thanks me for making this all happen on such short notice.

"My pleasure! I think you're going to love the touch and tone." I then walk to the side of the piano to open the lid. Someone has set up the teleprompter screen a little too close and when I open the piano, the lid clips the thin glass. It breaks off, falls to the floor and shatters into a million little pieces.

"What was that?!" Elton is as startled as I am. My friend Clive Franks who's at the mixing console thinks this is the funniest thing he's ever seen and his laughter echoes throughout the empty auditorium.

With that commotion behind us, I sit down to demonstrate to Elton with my gram weights how beautifully the action is weighing out (49 grams of downweight and 28 grams up. Translation: keys are easy to push down but are quick to respond. The best of both worlds.) He immediately sits down and starts playing the piano. He soon starts nodding his head. "Lovely. . . . This is just lovely."

TUNED IN: MEMOIRS OF A PIANO MAN

I tell him I can get a similar touch on his other touring piano. He plays for a few seconds longer and pauses. He shakes his head. "Nah. I think I'll give it to charity."

And with that Elton John became a Yamaha artist.

It's years later, on a Thursday evening. But this is no ordinary weeknight. Elton is in town to perform at the Greek Theatre. This is the first of two consecutive sold-out nights. With 7,000 people streaming into the venue, the excitement is palpable. Billed as "A Special Evening with Elton John," it's all the more rare as there's no band. Elton's only other accompanist is his legendary, long-time percussionist Ray Cooper. Disney is set up to film both nights and edit them into a concert special. I've been given amazing VIP tickets and two all-access passes. I roll in with a date on my arm. Right off the bat, we run into my friend Greg Penny, who's producing the music that night.

"Hey Jim! Great to see you. You here to look after the piano?"

"Nah, just here as a civilian." I introduce him to my date Laura.

"You two wanna join me in the production trailer?"

I look at Laura, a girl for whom I've had the hots for ages. Surely I'm getting Mr. Cool points. "Sure!" She lights up, flashes a big smile.

I take her hand. Greg leads us through the inner corridors of the venue and out to the trailer where the video and music are being recorded. We enter the darkened room, illuminated by the dozen or more TV monitors in the video section. Laura and I squeeze past the row of people, then past the mixing board. Greg sets up two folding chairs for us just to his left.

If I had to script the perfect scenario to impress a date, this has gotta be hitting all the marks. I've been given special treatment before, but this is next level. I'm trying to act like this is nothing out of the ordinary, but inside I still can't believe I'm flying in this jet stream. I smile. I'm kinda feeling like I'm the man. Laura leans over and whispers, "What was it again you did to his piano?"

I lean closer, gently touch her hand. "I helped develop the MIDI-adapter that I installed in his piano. When he plays, he's triggering a piano sample off stage that the audience hea..." I was interrupted by the announcer.

Ladies and Gentlemen! Please welcome... Elton John!

Elton comes out in what appears to be a red vinyl suit. He bows, sits at the piano, and begins the intro to one of his most iconic compositions, "Your Song." The crowd roars in appreciation.

He starts singing the first verse, the audience slowly settles. A half minute later, I found it less than "a little bit funny" when the music stops, and Elton says, "I'm sorry. This piano has a MIDI-adapter in it and it's not working right."

My heart sinks. I turn to Greg, my look of terror is reflected on his face. Though I'm "off-duty," I can't just sit there.

I shoot out of the trailer and sprint full bore to the backstage area.

"What's the issue?" I ask Dale, Elton's road tech I've prepped to address this kind of stuff. Thing is, Dale isn't quite clear about the exact complaint. Between the two of us, we decide the safest thing to do would be to reinitialize the unit. This means playing a chromatic scale — all 88 notes depressed slowly left to right, one by one — to recalibrate the software. An otherwise routine procedure in an empty studio. But with no curtains and 7,000 people watching, it's as pleasurable as a root canal. Hearing the piano is becoming more difficult over an increasingly restless crowd. After ten excruciating minutes, we finish the calibration. We check it out, all systems go.

Elton restarts the show. I take a deep breath. He gets three more songs in, stops again, and walks off stage. I'm perplexed since everything we're hearing sounds great. No one seems clear on exactly what the problem is, so I think, hey, Elton's a mate, he recently invited me to his friend Bonnie's concert at The Bowl — I should be the one to approach him.

I find him backstage talking with his manager John Reid and a few others.

"Excuse me. Sorry, Elton. I just want to be clear on exactly what the issue is."

His frustrations have understandably reached a flashpoint. He moves *thisclose* to me and shouts, *"IT'S NOT THE SAME FUCKING SOUND!"*

My hair singes, my heart stops. I shrink to the size of a peanut and nod. "Got it, thanks," I mumble, and slither away.

Unfortunately, I'm still unclear on what the exact problem is so I recommend to Dale that we switch out the control head, which of course means that we'll have to — once again — reinitialize the new unit. This takes another ten minutes, but it feels like an eternity with the crowd getting more restless by the minute. As I'm feeling the flop sweat on my flushed face, I hear someone in one of the first few rows yell, "Hey Jim! Mine doesn't work either!" Turns out it was my pal Eddie Van Halen winding me up for a laugh. Thanks Ed. You're a laugh a minute, bro.

Clive Franks, who's been Elton's "front of house" mixer for decades, breaks protocol and — for the first time in his career — leaves his massive mixing console, positioned in the middle of the audience. He ventures backstage and into the garage, finding Elton with his hand on the limo door about to leave. Clive convinces him that everything sounds fine in the house. Elton returns to the stage and resumes the show, for good this time.

I return to the production trailer and sit back down between Laura and Greg. He looks at me and whispers, "What the fuck just happened?"

Without saying a word, I take a tape box, at the top of which someone has written "Greek Theatre." I take a pencil and scratch out the word "Theatre," and write "Tragedy." From then on Greg and I referred to that night as the Greek Tragedy.

After the show, I was so shell shocked from the earlier trauma, I dropped off Laura, went home and tossed and turned all night.

The next afternoon, my friend Dave Starkey – inventor of this Gulbransen MIDI-adapter – joined me at the venue and we installed an entirely new unit. Elton came out and thanked us profusely for coming.

Turns out there'd been one note in the middle that was intermittently double-triggering. Not that noticeable to the audience, but extremely distracting for Elton. He sat down and tried it out.

"Fantastic. When something's off, it's like driving a '39 Packard. Now it's like a brand-new Jaguar. I can't thank you enough. Sorry if I was a bit unpleasant last night."

I told him no apology needed. "I can't begin to imagine the pressure of performing for 7,000 people, cameras rolling, and having technical issues beyond your control. So very sorry you had to endure this glitch."

He made a lovely mention to that night's audience about "the crew being most helpful." The night went off without a hitch. The special turned out wonderfully and the two-night event raised a ton of money for AIDS awareness.

CHAPTER 18
London Calling, Again

"*The space shuttle just blew up!*" Phil ran into the lobby of the recording studio outside of London and quickly turned on the TV.

Obviously, he's confused the facts. The shuttle can't have "blown up." Phil, Howard, and I gathered 'round and watched in disbelief as it became apparent that he, indeed, had it exactly right. It was horrifying.

Just a couple of months before, during my first visit to the UK, my company had approached Phil Collins's team about possibly MIDI'ing his piano. There was interest, but the timing wasn't right. Naturally, immediately after my return to LA, we got the call from his tech "Pud," aka Steve Jones.

"How soon could you MIDI a Steinway concert grand and four Yamaha CP-70 electric pianos at the Genesis studio?"

"Sorry man. I'm back in LA already."

"No worries. We'll fly you back and put you up. How soon can you get here?"

It's January 1986. Fisher Lane Farm, or "The Farm," as Genesis calls their studio here in the lush, green countryside of Chiddingfold, Surrey, was once upon a recent time a cowshed where the former owner, a dairy farmer, milked his herd. A winding path leads from the studio to a charming English cottage a stone's throw away. It's here where I'll be sleeping during my week-long stay.

This morning's rainy, overcast skies mirror the gloom of the shuttle disaster. After a couple of hours of everyone watching replays in incredulous horror, I have to return to my work.

Once I'm finished with one CP-70, "Bison," the band's roadie and studio tech, tears it down, removes it and brings the next patient into the studio lobby where I'm doing my work.

TUNED IN: MEMOIRS OF A PIANO MAN

Every evening at 6:30 p.m., supper time rolls around, and I join the gang for a catered meal at the table — which is also in the studio lobby, just 20 feet from my command post.

"Care for another glass of wine?" Phil is being a gracious host and passes the bottle of French cabernet to Mike Rutherford, the Genesis guitar player, who passes it to keyboard player Tony Banks, who refills my glass. The guys have a collegial camaraderie and love sharing a laugh. Phil breaks out a limerick. The volume of his voice diminishes with each whispered word:

"There once was a man from Bombay,
whose voice was fading away..."

(After the second line, his lips keep moving with no sound coming out.)

Tony groans, Mike chuckles, I laugh a little too loudly. My face feels flush with embarrassment. By some bizarre circumstance, I've rightfully earned a seat at this table, but I still feel like the outcast kid who's imposed himself on the popular crowd at the school cafeteria table.

After everyone leaves for the evening, I sneak into the control room, at the center of which is a massive SSL mixing console — the Rolls-Royce of its ilk. Stuck to the studio wall are numerous rows of five-foot long strips of console tape, with dozens of track names — one every couple of inches. Before the era of "recallable mixing automation," you'd put a strip of console tape beneath the row of faders and use a Sharpie to label each individual track. When you moved on to the next song, you'd take the labeled console tape and stick it on the wall just in case you had to have another go at that mix.

Also taped to the wall are a dozen notebook pages — one for each song of an album — with additional notes about the mix. Atop one of the pages is a slightly peculiar song title that piques my interest. I ponder for a minute what a song called "Invisible Touch" might sound like.

It's approaching lunchtime the next day and I drop into the control room, where Phil is producing a record for Howard Jones. From their seats at the mixing console, they both turn, smile, and nod. I give a silent thumbs up to the cool pop track they're listening to at full volume:

And you want her, and she wants you
No one, no one, no one ever is to blame

JIM WILSON

Howard's "No One Is to Blame" will go on to become a smash hit. But now, Phil is basking in a current chart success of his own. Over lunch, he makes an announcement.

"I just phoned Bish to congratulate him on 'Separate Lives'." Phil shows us the *Billboard* chart, at the top of which is the duet he's done with Marilyn Martin, written by his friend Stephen Bishop. In years to come, Stephen would become a close friend and we'd perform that very song to audiences around the world.

After lunch, I muster the courage to ask Phil to take a picture with me by the fireplace. He plays along with my concept for the photo. I'm holding open *The Sun* newspaper, pointing to a bare-breasted "Page 3" girl. We look at each other in mock indignation. With my black silk baseball jacket, the huge "LA Piano Services" logo embroidered on the back, "Jim" in cursive writing on the front, my spiky, frosted hair and closely manicured beard, I'm the poster child for '80s couture.

Phil and me at "The Farm"

115

It's a couple of days later and I'm working on Genesis keyboard player Tony Bank's Steinway concert grand. Bison, the roadie, tells me the interesting back story on how he got it.

"For ages, Tony had wanted me to drive him into London to the Steinway dealer, Jaques Samuel, so he could try out a bunch of Steinways. His schedule was so crazy that we could never find the time. A few weeks ago, we were on our way somewhere, driving down Edgware Road, when Tony said, 'Hey! There's the Steinway store!' We were late and there were no parking places, so I double-parked. Tony waited in the car."

Bison continues to tell me how he — a large bloke with a big, burly beard — burst into the store, which was elegantly appointed to suggest an air of refinement. A slightly startled salesman in a 3-piece suit approached him. "May I help you, sir?"

"Yes! I'd like to buy a piano!"

The stodgy salesman sized up the disheveled figure before him. "What kind of piano would sir like?"

"Big! . . . Black!"

The salesman pointed to a group of 6- and 7-foot pianos.

"No . . . *Bigger!*" Bison exclaimed.

The salesman cleared his throat. He led Bison to the "D", Steinway's flagship 9-foot concert grand model. "This is the biggest one we have, sir."

"Great!" Bison pulls out a business card, quickly scribbles on the back. "Here's where to deliver it. Send the bill to the address on the front!"

I soon wrap up my work for Phil and head into London, where I settle into my old room at the Kensington Hotel in Earl's Court. I decide to take Paul McCartney up on his offer to "give him a bell whenever I'm in the UK."

I spend an anguished afternoon working up the nerve to give him a call. Never mind being nervous about calling a Beatle on his private home line, I'm planning to make a very big ask. I have a rough song idea, and I'm going to pitch to him the possibility that we work on it together. I feel our kinship is strong enough that he'll at least entertain the notion. Audacious move, but I know I'll beat myself up for the rest of my life if I don't at least take a swing. For better or worse, this pattern of daring myself in the moment to avoid self-flagellation later is a driving force in my life.

I take a shot of tequila, dial his secret Batphone number. He picks right up.

"Hey mate, it's Jim. Back in London, just checking in." I grip the phone; I clear my throat. "So… how are you enjoying the piano at the studio?"

"I love it. I feel like a kid with a new toy that I can't wait to get back to every day. … Actually, come to think of it, as long as we have this great piano tech in town, maybe I should put him to good use and have him come work on my home piano."

"Keep me off the streets, is that it?"

"Yeah, that's the idea."

I ask him what he's up to this evening, he says he's making stuff out of plaster of Paris with his kids. "I never resist the opportunity to act like a 14-year-old!"

"Ah yes. I can see the *National Enquirer* headlines: *Paul McCartney Gets Plastered with His Children!*" I muster a small laugh out of him.

I take a breath. It's now or never.

"So… when I see you next week, I have, um… this song idea I'd love to play you. If you like the melody… well, it needs lyrics…" I put the receiver away from my mouth and finally properly exhale as quietly as possible.

He chuckles. "Oh, I see. Star piano tech comes here from LA and wants to start writing with a Beatle, eh?" He's enjoying winding me up.

We laugh. He breaks the tension. "I'd be happy to have a listen."

We say our goodbyes and hang up. I pump my fists in the air and to the entirety of London shout, "*YES!*"

A few days later, a big black limo picks me up from my hotel for the two-hour drive to the south coast of England. Paul is putting me up in a quaint country cottage in Sedlescombe so I can be at his house bright and early. I get settled in and enjoy high tea in the rose garden. I slow down and tune in to the peaceful chorus of birds celebrating a glorious late-afternoon sunset.

That evening, I enjoy libations and a spirited conversation over an amazing dinner in Rye with John Hammel, Hugh Padgham (or "Huge Pageant" as Paul affectionately calls him,) and a couple of Paul's band members. Hugh's been busy for the last few weeks producing Paul's new record, *Press to Play*.

TUNED IN: MEMOIRS OF A PIANO MAN

The day breaks, my mind aches. I might have had one too many glasses of wine last night. Limo arrives; we drive through the backcountry on tiny hedgerow-lined dirt roads barely big enough for one car. We round a corner; Paul's two-story house comes into view. I smell the grass in the meadow. Living in a home in the heart of the country indeed.

Both Paul and his lovely wife Linda come out and welcome me inside. Linda preps us some tea and "bickies." We take seats around the kitchen table. I mention how much I love their home.

"I planned it from scratch, using very basic triangle and half-circle concepts." Paul gestures, tracing the perimeters of the abode. Their house is unique but quite homey and unpretentious. It could fit in nicely in Hancock Park, an upscale LA neighborhood with lovely, 1920's 2-story Tudor homes. By rock star standards, Paul's and Linda's home is very modest.

We chat for 20 minutes, then Paul smiles and pats the table. "OK. Let's hear your song idea!"

He shows me to the music room, I sit at the piano. I take a quick breath and despite slightly trembling fingers, do a halfway decent job of playing my rough song concept. I'm kind of proud of the nice little modulation in the middle of the chorus. The only lyric I have is "I'll be here tomorrow," then I hum and mumble the rest of the melody. Relieved I've made it through without having a heart attack, I anxiously await his response.

"Very nice! So, what would we call it? 'Tomorrow'? I really like the one-word titles, like 'Yesterday'."

"Hmmm... title sounds familiar. Could you hum a few bars?" He gives me the patented McCartney raised eyebrow and a wry smile.

We spitball for a minute on production and lyric ideas.

"Actually, there's a harmony that would go well with that. Play it again."

I launch in again and he nails this great harmony right out of the gate. Bloody hell. Paul McCartney is accompanying me on my rough song idea. Somebody pinch me.

"So, how'd you like the modulation in the chorus?" I'm dying to hear if he's impressed with my clever idea.

"It modulated?"

"Yeah, you know… it starts out in the key of C, then I do a '2 - 5' chord change up into Eb, then a '2 - 5' back down into C." I demonstrate the changes again.

"Yeah, I like it when it sort of moves from the white keys to the black keys." His face betrays nothing.

Realizing he's serious, I'm now rethinking all my years of studying music theory. Here's one of the greatest songwriters in the history of … ever, who clearly understands and utilizes modulations in his songs — the fantastic key change in 'Penny Lane' comes to mind, among many others. But he *feels* it on a visceral level. A command of music theory is a great tool but it's a guarantee of nothing — tools aren't rules. It drives home the point to me that the bottom line isn't a person's education, it's their creative ability.

I follow Paul's request and play the song a third time, this time making a cassette copy of the tune to leave with him.

Though nothing ever came of it, I have no regrets. Just the experience of being in that creative zone with him for half an hour had a profound effect on me. There's a Sanskrit word, "Shaktipat," which refers to the process of transmitting spiritual energy from one person to another. The idea is when you are in the presence of an enlightened master, your vibration level rises. Just like when you strike a tuning fork, other tuning forks nearby begin sympathetically resonating with that frequency. At a profound level, I was struck with the realization that it's possible to tune in to another reality.

Looking back, it's clear that from this encounter going forward, my writing went to another level. My melodies got stronger and started coming from a more spiritual place. I shifted my focus from trying to craft a hit song to creating compositions that felt connected to deeper emotions seeking a means of expression.

Paul and Linda have to go to London on business, so they leave me there to work. "Help yourself to whatever's in the fridge." (It would turn out to be mostly stuff like sprouts, garbanzo beans and veggies — hard pass.) "Feel free to take a break and stroll around the farm." Paul smiles as he walks out the door.

I have a full day of work ahead, but I have to take a second to sneak a look at all of Paul's works of art around the room: a painting in progress on an easel with tubes of color on a nearby stand, a completed painting hung on the wall, a few leaning against a chair. Mostly colorful, abstract, impressionistic works. Very evocative. This guy has enough money that he, his children, and their children will never need to work if they don't want to. But that's hardly the point. He's driven by a life-long desire to create, to answer to the muse. "Ars Gratia Artis," as the expression goes. One of the greatest joys art has to offer comes from the simple act of creating it. What a beautiful space to live in.

Throughout the day, one by one, each of his four kids come in and talk to me while I work on the piano: Stella, Mary, Heather then James. Each of them is gracious and genuinely curious about the process. None of them are afflicted with the sense of entitlement I've seen with many children of celebrities.

Late afternoon turns into early evening. I'm finally winding up my work when Paul and Linda return. "Wow. Quite the project, eh?" He gives me a pat on the back.

"Take it for a spin!" I stand up, offering him the bench.

He sits down, plays a few chords — he loves the new way it feels and sounds. He starts playing the classic intro to "Lady Madonna."

"Oh man, I love that riff! Would you show me how to play it?"

"Sure. It's just this line in the bass ... and these chords in the right hand." He plays it again slowly a couple of times, breaking down the left- and right-hand parts. I can't believe I'm getting a piano lesson from Paul McCartney.

Earlier, I'd found the remnants of a resin-stained, mostly smoked joint inside his piano. "It's only fair to tell you I've already alerted the Japanese authorities. They're on their way." I set it on the music desk in front of him.

He laughs at my reference to the recent legal trouble he'd had in Japan when customs found pot in his luggage. Days later, when he finally landed in LA, the press asked how he resolved the issue. He said, "I promised I'd never do it again," smiling with an exaggerated wink into the camera.

As I'm leaving, his feisty seven-year-old son James and I are having fun, horsing around in the entryway. He's mock-slugging me and I'm pretend-slugging him in return. Then without warning, I feel this incredibly sharp, overwhelming pain in my groin. Paul's sheepdog Murdoch thought I was trying to attack James and bit me hard, precisely in the center of my existence. I let out a piercing yell. Paul and Linda rush in. I'm hunched over with both hands over my crotch.

"What on earth happened!" Linda moves towards me. Murdoch barks.

I lurch back. "Murdoch just bit me in my manhood!" I'm not about to tangle with those fangs again.

"You better go check to see everything's still intact!" Paul gestures to the bathroom down the hall.

After I return — fortunately unscathed — and the initial shock is wearing off, Paul lightens things up. "Oh, come on Jim, that's the best you've felt all day!"

"Yeah, I guess you're right." I turn and face his pooch. "Did the earth move for you too, Murdoch?"

A few years later, Paul will remind me of this incident in an unexpected setting.

"Jimmmbo!!"

I can tell you with absolute certainty that few things in life will ever compare to the feeling you get when Paul McCartney shouts his nickname for you into the microphone during soundcheck, and your name echoes under an afternoon sun throughout an empty Hollywood Bowl.

It's April of 1993. Paul's personal manager, John Hammel, has called me from the road. "We'll be coming to LA doing an Earth Day benefit at the Bowl and I thought that might be a good opportunity to have you check out the Sgt. Pepper piano. We're not using it that night and we could set it up backstage for you. And of course, you're welcome to stay for the show."

Well, that's a no-brainer. The afternoon of the concert rolls around, I head up the long drive to the historic venue, parking in the VIP section just behind the Bowl. Once backstage, I head towards the sound of Paul's vocal echoing through the empty amphitheater. He turns around, sees me, shouts my name. He sets his guitar down, walks over, gives me a hug. Even if he weren't the icon he is, I'd still have lit up seeing him. He's just a great dude.

"Murdoch sends his love." Paul grins, gives a wink and a nod.

"Please tell him I think of him often. Fondly. We'll always have that … special moment." I give a wistful look, cross my hands over my heart.

He laughs. "Seriously, I kept waiting to hear from your attorney after that one."

Linda comes over, gives me a hug.

"Well done on your new vegetarian food line!" I give her a pat on the arm. We talk about the benefits of vegetarianism for a bit before I must head backstage and get started on the piano.

A while later, my friend Andrew Gold walks in as I'm finishing putting the piano back together. "Hey Jim! Fancy seeing you here. What are you up to?"

I debrief him on my mission. "Come check out Paul's touring piano, dude! He's painted it psychedelic colors and calls it the 'Sgt. Pepper' piano."

Andrew's a rabid Beatle fan. He plays a few chords of "Let It Be." "Wow. So cool!"

Andrew tells me he's part of that night's big surprise. At the very end of the show, each of the featured artists of the star-studded concert will join the grand finale, "Hey Jude." As they're being introduced, a huge choir — led by Andrew — will be ushered on stage to join in.

Andrew pauses, cocks his head, turns more directly towards me. "Actually, it's the same choir that you've sung with many times, Jim."

He's referring to the choir he and Debbie Pearl organize every December to sing Christmas Carols at children's hospitals. "Why don't you join us? You know all the singers. And I think you know the song!"

"Dude! Are you kidding? I'd love to!"

I finish my work, load my tools in the car and head back to the artist's tent where they're serving dinner. I chat with a few of the folks from VH-1 who are there taping the event for a TV special. My all-access pass allows me to mill about the venue over the course of the evening, enjoying the fantastic concert from multiple vantage points. Andrew has instructed us to gather backstage when Paul begins his set. Over the strains of "All My Loving," "Blackbird," and "Live and Let Die" drifting from the stage, Andrew is quietly giving us last-minute instructions.

Paul is now finishing his set; we start lining up close to the stage entrance. With the first strains of "Hey Jude," a deafening roar rises from the amphitheater. My pulse is quickening. How the hell have I become part of this historic moment?

"Steve Miller! . . . Natalie Merchant! . . . Bruce Cockburn! . . . Kenny Loggins! . . . Don Henley!" Paul brings the guest artists on stage one by one. Then finally, the evening's big surprise guest: *"Ladies and Gentlemen . . . Ringo!"*

The crowd goes wild. That's our cue, it's *go* time. All 60 of us are led single file on stage, breaking into several rows across the back. It's a roll of the dice where each of us will end up. As fate would have it, I end up standing directly behind Paul. Holy shit. This is crazy. I'm singing with a Beatle on stage at the Hollywood fucking Bowl — a place that Paul last played with John, George, and Ringo 29 years ago in 1964. How is this my life? I feel like Zelig, randomly showing up in the middle of all these epic events.

I spot my friend Ed Begley, Jr. in the front row and thankfully suppress the impulse to wave and yell "Hey Ed! Dig who's standing right behind Paul fucking McCartney!" Instead, I do my best to be present and soak up the vibe of this amazing moment.

With VH-1 camera cranes zooming in, Paul comes to the climax of the song, singing *"Better, better, better, better . . . ahhhh!"* Then we all go:

Nah . . . nah nah-nah-nah nah, nah-nah-nah nah . . . hey Jude!

Lighters come out, thousands of people waving hands in the air, tears streaming down faces. Seventeen thousand of us singing at the top of our lungs, sharing a communal experience of being ignited by music deeply ingrained in our DNA. This glorious moment is emblematic of what drives me as an artist: the hope of creating music that transcends boundaries, that unites people, that speaks to the very essence of the human condition.

The next day, *LA Times* critic Robert Hilburn said the "Hey Jude" climax of the show "served on this special night as a moment of benediction for the city." I'll realize later it was a benediction for me as well. The 8-year-old West Texas boy who was first lit up by the Beatles decades ago had come full circle.

CHAPTER 19
London Still Calling

In the coming years, I'd be flown to the UK a dozen times, being offered royal treatment by one icon after another: Pete Townshend of The Who, Dave Gilmour of Pink Floyd, Chris Squire of Yes. The visits usually included an overnight stay at their home, sharing tales over dinner and wine. My trip to Keith Emerson's house south of London was incredibly special. I'd worn out *Pictures at an Exhibition* by Emerson, Lake and Palmer, among several of their other albums, and Keith was an icon to me.

Keith offered to send a limo for me, but I decided to have a go at "hiring" a car, driving to his place on my own. In the days before GPS, driving on the left side of the road for my first time, on English back roads, navigating their "roundabouts," was no small feat.

"Hey, I only got lost four times!" I've shown up over an hour late, but Keith is most gracious and enjoys showing me around his historic English Tudor home. With its huge, arched doors of weathered oak and massive iron rings for door handles, the decorative half-timbering and intricate leaded glass windows, the clay chimney pots atop the steeply pitched gable roof, the uneven, worn brick walkway, this is the real deal.

"Hundreds of years ago, this house was owned by the county tax collector. People would come here from miles around to pay their fees owed to the Crown." Keith leads me inside, down a dimly lit hallway, gesturing to me to watch my head on the low door jams — reminders of an era when people were much shorter.

I smile and shake my head. "Man, in America, we put historical marker plaques on homes built in the 1920s. This is amazing!"

Over dinner and a couple of bottles of a wonderful French cabernet, he shares stories of touring with ELP, his classical piano upbringing, how much music has changed over the years. The next day when I'm showing off the work I've done on his piano, for a laugh, I play the first few notes of "Pictures at an Exhibition." He quickly joins in, accompanying me on a nearby piano. Shit. He's called my bluff. I make it about three bars in before I have to throw in the towel, confessing I'm out of my depth.

In the coming years, Keith became a mate. We shared laughs over meals at his home a few times and would get together for lunch when he came to LA. An incredible talent, but more importantly, just a great, down-to-earth guy. His presence is sorely missed since his death in 2016, but what a legacy of amazing music he left behind.

Besides connecting me with world-class artists, my work was providing me with world-class travel opportunities.

"Do you have anything darker?" I speak slowly, over-articulating my words. I thumb through my English-to-German translation pocketbook, direct the salesperson's attention to the word closest to my meaning: *"Dunkelblau?"*

I'm trying to find the exact shade of blue ink in which an agent had handwritten on my Eurail Pass. The clerk in this Zurich stationery store is helpful, bringing out a half dozen pens. After auditioning them all, I find the closest color match. I do several practice strokes on a blank piece of paper, steady my hand, and carefully draw a backwards three on the pass, turning the three of the expiration date into an eight. *Voila!* I've just extended my 21-day Eurail pass another 5 days.

Several weeks earlier in London, I'd gotten a call from Chris Squire of Yes. "We're going to record our new album in an ancient stone castle north of Milan that's been converted into a state-of-the-art recording studio. Would you be up for going there to install a MIDI-adapter in their piano for us? Of course, we'll fly you business class and they'll treat you like a king while you're there."

Uh, yeah.

What an incredible opportunity to finally see the continent of Europe. I pore over maps of Italy, Switzerland, Austria, and France and concoct a plan to parlay this work trip into the holiday of a lifetime. I pick up several translation books and start learning a few key phrases in Italian, German, and French.

"Molto bene!" and "sehr gut!" come easy. And of course, I already have *"Voulez vous coucher avec moi, ce soir?"* down cold. I'm good to go.

After finishing my work in Milan, I phone a sweet girl I'd met on the plane flying into Italy. Laura — with "silky smooth skin the color of café au lait" — is glad to play host, proudly showing me several of the amazing sites around her hometown: Il Duomo, lunch near the Piazza del Duomo, then finally a 50-kilometer drive north to Lake Como. Absolutely gorgeous. The lake also.

The next morning, she takes me to the train station and plays interpreter for me, assisting me in getting my Eurail pass.

"Mille grazie, Laura!" I blow a kiss and wave goodbye to her out the train window. I'm off on a grand adventure: I throw coins in the Trevi Fountain in Rome; climb to the top of St. Stephen's Cathedral overlooking Stephansplatz in Vienna with my old high school friend Heidi Gabriel; walk up the Olympic ski slope at night in Innsbruck; clink toasts with new friends in beer halls in Munich; commit forgery in a stationery store in Zurich; listen to "Invisible" by Alison Moyet on repeat on my Walkman headphones while steering a rented motorboat around Lake Geneva on a picture-perfect day; scuba dive off the coast of Cannes, seeing my first octopus up close and personal; watch artists in front of easels creating amazing pencil drawings in the cobblestone square atop Montmartre; look out onto the Seine River and colorful rooftops of Paris from atop the Eiffel Tower.

As soon as the train dropped me off in each new city, I'd get money changed into yet another currency, then head straight to the information kiosk. Some kind person would help me find lodging nearby, offering directions in broken English accompanied by exaggerated gesticulations. I'd settle into the hotel and venture out "on God's good humor," soaking up as much of the local culture as possible, connecting with as many people as possible. I absorbed more understanding of European geography and culture in this short period than I ever had in all my years of school.

Each of the dozen times I'd travel from LA to London for another artist, I used it as a springboard for an adventure onto "the continent." Once when flying to Geneva, the pilot let me sit in the cockpit with him and his copilot.

"That's Mt. Blanc in the distance." He nodded his head toward the snow-capped mountain as he flipped a couple of switches. They let me stay with them right up to the last minute before landing. Ah, the days before 9/11.

The travel opportunities that kept pouring in were insane. I felt like I was in a fairy tale. My unique position of being the guy exclusively offering this cool, new "must-have" MIDI-adapter for piano whisked me to all parts of the globe. A new country, a new adventure, making friends and learning about their cultures along the way. When you have no agenda, magic happens.

In the last few years of my twenties, I explored Stockholm with beautiful Susanna; dined al fresco in Aix en Provence in the south of France with Jean-Jerome and Anne Dominique; strolled on the beach in Ipanema; worked in Rio for Little Richard; and was welcomed in Santa Margherita Italy by Marco and Anna — a random couple on the street I'd asked for directions, who later insisted I stay in their guest bedroom. Both were working the following day, but demanded I take their VW station wagon. "You MUST see La Spezia — the drive is one of the most beautiful anywhere." Each new adventure, each new person I connected with, expanded the boundaries of my worldview, and deepened my appreciation of our shared humanity.

It's a stunning afternoon at the country villa where I'm visiting in the south of France. British composer Michael Nyman is writing the music to the film *The Piano*, starring Holly Hunter. He's flown me here to MIDI the piano in his remote villa — "remote" being the operative word. To get here, you fly into Toulouse, then take an hour-long train ride to Faget-Abbatial, a tiny village with a population of 200. You then hail a cab, driving another 30 minutes to Michael's villa.

"My nearest neighbor used to be a piano tuner," Michael tells me. "He's fascinated to see what it is you'll be doing to the piano. I hope you don't mind that I told him he could come watch you while you work?" Michael's been a gracious host, I can hardly object.

Soon, across the field, we see Michael's friend approaching. I squint my eyes. The closer the neighbor gets, the stronger my sense that I recognize this tall, slender, dark-haired figure. He comes a few steps closer, I jump to my feet.

"*Bruce?* . . . What the *hell?*" I smile and shake my head in disbelief.

Turns out his nearest neighbor — a mile to the west — is Bruce, the French-Canadian with whom I'd attended piano tuning school in Cleveland. Though we'd become friendly back in the day, he hadn't really crossed my mind in the decade or so since we graduated.

"Oh … my … God. I can't believe I'm running into you, in the middle of the boonies, on the other side of the world." I throw my arms around him.

Bruce laughs, pats me on the shoulder. "After tuning school, I returned to Toronto, married a French woman and we moved to the hotel that's been in her family for several generations." He nods to the west, in the direction of his home.

We soon head to the piano where Bruce watches intently over the next few hours as I take apart the piano, disassemble the action, install and adjust the sensor strip beneath the keys, mount the sustain sensor and CPU inside the piano, and connect it all together. We summon Michael, who's delighted with the end result.

Bruce picks me up the next day. We spend the afternoon driving high into the Pyrenees, looking into the rolling mountains of Spain. He takes me to an abandoned church out in the country, with the sole intent of showing me this ancient, massive oak tree in front. I stretch out my arms and wrap them as far as I can around the tree. Bruce grasps my hand, continuing the reach. We'd have needed at least one more person to encircle the tree.

"This tree is estimated to be over 400 years old. It was around during the Renaissance and the French Revolution," Bruce says, both of us taking a second to imagine the history that unfolded in the lifespan of this tree.

Bruce and I kept in touch over the coming years, exchanging postcards. Each card a reminder of the simpler, laid-back life he'd chosen. Perhaps such a life was waiting for me, but for now, I had "miles to go before I sleep."

CHAPTER 20
Go for it, Jimmy

"Hey Jimmy... is that *you?*"

Who the hell still calls me *Jimmy?* And what are they doing in this bar, in a New Mexico hotel, in the middle of this blizzard? I turn to my left, squint my eyes. Across the crowded, smokey room, I make out a familiar face.

Only two hours ago, en route from LA to Amarillo for Christmas, I was boarding the plane in Albuquerque when the Southwest flight attendant announced, "Sorry folks. We just got word that the Amarillo airport has shut down due to a massive blizzard. This flight's been canceled." Over a collective groan from the travelers, they announced they were putting us on standby for the first flight in the morning and giving us vouchers to stay at the nearby Amfac Hotel. I caught the shuttle, got checked in, headed to the bar.

Of all the gin joints in all the towns in all the world, my cousin Dudley — who could pass for Danny Devito's taller brother — just so happens to be stranded in the same middle-of-nowhere as me. He's an eccentric character who grows his own pot and plays left-handed guitar. But most notably, Dudley's a hot-shot helicopter pilot. Have chopper, will travel. Need a pilot for fighting forest fires in Idaho? Flying an Arab prince in Saudi Arabia? A mercenary for hire in Vietnam? He's your man.

"Dudley! What the hell are you doing here?" I give him a big bear hug. We take our drinks, grab a table and over the din of the raucous crowd, Dudley debriefs me about his crazy, clandestine mission.

"A couple of El Salvadoran CIA operatives bought a helicopter in California. They've hired me to fly it cross-country to Miami where it'll be outfitted with gun turrets."

I reach for my drink. Did he just say *gun turrets?*

"After that, I'll fly it under radar down to Nicaragua, where they'll give it to the Contras. All of this, by the way, has been paid for with Ollie

North drug money."

Alright then. I think I'll have that second screwdriver now.

Then Dudley throws out an invitation. "I'll have to run it by the two other guys, but Amarillo is right on our way. We have an open seat and can drop you off if you want."

Old helicopter, sketchy-sounding passengers, intense winter storm, daredevil pilot — this has all the makings of *The Buddy Holly Story, Part Two*.

"Uh… wow … *man!* … thanks so much for the offer, Dudley, but I think I should play it safe and just…"

He sees my apprehension and before I can decline his offer he smiles and looks me square in the eyes.

"Sometimes ya just gotta go for it, Jimmy."

I didn't realize their effect on me at the time, but the sound of Dudley's gravelly voice uttering those words would echo in my head many times over the years. An incantation inspiring me to push through and achieve my goals.

Cut to the following morning on the Cutter Airport tarmac. Dudley has cleared this impromptu plan with the El Salvadorians (let's call them ES1 and ES2) and on a crisp, sunny December morning, we exchange pleasant nods and all pile into the helicopter. Dudley's in the pilot seat, ES1 flying shotgun; I'm directly behind Dudley and to my right is ES2 – – at whose feet is a black briefcase. Dudley would later tell me it held a million in cash intended for weaponizing the helicopter and funding the Contras.

Dudley is now running through his pre-flight checklist, flipping switches, tapping gauges. Rotors up to speed, everyone strapped in. Dudley turns and peeks at us from over the top of his aviator sunglasses. We all have our headsets on and over the deafening roar of the engine, Dudley barks, "ALL SET?" We give a thumbs-up. Up and off we go.

The next hour is pretty sweet, hovering happily over I-40, watching the trucks far below. Beautiful sunny day. Life is good.

Then far on the horizon, a massive wall of clouds as black as night comes into view. The closer we get, the more ominous they become. Dudley doesn't bat an eye and flies directly into them. Instantly, the intense winds start violently jolting our little aircraft. ES2 flinches. Ice collects on the blades, slowing their speed, decreasing our altitude. I'm now making out license numbers on trucks that were tiny specks only 20 minutes ago.

Trying to shake ice off the blades, Dudley takes the stick and rams it back and forth a few times, slamming the helicopter up and down violently. ES2 freaks. He shouts to Dudley, "LOCO! PUT *DOWN!*," wildly gesticulating his thumb downwards. Not a great way for my life to end, but the news article announcing my demise is going to be pretty fucking cool:

Recovered body ... aspiring musician ... smoldering wreckage ... suspected CIA operatives ... family requests that you respect their privacy at this difficult time...

Even Dudley is now realizing the gravity of the situation and is looking for a place to "put down." Just ahead through the swirling blizzard, a mirage begins emerging on the horizon. It's the glowing lights from the only building for miles — a Stuckey's roadside stop. Slowly, unsteadily, we descend into the vacant parking lot. ES 1 and 2 and I all exhale for the first time in 45 minutes.

I bundle up and run inside. There at the counter stands the solitary customer. He notices me as I walk in. I smile and nod. "Hey, you wouldn't happen to be going through Amarillo would you?"

"Sure am. Need a lift?" I run back out, inform Dudley of my luck. He tells me to go ahead, but they have to stay behind with the chopper. I grab my things, and my Stuckey's savior and I pile into his car. He shares one of his pecan pralines and drives the remaining 27 miles to Amarillo, dropping me at my mom's house just off I-40. Journey complete.

Years later, we would lose Dudley to Agent Orange-related cancer. I would often think back to this chance encounter with him in a bar in the middle of nowhere, reminding me of his daring, gonzo spirit. His "life's too short / fuck your fears" attitude would inspire me long after his passing. Whenever I would hit a brick wall of trepidation, I could hear him telling me "Sometimes ya just gotta go for it, Jimmy."

CHAPTER 21
Paul

I can't shake the sense that something in my universe isn't quite right. It's a Saturday night. I've gone to the Grauman's Chinese Theater in Hollywood to see *River's Edge*, a movie about these teenagers who find the naked body of a dead girl beside a river. The dark drama is disturbing but the unsettled feeling I have seems rooted in something more. I'm not exactly enjoying the movie, but I can't bring myself to walk out. When I get home, there are four messages on my answering machine, all from my Aunt Billie urging me to call my mom right away.

"Are you sitting down?" Mom sounds hoarse, her voice is breaking.

"Mom, what is it? What's happened?" My mouth goes dry, my heart races. Whatever it is, I know instantly this is what my unsettled feeling has been connected to.

She takes a long pause.

"Paul's dead."

"Wait... what? ... *How?*" I feel my face grow flush.

"He ... died of a heroin overdose a couple of hours ago."

I feel like someone's kicked me in the stomach. I can't speak.

"Paul, his friend Jon, and I had a nice quiet dinner here at home. Paul got news of his 4.0 grade average in the mail today. We were celebrating." Mom is doing her best to speak through tears. "Paul and Jon went back to Paul's bedroom. Later, I was watching *Golden Girls* in the living room when Jon came in and said, 'I think you might want to go check on Paul.'"

Mom's voice is trembling. Only six weeks earlier, Mom's husband Lou, my stepfather, died of cirrhosis of the liver. She's been a mess ever since. Now this.

"When I went in, Paul wasn't moving, and his body was cold." We're both sobbing. She blows her nose. "The paramedics came 15 minutes later and performed CPR on him. The paddles were useless. He was gone."

Words evade me, my stomach is in knots. I tell her I'll be on a plane tomorrow. I call Paul's friend Jon. He levels with me. Earlier that afternoon, Paul hocked the Rolex watch he'd inherited from our Uncle Cliff. He used the money to buy some smack. After dinner, Paul shot up, then he and Jon went to Paul's room to listen to music. After a while, Paul went to the bathroom again. He came back and said, "I just did some more." Paul put his headphones on, sank into his chair, and drifted off into the ether.

"Later," Jon elaborated, "I noticed he hadn't moved. I went to shake him, and he didn't respond. That's when I went to tell your mom."

I'm gripping the phone so tightly my knuckles are white. I want to fucking punch Jon for not having acted sooner, but deep down I know that as a kid, I'd probably have done exactly what he did: get the hell out of there. Little by little, it's sinking in that there's nothing I can do or say that will change reality.

My little brother is gone.

I grit my teeth. I thank Jon. I hang up. I sit in dazed silence for a minute, then yell at the top of my lungs. ... *"GODDAMN IT!"* ... I clench my fist and punch a hole in the wall. I cry in my bones.

How can something so fundamentally unfair happen . . . now? Paul had *just* discovered his mission in life, he was lit up with purpose. After floundering for several years, he'd enrolled in Amarillo College, majoring in Broadcasting and Video Production. He became the top scoring student in his class.

It's the day of the funeral, the family is gathered in Amarillo. The black limo delivers us to Boxwell Funeral Home. People are already seated as we're escorted to our pew on the front row. "Imagine" by John Lennon, one of Paul's favorite songs, is playing on the P.A. system. I'm in a haze as one bittersweet memory after another comes to mind. It comes my time to speak.

I thank everyone on behalf of the family for coming. I talk about Paul's love for traveling, skiing, and reading. About his and my shared sense of humor, how we were both spiritual seekers, how we'd learned Transcendental Meditation together. About how, though nine years apart, we had very similar childhoods, with sometimes troubled emotions, and the intense need for acceptance of our friends and peers. I say how happy we've been that he finally found his path in life.

I pause, fidget with my notes. "I think Paul might have been finding it difficult to deal with his newfound success. He knew he would have to change some old ways of thinking about himself, and that's not easy. Paul had said, 'Sometimes it's easier to just live up to people's expectations of you than to change.'

"I've been trying really hard in the past three days to make sense of why a 23-year-old in the prime of their youth with a newfound purpose would be 'taken out of the game.' While my sense of loss cuts to the bone, and I still have many unanswered questions, I know Paul's brief life was not in vain. I resolve to carry Paul's memory with me as a constant reminder of how fragile life is; how important it is to not take life for granted; to live each day like it's my last."

People hug us afterwards, offer condolences, fumble for the right words. But especially for my mom and dad, there are no right words. It's just not in the natural order of things for a parent to have to bury a child.

After the funeral, I sit comatose in a folding chair in my mom's backyard. The shock is wearing off, the grief is setting in. I look at my drink on the table just to my right. I can't muster sufficient energy to lift my arm and reach for it. I haven't properly slept in days and the *What Ifs* and demons of regret are beginning to weigh on me.

Would Paul's life have gone another direction if I'd have used my influence with him to dissuade him from drugs? Or would trying to dissuade him just have made it more taboo, making it even more desirable? My mother said he worshiped me. Had I set a bad example for him? The layers of sadness and remorse were caving me in.

I thought back to when Paul was living with me. Specifically, the time I could tell he was high, and — in an effort to be less controlling — told him it was OK if he had smoked some weed. When he swore he hadn't, it turns out he was telling the truth. No, it wasn't pot I was detecting, it was fucking heroin. He must have laughed to himself about the irony. I now know the difference: pot gives you red, bloodshot eyes. His were glassy and his skin was pale. I'd later find an entry he'd written in his diary: "it took me six months to find a heroin connection in LA." He was doing smack right under my roof and I had no clue.

For months after his passing, I'd see Paul in my dreams. He'd lay a joke on me and we'd both laugh our asses off. I'd wake and reach for the phone to call him. Then the crushing heartache would return. His death wasn't a dream. He wasn't coming back. While I was eventually able to partially compartmentalize the pain, I don't think Mom or Dad ever really did. Mom especially was devastated by his loss and carried a trace of sadness in her eyes for the rest of her years.

Long after Paul's overdose, an idea sat in dark isolation in a dank, secluded corner of my mind. One of those ideas that seems perfectly reasonable until it's finally drawn out into the light of day. I'd held onto the notion that "one day, I'll try heroin just to see what it was my brother was so drawn to." I'll come away from the experience with more compassion and understanding of what lured him so. I'll think of Paul, smile, and say, "I get it, little bro."

Then I met someone who had been a heroin addict — an incredibly smart, high-functioning engineer who'd been on the team designing parts for the space shuttle. As I related my intention to him, the words sounded utterly inane as they left my mouth for the first time.

He took a beat.

"Don't you fucking dare." He glared at me with laser focus. "Let me tell you how it'll go down. You'll try it that one time. You'll feel an incredible sense of well-being, like you're being held in the arms of God. Then six months later, you'll think 'I did it that one time and was able to walk away — maybe it could be a Saturday night thing.' Then it becomes a Friday *and* Saturday night thing. Then Thursday rolls around and 'why not get a head start on the weekend?' This is how I started, and it eventually became a thousand-dollar-a-day habit that destroyed my life and put me in a hole that took me years to climb out of."

His words were a cold, hard reality-slap across my face. In all my youthful mischief, I'd somehow avoided the rocky coastline to which my brother ventured too close. The same sirens that called to me, ultimately drew my brother to his demise.

To this day, I'll see someone who reminds me of my little bro and think of the Paul that could have been. Would he be a video editor? A cameraman for a news affiliate? Perhaps even a successful movie producer? It can be a dark rabbit hole.

CHAPTER 22
You've Got a Road Trip

I love the MIDI-adapter you installed in my piano in LA and was wondering if you'd be up for doing the same thing to the piano at my ranch in Idaho."

Holy shit. One of the greatest singer-songwriters of all time just made me an offer I can't refuse. And it gets better...

"I have to drive a U-Haul trailer up there soon. If you want to keep me company on the two-day drive, you could do the work, then hang out at the ranch for a week. I'll fly us both back first-class."

I'm still grieving over Paul's death. A road trip will do me good.

A couple of weeks later, Carole King pulls up to my apartment in North Hollywood, U-Haul trailer in tow. I throw my work stuff and suitcase in the back. I hop in, pull the door shut, we're off.

"Ah... a nice long road trip. Just what the doctor ordered." I exhale slowly and fasten my seatbelt.

"Everything OK?" Carole senses that my words might be loaded.

I contemplate glossing over the subject, not wanting her to think she's going to be trapped in a car for two days driving 933 miles with Mr. Morose. *What the fuck. Are we going to talk about the weather for the next two days?*

"Well actually ... I lost my brother recently and I've been struggling to deal with the pain. A road trip and time in the mountains is probably just what I need."

She pulls the car over, touches my arm. "I'm so sorry, Jim. I had no idea."

We've barely made it four blocks and we're already diving headlong into the heavy shit. For the next several hours, we discuss our spiritual beliefs, ideas about what happens after people die, the meaning of life. You know, light stuff. A resilient conversationalist and a thoughtful, caring person, she doesn't think twice about "going there."

"I believe in the *idea* of reincarnation," I say, "but the whole question of *exactly* what persists when we shake off our mortal coil is a mystery." I pause while I remember a favorite lyric. "As far as the wrestling with the looming riddle of what happens when people die, I think Jackson Browne summed up best:

> *It's like a song I can hear, playing right in my ear*
> *I can't sing it, but I can't help listening*

Carole shares some of the basic tenets of Judaism and the focus on the importance of doing good deeds while you're alive, and less focus on the afterlife.

"Well, what do *you* believe happens when people die? Do you believe in reincarnation?" I turn slightly more towards her.

She pauses, focuses on a point in the distance, draws a slow breath. "I think the *essence* of us does carry on . . . somehow. Maybe it goes into the ether, then sort of ... mixes with other's essences and lives on in another form."

I tell her about a book that someone recently gave me that I found comfort in, *Life After Life* by Dr. Raymond Moody. "What I love about it, is that it isn't religion or philosophy. It's simply interviews with over 150 people who've had the experience of dying and coming back. The commonality of their experiences was too much for my skeptical mind to dismiss."

Carole glances at me, then back to the road. She nods as if to say, "go on…"

"The composite experience went something like this: people come out of their body, they look down on the hospital bed, or crash scene, etc., are greeted by the essences of friends and family who've died before. They're then drawn towards a radiant light at the end of a long, dark tunnel. Finally, they're greeted by some kind of omniscient presence and together they objectively but compassionately review the person's life. It was kind of like, 'so how did it go for you?' For some it was a scene-by-scene 3D movie. For others it was selected highlights. For all of them, it was a blink of an eye. And then, in an instant, they were back in their bodies as it wasn't quite their time to die."

The miles and hours roll by, but we continue the contemplative, existential theme. Against the backdrop of Mt. Whitney and the majestic Sierra Nevada mountains to our left, we kick around ideas about the meaning of life, about each religion's take on the afterlife.

I tell her I think the concept of infinity and the question of whatever lies beyond this life is so far beyond our rational mind's capacity to comprehend that we grasp for some kind of narrative that makes sense of it. "There are countless religions, with countless explanations about how it all works."

"Yes," she says, "but at their core, they're all some variation on the Golden Rule: 'do unto others as you'd have them do unto you'."

I smiled and nodded in agreement. "There are many paths up the mountain, and I respect that everyone has to figure out what works best for them."

We stop in Lone Pine to grab a couple of sandwiches for the road. We nip into the general store. Carole grabs a few bottles of water, some chips and a couple of packages of peanuts.

"That'll be $8.68, please." The lady behind the cash register barely looks up. I want to say, "Hey! Don't you know who you just sold road snacks to? This woman sold more records than any other female singer-songwriter! Ever heard "I Feel the Earth Move Under My Feet"? . . . "It's Too Late"? . . . "So Far Away"?"

"Here you go. Thanks so much." Carole puts a ten on the counter, smiles, tells her to keep the change.

Back on the road, we soon leave the gorgeous country along Route 395 and are now headed east out of Bishop into no man's land — mile after mile of featureless desert. We try tuning into a local AM radio station or two but mostly get static. We talk about everything and nothing.

Carole casually mentions that she's looking for an assistant — someone who can make calls on her behalf, handle correspondence for her. I tell her I'll give it some thought. Then a few miles down the road, a light bulb goes off.

"Carole! I have the *perfect* person for you. Lorna Guess. She used to work for me. Super smart, great communicator. She's exactly who you need."

"Sounds great. Let's set up a meeting when we get back."

I would later introduce Carole to Lorna, who went on to manage Carole for 24 years. Lorna's husband Rudy played in Carole's band for years and became a producer for Carole. Looking back, I get a huge sense of gratitude when I'm at the right place at the right time to connect people I care about with each other.

Pitstop en route to Idaho. Note the gas price.

The shadows are growing longer, casting a muted, lavender veil across the desert landscape. We decide to stop for the night in Ely, a quaint Nevada mining town. We grab dinner at a funky diner, check into our respective rooms, and call it a day.

The next morning, sufficiently caffeinated, we're back on the road and the endless stretch of vast, featureless landscape continues. I'm dying to know about her musical background and how she got from her humble origins in Brooklyn to becoming one of the most successful songwriters of all time. The miles and hours pass.

We talk about her mom teaching her to play piano starting at age three, about being fascinated by pop songs on the radio, writing with Paul Simon when she was in high school, then meeting and marrying her songwriting partner, Gerry Goffin. Carole and Gerry had day jobs and wrote songs at night. Then in 1961 the big break comes — they have a number one hit with their song "Will You Still Love Me Tomorrow" by the Shirelles.

"Wow. That must have felt amazing to have finally punched through like that." I'm thrilled to be treated to these incredible stories from a legend, but I'm trying not to sound too much like Gomer Pyle.

Carole nods and smiles. "Time to stretch our legs!"

She's pulled over to a rest stop. We get out, do some jumping jacks, shake out our hands. We hit the bathrooms and jump back in the car for round two.

Back on the road, I gently restart my *This Is Your Life* query. I sense she's enjoying sharing her amazing narrative with a curious soul. I ask her what it was like writing in the Brill Building, the famous office complex at 1619 Broadway in New York where "On Broadway," "Stand by Me," "Jailhouse Rock," and a zillion iconic pop songs were written. Think sweat shop for hits.

"We'd squeeze into these tiny cubby holes that barely had room for a piano and a bench," she told me. "You could hear another songwriter next door also searching for the next hit. It was claustrophobic but great fun."

By "another songwriter next door" she means music titans like Neil Diamond, Burt Bacharach, Leiber & Stoller, Barry Mann & Cynthia Weil, Neil Sedaka, Phil Spector, Jeff Barry & Ellie Greenwich, and a dozen other writers, all of whom would go on to create some of the biggest hits of all time.

We talk about everything from Carole having met my personal hero James Taylor at a party in Laurel Canyon in '69 to her astonishing track record of something like 500 songs published, 300 songs recorded and over 100 hits.

But the coolest thing is her telling me about a tough decision she had to make in 1970. She was at the top of her game as a behind-the-scenes songwriter with massive hits under her belt such as "The Loco-Motion" (recorded by their babysitter Little Eva!), "Up on the Roof" for the Drifters, "One Fine Day" for the Chiffons, and "Pleasant Valley Sunday" for the Monkees, and "A Natural Woman" for Aretha Franklin. She was killing it, so why rock the boat?

But she was being encouraged by the legendary music producer Lou

Adler to release a record under her own name and branch out as an artist. On my own, much smaller level, I could relate to people thinking of you in a certain way and how scary it is to risk losing face.

The courage she found in stepping out was rewarded beyond her wildest imagination: her album *Tapestry* won several Grammys, blasted through the top of the *Billboard* charts — stayed at #1 for 15 consecutive weeks, then remained on the charts for nearly six years. It went on to sell over 25 million albums — one of the greatest selling records of all time. Just phenomenal.

I'm so engrossed in the story I only now notice that we're driving through the gates of her ranch.

"This is it!" Carole steers the car down the long gravel road through the slice of heaven that is her property. Geothermal pool to our left, massive western lodge and numerous guest houses nestled against a mountain to our right. Her 128-acre spread is surrounded by national forests and has rivers running through it. "Welcome!"

Over the next several idyllic days, we have dinner with her husband Rick, we ride horses, fish in a portion of the Snake River that runs through her property, skinny dip in her hot springs pool and oh yeah, I work on her piano.

I've wrapped up the MIDI installation. I call her in to try it out and show her how to use the features.

"How cool!" She plays a few chords, breaks into a smile. "Can't wait to write with this."

I pick up a guitar sitting next to the piano and start playing the intro to James Taylor's version of her iconic song, "You've Got a Friend." She looks at me, cocks her head and raises an eyebrow.

"No way I'm singing that song with you!" Her smirk slowly turns into a half-smile. I keep playing. I'm not letting her off easy. I restart the intro. I grin, chuckle, and return her raised eyebrow.

"Aw, c'mon. You got something better to do?" I play the intro yet again.

She rolls her eyes, smiles, and starts singing, "When you're down, and troubled…"

CHAPTER 23
Part of the Plan

"I could tell when we first met we were gonna be buds." He looks at me and smiles.

This is yet another of my heroes. These words mean the world to me. A balloon of emotion is inflating in my chest and is working its way to my throat. I take a sip of wine. We're standing in his kitchen chatting as he's preparing his special chili relleno dish. The aroma in the air is intoxicating, as is my second glass of cabernet.

"This recipe's one of my favorites. The clove gives it a special kick." He places a wooden spoon on a stone inset by the stove. I grab a stool, take a seat, and enjoy watching a master at work. He loves to cook and is a consummate chef.

From his kitchen window, looking beyond the barn housing his horses, past the wood fence bordering his ranch, the sun is setting on the majestic San Juan mountain range towering in the distance.

My mind drifts back to 1977, when I first heard his music. During my stint in piano tuning school in Cleveland, I was browsing the aisles of a Peaches record store when a haunting ballad with harpsichord and layered harmonies literally stopped me in my tracks. Ethereal and angelic, I'd never heard anything quite like it. Then someone turned up the volume. Clearly, they wanted to share this treasure. The hair on the back of my neck stood to attention, I got goosebumps. I stood there spellbound until the final note faded. I dashed to the counter and got the clerk's attention. "That was incredible! What was that song? Who was that artist?"

"That was "Scarecrow's Dream" by Dan Fogelberg. It's from his new album *Nether Lands*."

I couldn't get home fast enough with my newly-purchased discovery. I'd heard his name before, but he was barely a blip on my radar. I pored over the liner notes while I listened to the record on repeat. I soon bought his first three records and devoured them as well. How had I not known about this phenomenal artist?

Now, here I am a decade later standing with him in his kitchen in his incredible mountain retreat on his 600-acre ranch in southwest Colorado. This is my second of what will eventually be seven trips up to his ranch, each stay lasting just under a week.

The first time I came up here was only a few months ago. I'd coordinated my trip to Dan's ranch with a ski trip with my pop. From LAX, I flew into Albuquerque, rented a car, and headed to Taos, New Mexico, where I joined my dad. Taos had been a favorite ski area of my family's since I was a kid. After a weekend of skiing with my dad, I drove the 140 miles through the gorgeous Carson National Forest, past Apache Nation Reservation land to just south of Pagosa Springs, Colorado. From there, it's still another 20 to 30 minutes to his ranch on unpaved roads. It was extremely remote and to get there meant following a long list of written directions — quite the challenge in the days before GPS and cell phones. Dan took his need for isolation seriously.

Once you finally got to the gate of his property, there's still a mile and a half to go. I began winding my way through the forest up the steep dirt driveway. The rays of light coming through the tall pines lining his drive were awe-inspiring. I finally rounded a corner and there in the middle of an enchanted forest was his castle — the answer to the question, "What if Daniel Boone built a grand-English-country-home-meets-rustic-log-cabin-on-steroids mansion?" Throw in a few tall spires, steep roofs, and a romantic old-world gazebo, and it was a majestic sight against the lush, dense forest. Getting out of the car, I drew in the fresh, pine-scented air and shook off the road fatigue. I trundled up the steps, knocked on the door.

"You made it! I know it's an ordeal getting here." Dan greeted me with a hug.

"It was definitely over the river and through the woods, but well worth the trip — what an amazing sanctuary you have." I took off my coat, he hung it up for me.

"When my manager first told me you wanted to coordinate your trip up here with a ski trip with your dad, I thought, 'a man after my own heart'."

I was in awe meeting Dan, a multi-platinum recording artist whose albums I'd scrutinized more closely than the Zapruder film, whose songs

I'd worked up on guitar. But his casual attire of jeans and moccasins along with his broad, welcoming smile put me at ease. Beyond knowing his music by heart, he felt familiar to me. We chatted for a bit about his ranch and our love of the mountains before he showed me to my guest quarters.

En route, he gave me a brief tour of his amazing house. The upstairs hall was lined with framed pencil drawings. Dan noticed me observing them. "Toulouse-Lautrec." Dan gestured to them as he continued the tour. Shit. Was he saying these were *of* him or *by* him? I was too embarrassed to ask. He then led me down to his studio in the basement.

"Here's the Yamaha C7 I want you to do your magic on. It's the one I've been touring with." I gave a quick listen. The tone was harsh, and the touch was heavy. I had my work cut out for me.

"But that's for tomorrow. Join us for dinner in say, an hour?"

I looked forward to each night's dinner and the spirited conversations that extended well into the midnight hours. Dan's a true Renaissance man with an impressive command of many subjects. He's also a great listener and lit up with each passion we found in common: skiing, diving, musical influences, and twisted senses of humor. By this time, I'd met just about all of my idols, but Dan was unlike the rest. He felt more and more to me like family, like a big brother. We were kin.

After dinner, we'd adjourn to the den. If there wasn't a ski race or football game on TV, he'd pop in a VHS of one his fave movies: Scorsese's documentary about The Band, *The Last Waltz*, Monty Python's *Life of Brian* (which he could quote line for line), or *Waiting for Guffman*, which had me howling with tears of laughter.

But, as with each visit to his ranch, the highlight of each evening is listening to music. Against one wall of the den is Dan's immense vinyl collection. He pulls out one record after another and pops it on to the turntable: *Graceland* by Paul Simon, *Big Circumstance* by Bruce Cockburn, the new Robbie Robertson album, or perhaps some old B.B. King records.

But I especially light up when he pulls out the single by The Left Banke, "Walk Away Renee." A favorite for both of us, we listen to it repeatedly.

"This one absolutely slays me. Those bittersweet lyrics, that cello part, that pedal tone harmony. ... Turn it up!" I hold my hand to my heart, growing more animated each time he plays it.

There are certain songs that bore deep into a writer's genetic code and hold hostage emotions you felt when you first heard it. The song's sentiment will do its damndest to seep its way into music you create — no matter how many years or decades it takes. Sharing this song and that experience with Dan is a moment that transcends time and words.

With each of those listening sessions, Dan is making me stop and properly enjoy a record, pore over the liner notes, relishing every detail — something I used to do as a kid. It becomes our ritual that with each visit, I bring a CD by an artist he might not have heard of yet: *Steady On* by Shawn Colvin, *Little Earthquakes* by Tori Amos, *The Way It Is*, by Bruce Hornsby, *Le Mystère des Voix Bulgares* by the Bulgarian State Television Female Vocal Choir. He particularly digs Shawn and begins playing her CD over the sound system as people are taking their seats before his concerts. And I later suspect I can hear the influence of John Leventhal, Shawn's guitar player, in Dan's subsequent records.

The bottles of wine he retrieves from the cellar get progressively better as the night goes on. Each successive night of the visit creeps longer and longer into the wee hours until we finally end up throwing in the towel around 4 or 5 in the morning. As one of Dan's favorite artists, Bruce Cockburn sings, we'd "kick the darkness until it bleeds daylight."

One night among many stands out in my memory. It's well after 3 a.m. but the conversation is still going strong. He goes to the wine cellar and returns with a vintage Caymus Vineyard Cabernet Sauvignon.

"This is from my special reserve." Dan smiles as he opens the bottle. As the wine is breathing, he tells me the story behind the wine glasses we've been drinking from.

"These aren't just any glasses. Riedel had the idea that the shape of the glass could enhance the flavor of the wine." Dan points out the wide belly of the glass leading to the small, thin opening. "Riedel tried numerous times to show his special wine glasses to a prominent winemaker. Once he finally gave a proper demonstration, the winemaker was so blown away he instructed his staff to destroy all the glasses they'd been using and replace them with these Riedel Bordeaux glasses."

Dan pours us each a glass of the vin extraordinaire. He demonstrates how to appreciate the viscosity of the wine by swirling it in the glass, then watching the 'legs' develop as the wine drains back down. I prolong the experience, slowly inhaling the bouquet, trying to pick out the different notes. All while Dan is playing the role of DJ.

After one album finishes playing, Dan gets up and combs through his vinyl collection, tracing his finger along the spines. "Here we go! *The Wheatstraw Suite*, by The Dillards!"

"The what ... by the who?" I've given up pretending to know every artist he's turning me on to. Dan's clearly enjoying edifying me, as much as I'm enjoying embracing the student role. His musical interests are vast and deep and he's forcing me to broaden my limits.

"You've never heard of *The Wheatstraw Suite*! This album was the *Sgt. Pepper's* of country music! The Dillards blazed a trail with their major second harmonies, among other things."

As we listen, he points out favorite phrases, singing along with harmonies he wants me to notice. He savors them like a fine cabernet.

As the album is wrapping up, Dan calls me to the window, pointing out how brightly the full moon is illuminating the landscape. "This would be a great night to break out the telescope."

Among the many things I admire about Dan is that he's a "right now" kinda guy. You got an idea to do something? There's no time like the present. It's coming on 5 a.m. but the moment to view the full moon is *now*. We carry his huge monstrosity of a telescope onto the porch, set it up and aim it into the night sky. Once focused, he steps aside. "Check it out."

I move into position, close my right eye, and look into the eyepiece.

"Wow. The detail is amazing!" His telescope is so powerful I can actually see the moon moving through the image. Far less powerful is my brain the following morning. But my fierce hangover was a small price to pay for one of my most treasured memories.

Dan, Me, Equine.

Other fond Dan memories are out of sequence, but this is how I remember them.

It's a picture-perfect day for skiing — a bit overcast, but no wind and not too cold. Dan and I are standing at the top of a steep run at Wolf Creek, a great ski area just 45 minutes from his house. With us are Dan's then-wife, Anastasia, and his dear pal, Todd Pasquin. Dan has long 210-centimeter skis, and favors fast "giant slalom" style runs. He looks down at my 140-centimeter freestyle skis, then up at me. "Those look like fun but I'm just letting you know we're not going to be waiting up for you."

"No worries. Lead on!" I point my pole down the slope. He and Todd race off. Over dinner that night, he laughs as he recounts the tale of what happened next:

"So, Todd and I blast down the slope, leaving Wilson in our rear-view mirrors. Next thing I know, he comes flying past us on his tiny freestyle skis tucked into an egg position. Well done buddy!" Dan clinks his wine glass to mine. It's gratifying to get an 'atta boy' from my pal.

Todd Pasquin, Dan and me, about to carve some turns in Wolf Creek.

The next time we'd race down a mountain was not on skis, and I had far less control.

—

"This is among the largest groves of aspens anywhere." Dan gestures from atop his horse to the massive aspen forest we're approaching. Dan, Anastasia, and I have saddled up three of his horses and are riding through the backcountry of his 700-acre ranch. "If you want, next time you come up we can do a backpacking trip back in there."

Dan would make the offer a couple of times, as well as to come for a visit at their place in Maine. I'd forever regret not having acted on those invitations. If only I'd known how limited his time on the planet was to be.

We ride over streams and astride a levy, eventually coming to an old deserted one-room cabin on the back side of his property. We circle it a few times, then start heading back. Dan and Anastasia's horses begin picking up speed, then break into a dead heat. I have no choice but to match their pace — my horse is following their lead. As we jump over streams and race back to the barn, I'm hanging on for dear life. I'm scared shitless but we make it back in one piece. Even though I'm a Texas boy, I didn't spend my youth in the saddle. The fear of death seared this memory into my consciousness like a brand.

Dan and me, after the long ride to the back side of his property.

But that wasn't the last adventure with Dan that involved what felt like a near-death experience.

"Well . . . we could go *now* if you want." Dan looks at me, gives a wry smile.

Dan's been telling me about these awesome sledding events he hosts, using his mile-long driveway as the icy run. I've just missed one such party by a weekend and tell him how much I'd love to do that sometime. It's well past midnight and I'm leaving the following morning. When he makes his offer, my eyes light up. "Seriously?"

Minutes later, we're rifling through his closet for the warmest clothing we can find.

"Here. Put this on." Dan throws some coveralls at me, then scarves, a wool cap, and gloves. We go to the barn and throw the sled into the back of his jeep. We drive a few hundred feet down the driveway where the road begins its descent. I pop out and grab the sled.

"OK... now remember there's a steep, icy section near the very bottom with a hairpin turn at the end. You'll want to start your turn early from the left side and turn hard to the right. I'll be just behind you in the jeep. You ready?" Dan smiles, knowing what adventure is ahead for me.

"I was born ready. Let's do this!" I lie flat on the sled, grab the handles, and shove myself forward. I begin picking up a nice little clip. My smile grows wider as I take in this epic moment: the cold wind on my face, the scent of pines filling my lungs, the full moon illuminating the massive trees that line the road on either side — all with my buddy following just behind. Over the sound of the sled blades clattering against the icy drive, with the glee of a 10-year-old, I let out a *"wooooohooooooo!"*

I come to the top of the steep section and take a deep breath, steeling myself for the upcoming plunge. I hang on for dear life as my sled starts rocketing down the drive, my face inches from the snow. I'm bouncing wildly, terrified I'll fall off at any second. As my heart races with both exhilaration and terror, I feel like an astronaut blasting into outer space. Soon, the road begins leveling out — I'd survived!

Just as I'm wondering why I haven't encountered the hairpin turn he's warned me about, my sled glides on to the final section of the driveway. The previous section where I saw my life flash before my eyes was nothing compared to what lies ahead. This part feels like it's straight down. My sled starts shaking so hard I can barely hold on. I dig my toes into the icy snow as hard as I can to try to slow down. I round a slight bend and the slope gets steeper still, revealing the hairpin turn of Dead Man's Curve before me. ... *Ice berm! Dead ahead!"*

I veer as far left as possible, preparing for the critical right turn. At that speed, if I turn too sharply, I'll flip the sled and slam into the wall of ice. A brutal way to go, but at least it will make an awesome story at my funeral. I feel my heart pounding through my chest as I speed closer and closer to the ice wall ahead.

My left sled handle *just* clears the berm. My grip loosens, I finally exhale. The road finally levels out, but I have so much momentum my sled shoots all the way across the cattle guard. I eventually come to a stop and roll off the sled. The headlights of Dan's jeep draw closer. Dan gets out, closing the door behind him.

"Pretty awesome, right?" Dan is laughing his ass off. My face is white as a ghost. I stand up facing him, knees quivering. I'm unable to form words for a few seconds before I hear myself say, "Let's go again!"

———

Many of our conversations are sorted in my mind by where they took place:

On the ski lift, where he told me about his plan to do an R&B arrangement of "Rhythm of the Rain" for his next record and sneak in a line of the Beatles' "When the Rain Comes" near the end. ... In the kitchen, by the pot-belly stove, where he pointed to the nook table where just a week earlier, Henry Diltz had done a photo shoot with him because Henry loved the natural light. ... In the jacuzzi with Anastasia and Dan under a night sky, where he told me about his dad's reaction when Dan first played "Leader of the Band" for him. ... In the living room, where he surprised me with his plans to retire after his next record.

But the location that was a favorite scene of many a great hang was at his Trident Series 80B mixing console downstairs in his studio. He'd play me rough mixes of whatever album he was in the middle of working on. From the first note to the last, we listened to his hot-off-the-press album, *River of Souls*. ... It was also by this console where he once asked me to engineer for him, punching him in while he played the piano part in the studio. He didn't believe in cobbling together takes and if he made a mistake, he'd start over from the beginning. Old school.

This mixing board was where we discussed a book Dan had read called *The Population Bomb*. Dan took the time to walk me through the basic conundrum: "As our population grows exponentially, so do our environmental problems. In 1800, when there were only a billion people, it wasn't a major burden on the planet. Now there are five billion people and in just another 30 years, there will be eight billion." He explained that each of those people creates their own carbon footprint and consumes their share of non-renewable resources. The more people, the bigger the strain it puts on the planet in the form of rainforest destruction, fished out oceans, rising global temperatures, and crop failures. "It's each individual's responsibility to make their carbon footprints as small as possible."

Years later, inspired by these conversations and by the Native American quote *We do not inherit the Earth from our ancestors, we borrow it from our children,* I wrote the song "Our Children's World."

This world isn't ours, it is our children's
We borrow their land, their sky and sea
We pass them the flame, they give their children
It's not too late, we can turn it around
We choose our fate, for the world that is in our hands,
Our Children's World.

Over a dozen people, including my buddy George Merrill, as well as most of the guys from Toto, played or sang on the recording of the song for me. My friend James Guthrie did a stellar mix of the song. I even started a non-profit organization called *Our Children's World Foundation*, raising money that went towards environmental education. It was at the Trident mixing board that this effort was born, and it was here where I'd later play this song for Dan, who was moved to tears by its message.

But it was sitting at a piano where my most treasured Dan memory would later take place.

―

Dan puts another log on the fire, stirs it with the poker and sits back down. He takes a sip of his cabernet.

"This is just phenomenal," I say. "Well done, pal." I hand back the journal he's just read a chapter from. "It's so visual. Would you read another?" It's a collection of handwritten short stories he's titled something like *Scenes from an Illinois Boyhood*. The chapter he'd just read was 'The Piano.'

He pauses, flips through the pages, nods when he lands on the section he's looking for. "This one's called 'The Ice Storm'."

He begins reading a story from his childhood about when the temperatures had dropped during an overnight rain, and he'd awoken to a magical world where literally everything was covered in ice. His phenomenal gift for words is taking me right into the picture he's painting. I can feel the crisp air on my cheeks, the white winter wonder of trees encased in glass, the feeling of everyday life being held in suspended animation.

"No idea what I'll do with these." He takes another sip of wine.

"Dude, these are amazing! If nothing else, this could be a book that's available at the merch table at your concerts."

He shrugs, pauses, and reads another chapter, before putting the book down, laying the subject to rest for now.

As the fire crackles away, I pick up a guitar. "Check out this new tune I'm writing." I start strumming the chords to his hit "There's A Place in the World for A Gambler."

"Sounds familiar." He gives a wry smile. I keep playing and nod towards a second guitar near him. He takes a beat and smiles. "Sure, why not?" He picks up the guitar and starts playing along. We do an abbreviated version of his classic song, each of us singing a verse. A scene I never could have imagined years earlier when I was transfixed, listening to his voice for the first time in a Cleveland record store.

I move over to the piano. There's a new composition I've been working on that I'm dying to play for him. I feel confident he's going to like it better than the song I'd played for him on my first visit to the ranch.

I had played him a demo of what I hoped could be a hit song, called "It's All Wrong, But It's Alright." Halfway through the tune, he stopped, handed me back my Sony Walkman and said, "It sounds very LA."

Ouch.

Looking back, he was actually being very kind. The song was a shallow, formulaic attempt to craft a clever title into a hit song. It had zero soul. It was crap.

But this new piece I'm working on is a different animal. It's one of a new batch of compositions I've been creating just for my own gratification. In between my efforts to hammer out the next big hit song, I'd find myself at the piano, composing pieces that drew from a kettle in which my varied influences were simmering: my James Taylor roots, some country riffs that my Easy bandmate Charlie Clinton taught me, mixed in with some Dave Grusin-meets-Aaron Copland-meets-David Foster voicings, along with a heaping portion of Celtic and Appalachia-flavored melodies that trace back to folk songs my mom sang for me when I was a kid. I didn't expect much of anything to come of these tunes, but it felt great to play them.

I start in on one of those new pieces. Dan comes to the side of the piano and listens intently. When I finish, he says, "What's *that?*"

"New thing I'm workin' on. You like it?"

He nods and gestures towards the keys. "Play it again."

I do it once more and Dan closes his eyes, really tuning into the melody. As the last chord is ringing out, he opens his eyes and turns to me. "I love it. Maybe I could write a lyric to it."

I somehow manage to contain my elation. This is way beyond the response I'd hoped for. "That would be awesome, but the B section in the middle would need a melody to hang a lyric on. Currently, the bass line carries the melody there."

He tells me to play it again and when it comes to that B section, he starts singing a great vocal line that's a perfect counterpoint to the bass line melody. We play the song on repeat for the next twenty minutes, Dan singing with more conviction each time. We record a quick cassette tape of the idea.

Though he never got around to writing a lyric to the song, the counter melody he came up with on the spot that night is note-for-note the melody that Eric Rigler plays on the Uilleann pipes on what would become the title track to my first CD, *Northern Seascape*.

―

February 1997. It's a beautiful, clear night. I'm once again at my favorite spot on Mulholland overlooking the shimmering LA skyline. I've come up here to reflect on my life, review my dreams. I had come to LA to become the next Jackson Browne and instead, became the next Jackson Browne piano tuner. Not exactly my original quest, but overall, my life is rolling along quite nicely.

I've got tons of prominent clients; I'm being flown around the world to work on pianos. I've won the affections of remarkable women, built a reputation for myself, earned the respect of my peers. I've been elected to the Board of Governors of the LA Chapter of NARAS, had several articles written about me, and I'm knocking down a nice income. I mean, life's pretty cushy, right?

Then why did I feel so... *unfulfilled?*

PART III
Tuning In

"Until you make the unconscious conscious,
it will direct your life and you will call it fate."
— Carl Jung

CHAPTER 24
Claude

It's an overcast winter afternoon. I'm just finishing up an all-day regulation on a grand piano at Cherokee Studios in Hollywood. Somebody pages me, it's a friend of Claude's.

"Claude is in the hospital! He's had either a stroke or a heart attack and he's unconscious. Come quick."

What? Claude and I just had one of our mastermind sessions a few days ago. He was in good spirits, he seemed perfectly fine.

I race to the Riverside Memorial Hospital in North Hollywood. There's a group of people there now, including producer David Foster, who considers Claude his go-to genius for synth arrangements. Claude's dear pals Scott Frankfurt and Doug Rider greet me and do their best to fill me in with the limited information they have. I knew that both Claude's dad and uncle had died of heart attacks at young ages. I couldn't help but wonder if Claude's bad habits were catching up to him.

While commiserating with friends in the hall outside his room, I see the nurse leave. If I ask to have a moment alone with Claude, I'll most likely be denied. If there's any time to say fuck the rules, it's now.

I sneak into his room. Standing beside his bed, I hold his hand, startled by how cold and lifeless it feels. I think back to the lovely afternoon I shared with him just a few months earlier. He'd just finished his first piano sonata and he couldn't wait to share it with me. He sat down at the keyboard, placed the handwritten score on the music desk and began playing. It was a gorgeous piece written straight from the heart — I could feel his very essence woven intrinsically into the notes. It moved me to tears. He planned to record this and other compositions he'd written and release an album under his own name. Known and respected as an arranger, producer, and songwriter, stepping out as a solo artist was a scary idea for him. I got it.

Now, here he lies, motionless in this hospital bed, with a breathing tube taped to his mouth. The mechanical sound of the ventilator clanking in and out punctuates the silence.

What the fuck happens to those beautiful dreams now? This wonderful life mission of Claude's is vaporizing into a million little invisible particles, floating into the ether. He's just 37 years old with so much life ahead of him. I feel the impact of Paul's death compounding into this moment. The scab is coming off the wound. That was a decade ago, but it feels like yesterday. The tears are welling up in my eyes.

I'd read books about people's near-death experiences. Is Claude already out of his body, hovering above, looking down on the scene? I decide to talk to him directly.

"Mon ami… thank you so very much for everything you've done for me. Know that you'll live on in my heart forever." I resolve then and there to do whatever it will take to accomplish my dreams in his honor. This moment would prove to be a profound turning point in my life.

At his memorial service at Forest Lawn, dear friends — including Cherish Alexander, David Foster and Paul Anka — speak of his gentle heart, his immense talent, and his deep love for his family. In my eulogy, I express how proud I am to have seen his incredible rise over the years: from the scrawny, new kid in town from Montreal, to one of the top arrangers in LA with hit singles to his name.

I play keyboards while Joe Pizzulo sings a song of mine — a poem by Clare Harner that I'd set to music:

Don't stand at my grave and weep
I am not there, I do not sleep

I'm a thousand winds that blow
I'm the diamond glints on snow
I am sunlight on ripened grain
I am the gentle autumn rain

When you awaken in the morning's hush
I'm the swift uplifting rush
Of quiet birds in circled flight
I am the soft star that shines at night

TUNED IN: MEMOIRS OF A PIANO MAN

Don't stand at my grave and cry
I am not there, I did not die

My brother's passing had leveled me. But Claude's death is devastating me in a different way, shaking my fundamental convictions. My mind keeps going over and over my numerous mastermind sessions with Claude. He had such complete clarity on the life he wanted. I'd always believed his level of certitude was an assurance of success — there was absolutely no stopping this guy. Claude was my guiding star.

His sudden passing is a hand grenade thrown into the bunker where I store all my core beliefs. I'm in a million pieces. I'm forced to realize there are no guarantees, that everything can be taken away in an instant, that there isn't a limitless reserve of tomorrows. Whatever it is you want to do with your life, get the fuck on with it.

I'd had the idea to cobble together the piano-based instrumentals I'd been composing purely for my own gratification into an album. I'd seen what George Winston had done with his solo piano albums — taking accessible melodies and presenting them unadorned. While my melodies and style differ from his, his success at least shone a light on a proven path for me.

But this means I'll now have to face my fears of stepping out as a solo artist. I've worked my ass off to earn my reputation as a respected piano technician. My clients are world-class artists and session players at the top of their game. Who the hell am I to declare myself an "artist?" My self-worth is based on the identity I've carefully cultivated. If I fail, it's the worst of both worlds: I'll lose the respect I've earned as a piano tech. And as an artist, I'll be branded an imposter, laughed at for having the audacity to reach for the brass ring. I'll risk losing it all.

But Claude's passing puts things in perspective for me. Dying with an unfulfilled dream in my heart is a far worse fate than momentarily losing face. The artists and session pianists in my world may be more accomplished at what they do than me, but only one person can express my particular artistic vision — me. And my priority now is less about having a million-selling album than creating art I'm proud of. I'm driven to create a recording that if I get that unexpected tap on the shoulder like Paul or Claude did, there'd be a lasting legacy of what music was in my heart. Even if it only connects with a handful of people, I'll have achieved my mission.

From that week forward, I throw my heart and soul into fulfilling this dream. I stop bullshitting myself and move into action. I'm finally being true to my purpose. And it seems the universe is responding in kind to my newfound conviction. Doors swing open, people come to my support, magic happens.

I have just enough compositions to comprise an album. There's the song I'd composed with Dan. Its Celtic influence gave me the feeling of standing on the Cliffs of Mohr in Ireland, looking out over the Atlantic Ocean. I named it and the album "Northern Seascape." And there's "Sierra Snowfall," a composition I'd written that was inspired by the movie I saw in my head just hearing the title of the book *Snow Falling on Cedars*.

"Paul's Theme," the song I'd composed for my brother, works perfectly for this collection, as does "Anna's Blue Skies" — a piece I'd written that was inspired by a poignant passage in Anne Frank's diary that leveled me when I first read it. From a tiny window in her final hiding place of two years, Anne could stand on a stool and look out over the horizon of Amsterdam. *"As long as this exists, and I may live to see it, this sunshine, the cloudless skies, while this lasts, I cannot be unhappy."*

One night, my engineer Jerrold and I have a listen to these first four pieces we've recorded, back-to-back. I feel like the album needs something lighthearted to balance out the collection. Not being a "write on demand" kind of composer, I blow off the idea. That night I dream I'm driving through a misty forest. There's a solo piano piece playing on the radio. I'm struck by its lighthearted but emotive melody. I reach for the dial and turn up the volume, listening intently to this lovely, wistful song. What artist can this possibly be? Just then, the radio announcer in my dream breaks in with his hyper-modulated voice: *And that's the latest from Sheryl Crow!*

I start waking up slowly, slightly baffled. Sheryl Crow releasing a piano instrumental makes no sense. The more I start waking up, I begin realizing this is a melody that's being given to me — from wherever. I slowly start going over and over the melody, trying to remember the shape of it, notating it in my head, but not letting myself slip out of that ethereal, dreamlike state. I know if I get up, the melody will vanish into the ether.

Once I go over the melody enough times that I can remember it, I get out of bed, go straight to the piano, and start fleshing it out. "Heart of

Innocence" becomes just the piece the album needs.

Other original pieces for the record I have are "Mon Ami Eternel" — my tribute to Claude; "Django's Hope" — a song I'd written on David Crosby's piano, for David and Jan who were expecting their first child; "Laura's World" — a piece inspired by the poignant character in *The Glass Menagerie*; "Illuminara," and "Restless Sea" — inspired by the vista point in Carmel overlooking the Pacific Ocean.

Fun fact about "Restless Sea": one night Jerrold and I decide my cat, Tuna Breath, should be included on the album. We hold Tuna in the air until he meows into a microphone. We take that recording, slow it down a couple of octaves, duplicate it, panning both samples left and right. At the very end of "Restless Sea", just underneath Lenny Castro's conga slide, you can hear Tuna. Using an anagram of his name, I gave credit to "Bret A. Hunta" for "Whale Song." A reviewer later called out "Bret" amongst the all-star cast of players on the album.

To round out the album, I do a cover of "Walk Away Renee" — a reinterpretation I worked up simply because it's one of Dan's and my favorite songs. I couldn't wait to play it for him.

With the solo piano tracks of all 10 songs recorded, it's now time to begin fulfilling my vision for the record, adding other instrumentation I'm hearing.

My first call is to Davey Johnstone, Elton John's guitarist for decades. Davey's a friend, but this is still a scary ask. It will require me, for the first time, declaring my intention of stepping out as an artist. My fingers tremble slightly as I dial his number.

"Hey Jim! How are you mate?" Davey's cheerful voice puts me at ease a bit, but I still have to muster my nerve.

"So, buddy... I was wondering ... I... I don't know if you're available ... but, I'm recording an album of original piano compositions and ..."

He cuts me off. "That's fantastic! You want me to play on it? I'd be happy to!"

I breathe a sigh of relief, my shoulders relax a bit. My pal is willing to take a risk and support my vision. And before I know it, I get similar enthusiastic votes of support from friends including legendary percussionist Lenny Castro, top synth player Robbie Buchanan, accordion player Brian Mann, as well as Charlie Morgan, Chris Standring, and Dave Koz pitching in on percussion, guitar, and sax respectively. I'd heard this guy, Eric Rigler, playing the Irish flute and "Uilleann pipes" — — sometimes called Irish bagpipes — at a nightclub in Santa Monica. I loved his featured playing on the Titanic soundtrack and thought it would be a perfect addition to my music. I'm thrilled when Eric says he'd love to play on my tracks.

Now it's time to mix the record. Through Claude, I'd met and become friends with Doug Rider, who'd done all of Claude's mixing. Doug graciously endured the crappy circumstances of my cramped studio, encountering numerous challenges with my cumbersome ADAT tape and Yamaha O2-R set up. After a two-week period of brutal 12-hour days, we emerge with mixes I'm ecstatic with. My friend the brilliant mastering engineer Bernie Becker puts the finishing touches on the record.

I put together packaging for the album and have a thousand CDs printed. I send a promotional flyer to the mailing list I've cobbled together of folks I hope might be receptive to this new effort. I sell a few hundred copies before coming to a profound realization: perhaps there are reasons major record labels have huge staffs of people running multiple divisions. Maybe getting a label to handle the record wouldn't be such a terrible idea after all.

Of all things, a kid who had lived in my apartment building in North Hollywood years ago is now working for Jim Brickman, an established piano recording artist. The "kid," Steve Steinberg, is now in his twenties. His parents are on my mailing list and buy my album. Steve loves my record and wants to do all he can to help. He gives my CD to the guys in the group Tangerine Dream. They have a tiny label mostly for distributing their own music called Sonic Images. They love my album and want to release it! Steve sets up a meeting with them and we drive to their house in Laurel Canyon.

"Congrats on a truly wonderful record." The label owner smiles and gives me a thumbs up. "We want to take it and run with it."

Turns out they want to give me $3,000. They'd own the master; I'd sign away all rights to it — "in perpetuity." Considering that the album cost me $27,000 to make, it's a hard pass.

But what that paltry offer does do is give me leverage. I get a copy of "The A&R Registry" which has the contact info for all the "Artists and

TUNED IN: MEMOIRS OF A PIANO MAN

Repertoire" reps of dozens of major and independent labels. I put a form letter together and fax it — unsolicited — to reps at 20 labels, varying it slightly with each letter:

"Dear [Fill in the Blank],

Just a heads up that tomorrow you'll be receiving via FedEx a package containing Northern Seascape, *an album of piano-featured instrumentals that Carole King calls 'a delicately-woven romantic classic, a magical musical carpet ride of melodic beauty', Dan Fogelberg says is 'a beautiful and inspiring work. I highly recommend it', Lionel Richie calls 'mystical and calming', and David Crosby describes as 'beautiful, melodic, emotional, delicious music.' Jim Brickman's manager feels the album has strong commercial potential.*

"There's an offer on the table from another label, but before we commit, we wanted to present the finished master to you. As there is a limited time window, we'd appreciate hearing from you at your earliest opportunity."

That letter, with its sense of urgency, its simple "yes" or "no" choice, the celebrity endorsements, and — if I may — a really good record, gets incredible responses. Seven of the 20 labels I send to respond with a yes. Of those seven, four "put paper on the table," offering attractive advances.

I need a killer lawyer to bring this home for me and I know just the person for the gig.

Cut to a few months before. Carole King has recommended me as a piano tuner to her attorney, Emily Simon. When I arrive at Emily's house, I'm shown to her office, where she's in the middle of a phone call.

She looks up at me and smiles. She nods and gestures that she'll be off the phone in just a minute, then points to an empty chair. I sit while she finishes her call. She's clearly talking to someone who's violated an agreement with one of her clients. I'm impressed by her ability to be firm and direct but never break a sweat. With no notes in front of her, she lays into this person, articulately reading them the riot act. She's powerful but civil. Then when it's their turn to speak, she listens and casually takes another bite of her lunch. This is effortless child's play for her. Wow. I haven't even met her yet and I already love her.

How I wish I had a fraction of her brain power and clarity. I shy from confrontation and would give anything to be able to stand and deliver so fearlessly. I never wanted to be on her wrong side. And I knew if I ever got a record deal, I wanted her to represent me.

The most attractive contender of the lot is Angel EMI, a division of Capitol Records. Emily takes over on negotiating and soon they offer a $50,000 advance.

"Holy shit! Let's take it!" I'm ecstatic.

"Hang tight. I think we can do better. They really want the record," Emily says. Over the next several weeks she drives the price and my anxiety levels up, negotiating better and better terms for me. She plays the other labels against each other, eventually getting them up to a $75,000 advance.

The principals of the label fly out from New York, and I sign the contract with Capitol Records in the iconic record-shaped building in Hollywood. It's one of the proudest days of my life. I'm now "label mates" with Norah Jones – who I'm told is selling 200k units a week – and Anoushka Shankar, whom I'd soon meet at an Angel-sponsored showcase. Of the three of us, I'm the only one who's not a child of Ravi Shankar.

The label gears up all the departments for a big release. They fly me to New York to meet the staff, put me up in a four-star hotel, then have a limo pick me up to take me across the Brooklyn Bridge to a deserted red brick warehouse in a funky part of town for the photo shoot. They spare no expense and — not including the label reps — there are no less than ten people involved: the photographer and his assistant, the stylist and their assistant, the make-up artist, the lighting director and their assistant, and the caterers.

I can't believe all this fuss is being made over me. Half of me is feeling proud — I've earned this, this is my rightful place. The other half is expecting the Fraud Police to come busting down the doors, waving badges and arrest me for scamming all these good, earnest folks.

Not helping with my insecurities is the young German photographer who exudes all the warmth and charm of Rudolph Hess. Angel has shown me several portfolios of gifted photographers. I've chosen this guy for his hip-looking work, so there's only me to blame. He stares at me, looking me over like I'm a marble statue. Then he gazes down into his Hasselblad camera, eventually snapping another picture. Other than the occasional "raise your chin… look left…" command, he offers little direction. There are long, vibe-killing gaps of silence between shots. I'm fighting a jet-lag headache. It's torture. But we end up with a couple of great images. The grueling day pays off in the end.

In the limo ride back to the airport during Manhattan rush hour, as the cacophony of honking horns and strident sirens echo through forests of towering buildings that reach skyward to infinity, I look up at a billboard promoting the new Norah Jones record. I sit a little taller in my seat. A smile grows on my face. This is the club I belong to now. A rookie member, but I'll work hard to prove that I belong.

This is still what's called the "Bricks and Mortar" era, where people go to a physical store to buy records and CDs. Angel ponies up for "end caps" (display racks at the ends of rows — prime real estate for which record stores charge a premium) and pays to have my album featured on listening stations in Tower Records across the country. They line up a little Borders Bookstore tour for me where I play a few songs on piano and autograph CDs.

Angel hires David Millman, a P.R. rep to work *Northern Seascape*. I'm still very anxious about doing any on-camera interviews. Later, he'll line up TV appearances for me in Dallas, San Francisco, and Washington DC, but it's the first one I'm most nervous about. I'm about to lose my on-camera virginity and I beg him to please make the first interview as low-pressure as possible. Perhaps a midday farm-to-market report in Hereford, Texas with six farmers and a couple of cows watching? I've joined Toastmasters and have been going to their weekly meetings to help get over my intense fear of public speaking.

"Dude! Just got you a shot on CNN!" David has clearly ignored my request. Before I know it, the camera crew is there in my home, getting footage of me playing the piano and the reporter interviewing me. Keeping my nerves in check feels like riding a wild horse with no saddle or reins. I keep putting my focus on Claude; that I'm doing this for him as much as me. If I focus less on how I look and more on how appreciative I am to have the opportunity for my art connect with people — an opportunity Claude never got — I'm OK. *Just.*

Then they have the idea that they should interview a couple of my celebrity clients and get their take on the record. David Foster and

George Duke step up.

"OK, let's get a two shot of you and Jim on the sofa," the director says to David at David's Malibu recording studio Chartmaker. If I can just make it through this without being carted off in an ambulance seized by a major panic attack, I'll consider it a success. Miraculously, an early morning Xanax helps me ride the bucking bronco that is my jangled nerves and do a passable impersonation of someone actually enjoying themself.

"Yeah, Jim's album is absolutely beautiful with a unique twist. It's got this great Celtic-meets-Folk thing. I'm kinda jealous, actually." David delivers the goods for me, as does George, saying "It's a really great record with strong melodies."

I'm racing through DFW a week later when I see the finished piece airing on CNN International. Flush with excitement, I look around expecting to see people with eyes wide in utter astonishment, a hand covering their jaw-agape mouth. "That's ...*HIM!*" they'll be whispering to their neighbor as they discreetly nudge them, while pointing to me, then the TV, then back to me — a real, honest-to-God, Ray-Ban-wearing celebrity.

Instead, I see a mass of people looking down at their phones, moms tending to their kids, folks taking pre-flight naps. "Don't you know who I think I am?!" I yell in my mind.

The following week, I pick up a *Billboard* magazine. I flip through the pages to find the New Age chart (which is the nearest category into which they can put my folk-meets-Celtic-meets-classical-meets-whatever record.) Holy shit! There's *Northern Seascape* — *my* record — at number 21! That's *my name* right beside Enya, Yanni, David Lanz, George Winston, Jim Brickman, and Mannheim Steamroller. I'm not crying, *you're* crying.

A week later, I'm in Whole Foods and while ordering some wheat grass juice, I hear a familiar piano passage on the sound system. It dawns on me that I'm hearing "Anna's Blue Skies" from my record. "Oh my god! ... That's ...*my music!*" I say to the girl behind the counter. Too verklempt to speak, I point to the overhead speakers.

She pauses and forces a smile. "Did you want one ounce or two?"

CHAPTER 25
Malls and Halls

It's the winter of 1998. It's now time to get my butt out there and tour to promote my album. I'm willing to do everything in my power to help Angel make this record a success. Angel has me on a Borders Bookstore tour, and that's great, but I need to jump into doing proper concerts. I'll have to confront my deep-rooted anxiety about performing, which on more than one occasion has led to paralyzing panic attacks.

But there's a bigger conundrum ahead of me: you can't develop a following until you get out there and perform for people, but you can't perform for people until you develop a following.

Enter Plan B.

I've made a new friend, Lisa Lynne, a gifted harpist who's having great success performing at malls and arts festivals. The venues don't pay you anything — in fact, some of them charge a fee. You make all your money off CD sales, which you have to ship to your hotel ahead of time. Over lunch, Lisa gives me the lowdown on the whole routine. I jot down info about her typical schedule and a sample breakdown of out-of-pocket costs in my notes:

SCHEDULE:
Leave on Thurs morn,
play Thurs afternoon thru Sun afternoon
Play 8 hrs / day Sat & Sun
Rtn Mon.

EXPENSES (I pay all):
Airfare: $400
Rntl car: $200
Hotel: $225

Food: $100
Shipping CDs: $125
Insurance: ($50 per gig: $200 per year)

Approx. Total: $1100
Plus Jennifer comm: 15% of gross

"Sorry, but I don't take on keyboard players. Also, you really need to have multiple titles to make it work financially." Lisa's booking agent Jennifer Reid is throwing the next roadblock at me. I pull out every trick in my persuasion toolkit. After 20 minutes of charming and humoring her, I convince her that I'll do whatever it takes to make this work for her. She reluctantly agrees to a one-time trial run. If it goes well, she'll consider taking me on.

I now have to pony up for a ton of gear on spec. Gear that I'll only use for these specific types of gigs: a 61-note Alesis keyboard, a hard-shell case for it, a keyboard stand and collapsible keyboard stool. Also, two Yamaha powered speakers, a portable CD player, a small Mackie mixing board, a bunch of 1/4" cables, a 50' heavy-duty extension cord, a microphone, a boom stand, and a blue velvet tablecloth. I design a 5' x 2' vinyl banner that will drape across the merch table. Just above my name it reads "ANGEL EMI RECORDING ARTIST." As much as I'm not crazy about Angel's cursive, lower-case logo of my name, I use it for brand consistency.

I design two custom-built travel cases that just hold all the above. In the pre-9/11 days, if you slipped the skycap a twenty, smiled and said, "hope you can help me with these," nine times out of ten they'd wink and let you slide on the excess, overweight luggage fees.

A couple of weeks later, I get a call from Jennifer. "OK, I got you set up for the Rosedale Center Mall in Minneapolis in three weeks. Let's see how it goes."

I jump on the case and book my hotel and rental car. Dad is super supportive of my music goals and volunteers to come help. I book flights to Minneapolis: mine from LA, his from Amarillo. Having my dad come support my dreams has meaning for me beyond words.

We make our way to baggage claim and schlep a couple hundred pounds of equipment and luggage to our rental car. We have dinner, check in and hit the hay early. I'm apprehensive about what the next few days hold in store, but it's comforting knowing my dad has my back.

Bright and early Friday morning, Dad and I find our way to the mall. Other than knowing I'm to "set up on the crosswalk on the second level across from Cinnabon," I'm short on details. And I don't want to pester Jennifer with questions, so we figure it out on our own. Eventually.

Besides being brutally cold, there's a ton of crusty snow and ice in the parking lot. By the time we haul all my equipment across the snow, make our way upstairs and set up, I'm exhausted. Jet lag kicks in and when I start playing, I make a bunch of mistakes. I'm distracted and self-conscious. I want to be anywhere but here, but this is what I signed up for. I strap in for what's surely going to be a long, rough weekend.

But my dad's salesman background kicks into gear and he starts pulling people in. *"Just $15 for one or two for $25!"* He closes the deal by telling people he'll "get the artist to sign it personally." I play piano for a bit, then play the CD and schmooze, trying to follow Dad's example. Stumbling over my words, I feel less like an artist than a carnival barker. "I'll think about it," they say as they give a patronizing smile and walk away. I'm pushing too hard. The laws of social dynamics are at work: we run from that which pursues us, we pursue that which retreats from us.

The first day is torture, but mid-way through the second day, I start to get the hang of engaging people and letting the music sell itself. I also notice a kind of mob mentality at work: when our table is deserted, people just walk by. But when a couple of people are engaged, two more stop to see what the commotion is about. We try and capitalize on that and when a couple of people stop, we quickly engage other passersby. It would go from no people for a while to six or seven trying to get in on the action, back to no one in a matter of minutes.

It's during one of these mad frenzies when I see Dad in conversation with a woman who's stopped to listen to the music. In the space of 30 seconds, she's gone from mildly interested to being enthralled by the music. Dad sees what kind of visceral reaction my music is having on her. He then points to me, and I overhear him say, "That's my son." I see him fighting back a tear. I've made my father proud. I think back to when I burned down his stables as a careless kid. It's taken decades, but

I finally feel the beginnings of redemption.

Together, we have to sell about 140 CDs to just break even on my trip expenses. In the end, we sell 289. I'm completely stoked. Above her 15%, I pony up a $200 bonus to Jennifer. Less dough for me, but I'm far less concerned with making a profit than finding a path for getting my music out there.

Which is exactly what these gigs do. They aren't as prestigious as doing proper concerts, but these mall gigs connect me with fans one-on-one, one-*by*-one. With each appearance, I add a couple hundred more names to my database. In the coming years it will add up to thousands of people to whom we can promote.

Mom pitches in too. Big time. She's gone from being slightly dubious in the beginning about my new life path — wondering why I'd risk losing my bread-and-butter piano tuning gig — to being my biggest champion.

"Just listen to that. Isn't it *beautiful?*" she says, as she thrusts a CD into their hand, then points to me. "That's my son and this is his music. … and that's Eric Rigler from the *Titanic* soundtrack," she says as she points to the speakers on cue. She won't let them leave until they purchase a CD. "I keep telling Jim he has to buy me a car like Elvis did for his mom." Once she gets them laughing, the wallets come out.

Back at the hotel, we begin tallying the money. We spread it out on the table and marvel at the day's haul like Bonnie and Clyde back from a bank heist. The first day's take is usually just enough to cover expenses. It's the next day or two where you earn your profit.

Over the coming years, when they can, Mom and Dad fly all over the country to help on mall gigs in Boise, Idaho, Minneapolis and Mankato, Minnesota and Boulder and Littleton, Colorado. They also join me on festival gigs in New Smyrna Beach, Florida, Washington DC, Dallas — where my Uncle Ray pitches in, Philly and Scottsdale. Once, I even fly to New York City for a performance at the prestigious Lincoln Center!

OK, fine. … At an arts festival, in the parking lot of Lincoln Center. But still…

I work my ass off doing these gigs. My typical routine means that early on a Thursday morning, I load up my car with two huge equipment cases, my keyboard in its hard-shell case and my carry-on suitcase. Altogether, it's no less than 200 pounds. Fight traffic on the 405 and head to Parking

TUNED IN: MEMOIRS OF A PIANO MAN

Lot C, a mile from LAX. Unload my equipment cases and keyboard at the shuttle pick up point, leave them sitting unattended while I race to find a parking place, then sprint with my carry-on suitcase back to the shuttle pick up point. Once the shuttle arrives, schlep all the above onboard as the fellow passengers grumble. Once at my terminal — hopefully close to the skycap station — quickly offload everything. Bribe the skycap. If no skycap, rent a cart and haul all this stuff inside, pay the agent at the counter the extra fees for the overage.

Once in the new city, rent another cart, retrieve the luggage from the baggage carousel, then hunt for the "Oversize Luggage" sign to pick up my equipment cases. Schlep all the above outside to board the shuttle to the rental car facility. Then offload everything from the shuttle, rent the car, reload all into the car, unload everything at the hotel, retrieve the hundreds of CDs I've pre-shipped now waiting for me at the front desk. Next morning, haul all the above to the venue, where I set up shop. Then, after three days of up to ten hours of playing and hustling, reverse the process, also lugging back whatever CDs I haven't sold. Then it's back to LA and my other full-time job of working in my shop and servicing high-end pianos.

And you thought the entertainment biz wasn't glamorous and exciting.

It's a brutal routine, but I don't think twice about jumping through all those hoops. It provides a step-by-step footpath up an otherwise unscalable mountain. A doable, albeit grueling, routine to build a fan base, one person at a time. I sell as many as 600 CDs in a weekend and I make a point of thanking and shaking the hand of every single person who buys one of those CDs. As I drift off exhausted on Sunday night, safe in my bed at home, I smile remembering the look of sincere gratitude on the faces of people my music has deeply connected with.

Not long after the first mall gig in Minnesota, I get the call from Gilbert Hetherwick, the manager of Angel EMI. "Everyone here loves your record and is impressed with your dedication. We're picking up your option for the second record."

Fan-fucking-tastic. I'm a proper recording artist now. I begin producing my next record out of my own pocket. I'm so inspired, the new songs flow out of me. Works that still have my style to them, but push the envelope a bit.

There's the spirited piece in 6/8 that has a sense of hope to it. As I'm playing it, I can feel myself sailing off the south coast of Africa and can hear light African percussion coming from the shore. It becomes the title track of the new record, *Cape of Good Hope*.

Dan Fogelberg sends me an email telling me how much he's loving *Northern Seascape,* and offers to sing or play on my next record. I must have reread the email a dozen times. I've earned the respect and support of a paladin. So cool. And I have just the perfect song for him to guest on. It's a piece I recently composed as the soundtrack to a mini-movie I saw in my head of Picasso walking the streets of Paris late at night, looking for the next image to paint. I send Dan backing tapes and he not only self-records an awesome vocal but surprises me by laying down some brilliant guitar work that takes the song to the next level. My friend Bob Clearmountain, the legendary sound engineer, had told me he loves my music and said he'd be happy to mix one of my tracks as a favor for me sometime. Well, do I ever have the song for you. This track has a ton of overdubs and is way more than my little home studio can handle. We spend a full day sculpting all 80 tracks into shape and I leave his studio with a stellar mix. That one becomes "Picasso's Midnight Stroll."

A couple of other tracks that round out the album are "Discovery" — an adventurous piece dedicated to man's quest for flight, "Home in the Heartland" — a tribute to my Texas roots and "Donna Lynn" — a love song for my girlfriend.

I'm deeply humbled and beside myself with joy when stellar artists step up and contribute their talents: David Sanborn on "Friend," Stephen Bishop on "Donna Lynn," Chris Botti on "Discovery" and "Picasso's," as well as A-list players Michael Landau, Steve Lukather, Steve Porcaro, Mark Portmann, Neil Stubenhaus, and Lee Sklar. Not to mention return appearances by Davey Johnstone, Eric Rigler and Lenny Castro.

Angel connects me with an incredible LA photographer, Beth Herzhaft, to do photoshoots for this next album. She knows her shit and has a killer portfolio featuring her phenomenal portraits of everyone from Jakob Dylan, Beck and Alanis Morrisette to Cheap Trick, Radiohead, and Meat Loaf. We meet with her stylist who hooks us up with tons of cool clothes. We do shoots with me beside a grand piano in an empty warehouse in LA, under the Malibu Pier, then on the beach at Malibu at sunset. All the locations yield outstanding shots, which will ultimately end up on the *Cape of Good Hope* CD. I dedicate the album "to the spirit of voyaging into the unknown in the quest for a better life."

―

By this time, I felt ready. Or at least ready to push myself, to graduate to the next level of performing: breaking into the performing arts center circuit. The beauty of that world is that they all have their own subscribers and the municipality they're based in usually funds them to a certain degree. So, they don't *necessarily* have to make a huge profit on every act they present. Of course, they want to book popular artists, but they also have the latitude to occasionally gamble on a lesser-known artist, providing their supporters with something new and interesting. Performing arts centers serve a beautiful function in their local communities by presenting a wide variety of art and culture.

I envisioned my concerts being a "Musical Travelogue" of my favorite places I'd traveled in the world. I called it *Around the World in 88 Keys*. I had an idea of creating "performance videos" — images coordinated with the music that would be projected above and behind me when I performed. This kind of multimedia would become common later, but no one was doing this at the time, and I had to figure out how to pull it all off.

I invested several thousand dollars in a projector and screen. I also had to accomplish this with the least amount of weight and size for transportability. My friend Mike Bundlie helped me produce a dozen of these performance videos and transfer them onto a tiny DV tape. In concert, someone (many times, yours truly) would hit play on a DV camera, which would send the video to the screen, some backing tracks to the audience, and a click track to my in-ear monitor to keep me coordinated with the video.

Around this time, I got an email from Deb Jelinek, who hosted LivingLegacy.net, a website devoted to Dan Fogelberg's music. Deb noticed that the title track of my debut album was co-written by Dan. As

Dan never co-wrote with anyone, this caught her attention. She went on to become an invaluable supporter of my music, becoming my Communications Director. She and her assistant Laurie Williams mailed out dozens of packages to performing arts centers on my behalf.

The materials we sent them sold the vision:

Over the course of an evening, Jim and fellow musicians transport concert audiences on a 'cinematic melodic journey' enhanced by evocative multimedia montages filling the stage behind the performers.

Jim weaves his musical themes around breathtaking visions of Ireland's Cliffs of Mohr, the majesty of the California redwoods, and enchanting moonlit visions of late-night Paris.

The hard part of breaking into this circuit is getting to the "presenters" — the person at the Performing Arts Center responsible for booking the talent. They get inundated daily with promo materials from artists so it's difficult to stand out from the crowd.

One way to get in front of them is through booking conferences. There are several organizations around the country hosting these conferences: WAA, APAP, Arts Northwest, among others. At these expos, artists can rent booth space and hand out materials to presenters. Better yet, if you get selected to do a showcase, the presenter can see the artist's act live and know instantly if the artist is right for their venue.

I'd gone to a few of these conferences and ultimately got several bookings out of them. But my first day at the Arts Northwest conference in the suburbs of Seattle is brutal.

I spend the day in my booth handing out materials — once again feeling like I'm selling magic elixirs at a carnival. Trying to hustle presenters to come to your booth just feels unnatural and awkward — the antithesis of being an artist. The day drags on and around 4:30, I go back to my hotel room to nap before going to the "pitch session" in the big auditorium.

5:30 p.m. I'm jolted out of a dead-to-the-world sleep when the alarm goes off. I splash some water on my face and race to the auditorium in a daze. The process goes like this: you put your name on a list and if you're called, you head up to a podium on stage and give a 60-second pitch about the act you represent to the auditorium full of hundreds of presenters.

I'm not at all in a state of mind to get up and address this crowd, but know I'll beat myself up later if I bail. Fuck it. I put my name down and pray I don't get called. They call out a few names and I'm just about to walk out the door, when I hear, *Jim Wilson. Come on up!* Ugh.

Wobbling a bit as I'm walking up to the stage, I realize I'm even more out of it than I thought. I'm tempted to take the exit on the left just before the stairs to the stage, when they call my name again. Whatever. Let's just get this over with. Hopefully it won't be that bad.

I get to the podium, move close to the mic. "Ladies and Gentlemen, I'd like to tell you about a truly wonderful recording artist with a really compelling show your audiences are gonna love . . . *me!*" I get a huge laugh.

It goes south from there. Quickly. The spark plugs in my brain stop sparking. The words stop ... wording. I get tongue-tied and tripped up on my spiel. My chest gets tight, I can't breathe. I get an instant case of cottonmouth. My kingdom for one fucking sip of water. The more I hear my choked words blasting out of the PA system, echoing through the auditorium, the more I implode on myself. I want to run. ... *Can. Not. Breathe.* ... I sound like I'm being strangled — literally. But *goddammit*, I'm gonna finish. As I retch out the last two sentences of my pitch, I swear I see a woman in the middle of the auditorium put a hand over her mouth in horror, as if she's witnessing a gory Freddie Krueger murder scene in Nightmare on Elm Street.

By some miracle, I make it through. People offer a light smattering of applause, partly out of sympathy but mostly out of relief that this Hindenburg-in-flames-on-the-ground catastrophe is finally over. Oh, the humanity.

I'd normally have patted myself on the back for having acted in the face of my fears, but I was beating myself up for cratering so miserably. I thought I was mentally prepared to bypass these kind of panic attacks, but dragons from my childhood were obviously still lurking in the shadows. Head down, I began shuffling my way back to my room. To hell with this. I don't need this kind of torture. I have a good, safe career as a piano tech. I'll simply work on pianos and not have to face this kind of humiliation again. I'm done.

Having made a firm decision that I was bailing on this stupid conference the very next day, I felt a huge relief. Yeah, the worst that could happen indeed happened, but I'm still here. I didn't die.

8 p.m. I head to the bar to lick my wounds, maybe even have a laugh about it. There's a line of people for the free drinks and I start chatting with the guy standing next to me. I have zero agenda and our conversation becomes lively. He introduces me to his friend and the three of us get a fun, loose banter going. I make some wisecrack that gets them laughing. We all get our drinks, and one of the guys turn to me. "Hey, you wanna join us at our table?"

Turns out I've been talking to a couple of the top presenters at the conference, and the friends at their table are also presenters for major venues. Having abandoned any agenda, I'm now engaging with them on a deeper level — talking about anything but business. They eventually ask what I do and when I tell them I'm a recording artist of piano-featured instrumentals, one of them says, "That's fantastic! We'd love to hear your music. We have a piano in our shared suite. Would you come play for us?"

Labels and managers pay big bucks to get their artists to perform at a showcase at these conferences with *hopes* there might be a few presenters in the crowd. And here I was being invited to give a private concert in their suite. Wine and conversation flowed. I played for them without hesitation or fear — I was just sharing my music with new friends.

I ultimately booked three venues from that encounter – a nice reminder that when I let go of agendas and expectations, magic happens.

Soon after I returned from that trip, I was blown away with the reviews that started coming in for *Northern Seascape*:

"Sweeps you away to that wonderful place that you hardly ever get to go." - JazzNow.com

"This is inspirational music at its finest." - Creations Magazine

"Wilson's captivating, intoxicating music continues to grow on you even after it's swept you away. … Wilson delivers a truly magical, luminous experience." - Retailer Magazine

"An excellent debut, Jim Wilson has presented his audience with a collection of compositions that will astonish you." - windandwire.com

TUNED IN: MEMOIRS OF A PIANO MAN

And the flood of glowing reviews from fans on Amazon were filling me with a deep sense of gratification:

"Stunning! Absolutely gorgeous... The entire CD is wonderful, as is evidenced by all the other reviewers that all gave it 5 stars." ... "Northern Seascape is a fantastic piano voyage that everyone should take." ... "Jim shares his soul in every track. This is one of the best recordings in my collection." ... "He crafts miniature masterpieces of chamber music from streams of satisfying melodic motifs and variations." ... "This is one of my most played albums."

Man, I was on a roll. I was so proud that I'd delivered the goods for Angel. I was making great progress on *Cape of Good Hope* and couldn't wait for them to hear it.

I'd gotten the green light from Angel to proceed with the next record but wasn't given many specifics beyond that. When they later learned I'd been spending out-of-pocket to produce the next album, I was told, "That's not the way it works. You're supposed to submit a budget, we then pay expenses directly — and only once approved. Send us whatever mixes you have ASAP."

Uh, OK. Not exactly the protocol I recall being informed of a few months ago, but no problem. I had turned in *Northern Seascape* to them as a finished master, exactly as I'd envisioned from the first note to the last. Which is what I was planning on doing with *Cape of Good Hope*. I was allergic to the idea of anyone having any say in my creative process, but I was playing their game now. I had to play by their rules.

One of the tracks I'd cut for the new record was my reinterpretation of one of my favorite songs, "Can't Find My Way Home" by Blind Faith. To give Angel something to go to radio with, my friend Rick Braun did a smooth jazz remix — separate from the album version — that featured Richard Elliot on sax. It turned out great. I sent Angel the only three songs I had mixes for at that point. I led with the smooth jazz remix. It wasn't emblematic of the rest of the record, but I wanted to show Angel I was a team player. Chart success will help drive sales. I've got your back.

A couple of weeks later I got the call. Bruce Lundvall, the head of the label heard the tracks and reportedly said, "We don't need another Dave Koz. We've already got Dave Koz." They were not picking up the option on the second record after all.

Shit.

I was now into this album to the tune of $45k. I'd just been dealt a hard left hook, but I wasn't about to step out of the ring. After healing my bruises for a bit, I decided to approach the other labels that had courted me during the bidding war for *Northern Seascape*. But having been jilted a year earlier by my decision to go with Angel over them, they now collectively offered me a cold shoulder. Though I had done my best with each of them to gently break the news of passing on their offer, I probably should have met with them in person to fully express my gratitude for their interest. Note to self: *Be nice to the people around you on the way up. You just might meet them again on the way down.*

One of the twenty labels I'd pitched *Northern* to a year earlier was Windham Hill. I'd gotten crickets from them but wasn't surprised by their non-response. I mean, they already had piano artists George Winston and Jim Brickman. Labels typically don't sign artists similar to ones already in their roster.

But I'd now played all the other cards in my hand, and I had nothing to lose. I sent a fax to Steve Vining — the current head of the label — giving him a heads up that he'd be receiving *Cape of Good Hope* the following day. A few days later, damn if I didn't get a call.

"What a lovely record. Well done!" Steve was genuinely impressed. We made arrangements to meet in person. The next week, I went to his office in a swank Wilshire Boulevard office high rise, where we discussed the possibility of me signing to Windham Hill. He loved the album as it was but felt the opening (title) cut would have more punch if it were a bit faster. I jumped on the case and my engineer and I sped up the track by 8 percent. Turns out he was right — that added more energy to the track, giving a better first impression of the album. I got it to Steve who thought it was perfect. "We'll get a contract out to you next week."

YES! From the ashes, the Phoenix was rising and I was now going to be a Windham Hill artist. I thanked my lucky stars that I'd pulled off yet another miracle. The contract negotiations went forward but at a snail's pace. We weren't being difficult on our end, but we'd seek clarifications about what was or wasn't recoupable, try to restrict "cross-collateralization" against possible future releases, or request to remove a paragraph about "breakage" — a clause dating way back to when they sold vinyl 78s. There were weeks in between their responses.

After four anxious months, there it sat on my desk: a contract from Windham Hill. Hell yeah. They were offering an advance of $40,000 — a bit less money than I had in it — but I was ecstatic. I signed and returned the agreement and now all that was left was for them to sign on their end. Done and dusted. I called Steve Vining to celebrate.

I could already tell from his "hello" that something's off.

"Bad news, Jim. I don't know if you've read the trades this morning, but there's been a big shakeup. I'm leaving Windham Hill and the new people aren't interested in signing any new artists. Sorry, but I know you'll land on your feet. Best of luck."

Fuck.

CHAPTER 26
Green Hill

"That's my son's music!" My mom points to the TV with one hand, waving her second glass of chardonnay with the other. The fellow attendees at this Sunday afternoon open house at her local PBS station discreetly roll their eyes. Then sure enough, when the credits roll, there's my name.

There's that Power of One idea again — how one moment in time can create a massive domino effect. Because someone at UNC-TV, the PBS affiliate in Raleigh-Durham, North Carolina *just so happened* to have purchased my CD *Northern Seascape*...

And they *just so happened* to think it could be the perfect underscore to the 4-minute piece on the historic Biltmore Estate they were producing to show off the new "hi-def" format...

And because my mom *just so happened* to be at an open house on a Sunday in February of 1999, at which they *just so happened* to be playing that Biltmore video, and the station's director *just so happened* to be standing next to her ... I now have two PBS concert specials to my name.

"So that's your son's music? It's lovely. And you say he's from here?" Joyce Herring, the director, was interested. "Maybe we should do some kind of piece on him."

I soon get a call from Ellen Robertson Neal, a well-known TV figure in Amarillo. Ellen's an Executive Producer for Amarillo's PBS affiliate, KACV, and oversees several specials for them. Now she's calling to see if I'm interested in them producing a one-hour concert special featuring moi.

Holy shit. In just six months, I've gone from the highest high, to the lowest low, now back to the highest high.

I'm also flying high because I've just signed with Green Hill — a record label out of Nashville who're big in "non-trad," distributing music through gift shops and other non-traditional marketing. The manager,

Greg Howard, had reached out to me when I was signed to Angel EMI. He'd heard *Northern Seascape* at a Tower Records listening station in New York City. "I hate that Angel found you first. I could have sold a lot of records on you."

Aw… how sweet that a label I've never heard of is courting me, a hot-shot, big-time artist signed to a major label. Thank God I kept those arrogant thoughts to myself at the time. Because here I am a year later with hat in hand, seeing if Greg is still interested in "selling a lot of records on me." He not only picks up *Cape of Good Hope*, but *Quiet Shadows* — a CD of solo piano covers of some of my favorite songs that I've been selling at gigs, as well as *Northern Seascape*. My friend and amazing lawyer Emily negotiated with Angel EMI / Capitol Records to return the ownership of my master to me, convincing them that if they weren't going to do anything with the record, at least let Jim try.

Whatever preconceptions I'd had about this little non-trad label out of Tennessee go out the window as soon as I see how earnest they are about working my music. They fly me to Nashville, have me perform for their sales staff, they treat me like royalty. They don't have the big Angel EMI advance money to offer, but they'll go on to sell more records in a couple of months than Angel had in a year. And unlike major label contracts, their agreement doesn't require a PhD in calculus to work out what my royalties will be: they pay artists a no-bullshit, generous flat fee per CD sold. Furthermore, I'll retain ownership of the master and lease it to them for a four-year period. They're sincere, kind people who genuinely love my music. I'm home.

And now I'm not only giving Green Hill three solid records, but soon, free promotion from a PBS special in the works, as well as some great celebrity endorsements they can use in marketing.

Besides the previous endorsements from Dan, Carole, Croz and Lionel, there's now one from Phil Collins, who left a message on my answering machine ("Hello Jim, it's Phil Collins. Hope you remember me. I'm just calling to say I put your lovely album *Northern Seascape* on and absolutely loved it. It's really, really lovely. … Just lovely. … Did I mention that I think it's lovely?") I've also just gotten a wonderful endorsement by my long-time client and friend, music legend Burt Bacharach: "*Cape of Good Hope* makes a classy, artistic statement."

Now on to crossing the finish line with this PBS special that KACV is working on for me. They have a great design concept for it. They're going to dress up the second story of an old warehouse in downtown Amarillo, that in its former life in the '20s had been a car dealership. They'll decorate it as an intimate nightclub setting with small round tables and candles. KACV will advertise a free concert, fill the joint and do a 3-camera shoot. Intersperse that footage with some interviews with me offering a little background about each song, and voilà — you've got yourself a concert special.

The Yamaha corporation has recently endorsed me, and they're on board to ship in a 9-foot concert grand. The plans call for me putting together an LA band to come back me up for the concert. KACV's fundraising team have pulled together donations from all their usual suspects but are falling short of the target needed to pull off this grand vision.

Turns out, Mom is dear friends with Don Paxton, whose family had the good fortune of being one of the early investors in a new little startup company.

One night, Mom and I go to the Paxtons' Christmas party. After we all sing a few Christmas carols, eggnog flowing freely, they ask if I'll perform some of my compositions on their Bosendorfer grand piano. They're really moved by the music. Don's wife Dean sits next to me on the piano bench, smiles and puts a check for $4,000 on the music desk in front of me. "Don and I love your music and we want to help make your concert special happen. Also, Don would be happy to come pick up you and your musicians in our jet."

That little startup the Paxton family had invested in? Word was it was an internet-based company that rhymes with "wa-hoo," which is precisely what I say to myself when they offer their support.

Mom and I wait until we walk out into the lightly falling snow to hi-five and hug. My tears of joy soon crystalize in the cold December air. We laugh all the way home.

I spend the next few months in mad preparation for the big event: working up the set list, making charts, putting together my band, and rehearsing them. I have several sessions with acting coach Kate McGregor Stewart, working on feeling more at ease doing on-camera interviews. The months fly by.

———

I smile and playfully salute to Don as he descends the steps of his private jet onto the tarmac at Van Nuys Airport. I give him a big Texas hug, then step back to admire his plane. "Man, she's a beauty! What is she?"

Don, who could pass for Ken Burns' darker-haired brother, always took a moment before he responded. But he'd then look you directly in the eyes, and speak deliberately, with a faint suggestion of a Texas accent. "She's a Dassault Falcon 2000. We sure do like 'er. Wanna have a look?"

I follow him up the steps and catch my breath as I take in the lavish interior of this world-class, 20-million-dollar plane: all 12 passenger seats are upholstered in plush leather, can pivot 180 degrees, and have their own window and private TV monitor. The soft carpet and burl wood trim add an extra touch of elegance. The smell of roasted nuts fills the air.

"We're not gonna be outdone by Southwest!" Don's wife Dean hands me a bowl of mixed nuts she's just warmed up in the kitchen.

"Man, I could get used to this!" I turn to introduce Don and Dean to the rest of my posse, now coming onboard. I speak into an imaginary mic and give them all hyped-up stage intros:

"From London *Eng-ah-lund*, a bloke who'll strum his guitar like none other, please give a warm welcome to my dear mate, *Chris Standring!* ... You heard him on the Titanic soundtrack, and you'll soon hear him asking for a fourth helping of nuts – give it up for renowned Irish flute player, *Eric Rigler!* ...Fresh off gigs with Bonnie Raitt and Jackson Browne, let's hear it for percussionist extraordinaire, *Deborah Dobkin!* ... And on synths we have the indubitably inimitable, *Quinn Johnson!* ...Tonight, the role of Stephen Bishop will be played by ... *Stephen Bishop!* ... And let's not forget my recording engineer *Jerrold Launer* and tech director *Mike Bundlie!*" Don and Dean laugh as they shake hands with everyone.

I go back outside to help load up gear. I drive my car right up to the plane, drop off my stuff and park my car in a parking place 50 feet away. Man, talk about living the life.

A few minutes later, we're wheels up and Amarillo-bound. Between sitting up in the cockpit with the pilot and playing cards with my pals while sipping on champagne, the trip is over in a heartbeat. With traffic, checking bags, security hassles and plane changes, flying commercially from LA to Amarillo eats up the better part of a day. Via Air Paxton, it's an hour and 45 minutes flat.

My old high school chum, Billy Krause, a walking Teddy Bear with an ever-present smile and a peculiar obsession for all things red — red shoes, red cars, red carpets, red ... *everything* — and his lovely wife Danna, who's also wearing red, have volunteered to pick us all up. They take us to the Ambassador Hotel, which is putting us up gratis.

After a quick recon visit to the venue, we finish off the evening with a celebratory dinner with Ellen, Joyce, Hilda Patterson, and the rest of the KACV gang. Though it's a great Mexican food restaurant, it's not conducive to intimate conversations. Between my having to shout over the festive patrons and allowing myself to stress out earlier over details beyond my control — missing luggage, a wrong piano bench, impending interviews — I start losing my voice. By the time dinner is over, it's clear we have a problem. I can't speak. Not good for someone doing interviews the next day.

Billy hops into action and finds someone who'll give me a steroid shot — his veterinarian. Billy drives me to the vet's office and as I look up at a detailed diagram on the wall of horse anatomy, I drop trou and the vet jabs me in my right haunch. I stomp my hoof twice to indicate my gratitude. I fortunately have just enough of a voice the following morning to do the interviews.

Showtime finally rolls around and I'm now standing at the back of the audience of 300. Many of my high school friends are there, as are Mom, Dad, stepmom Andi and Aunt Billie Jo. The place looks enchanting — they have soft blue lights shining on the windows from the inside. They've rigged sprinklers on the outside to give a rainy night vibe.

My dad gets up and gives me a beautiful intro. "...I always believed my son could achieve anything he wanted to." I fight the lump in my throat. Cameras are rolling. I feel my heart pounding in my chest. I so want this to go well. They announce my name, the crowd cheers wildly. I dash to the stage where the band is waiting to play the first note. I have a seat on the piano bench, draw the mike closer.

TUNED IN: MEMOIRS OF A PIANO MAN

"Welcome everyone!" I launch into a minute-long intro about my love of travel that's necessary to set up the show concept. As I look out over the audience, I start feeling the beginnings of a panic attack. It feels like a Boa constrictor is closing around my chest. My mouth goes dry, my head fills with helium. Seriously? *Fucking now?* I'm determined to be bigger than my fears this time. I pause and take a breath. "I'm Jim Wilson and I'll be here in a minute!"

The laugh from the crowd gives me a tiny window to get a grip. I take a drink from my water bottle and remind myself of my pre-performance bullet points: *"Breathe ... Focus ... Unconditional Gratitude..."* I take a slow, deliberate breath deep into my belly and dive back in. I've gotten myself just enough back in present time to get the train back on track. The band performs flawlessly and Stephen, the evening's special guest, is in rare form singing his classic hit, "On and On." I feel a mixture of pride and relief as we play the final chord.

After the show, I go with a few of my old high school buddies and members of my band for a celebratory 1 a.m. breakfast at Denny's. Sharing the familiar embrace of this old late-night hangout with time-tested friends and my LA musician pals is a perfect punctuation to this life milestone.

A couple of days later, Don gave us all a lift back to LA in his jet. This time, my mom and dad joined us, just for fun. Right after takeoff, the pilot took a little detour, flying low to give us views of Palo Duro Canyon — "America's second-deepest canyon" — just a few miles from the airport. I flashed back to all the camping trips I'd taken with Mom and Dad as a kid, as well as other types of trips I'd taken there as a teen. As those movies were playing in my mind, my words catch in my throat as I clinked a celebratory toast with Mom and Dad. It made me proud to make them proud.

KACV did a fantastic job putting together the special, which I dubbed, *Cape of Good Hope and Other Musical Portraits*. They later flew me back for the premiere, where the DVD of the special was being used as a "premium" for their pledge drive. I pitched in on the phones and did some live on-camera interviews. I was told it was one of their most successful pledge drives to date. An avid supporter of the mission of public television, I couldn't have been more honored.

KACV then gave a master tape to the PBS station in Nashville, which fed the special to the other affiliates. Over a hundred stations ran the show and I got emails from new fans from around the country. The timing of the special's airing couldn't have been better, coinciding with Green Hill releasing *Cape of Good Hope* and the awesome reviews that were coming in:

"*Cape of Good Hope is an ambitious, eclectic musical blend of wonderful, catchy, heartfelt melodies that come from the heart to touch the deepest hidden spaces of our emotions. Together they are magic.*" – Arizona Networking News

"*If you've ever wished that your life had a soundtrack, this would be it. Wilson speaks volumes on his second album, with hardly a word said. This is feel-good music, fabulous in any background, accompanying an evening glass of wine on the deck, or as an excuse for just closing your eyes and letting your imagination wander.*" – The NAPRA Review

"*Full of the optimism and wonder suggested by its title, Jim Wilson's* Cape of Good Hope *is full of elegant, layered arrangements that start with gentle piano melodies and build to grand adventures. Wilson draws upon timeless components to craft his arrangements. The resolution to these adventures is always one of strength, hope and gentle uplift.*" – Jazz Times

"*Wilson has gathered together a truly breathtaking collection of guest performances to support his beautiful, romantic, poignant, thoughtful piano lead melodies. David Sanborn, Chris Botti, and vocalists Stephen Bishop and Dan Fogelberg turn in tastefully nuanced ensemble performances that make the most of these tuneful odes to relationships and fantasies.... There are simply too many good Wilson originals to pick a few – enjoy them all.*" – NAV Magazine

---

Before the internet became the 800-pound gorilla it is today, one of the most sought-after avenues for promoting artists and selling CDs was the Quality Value Convenience Network, aka, QVC. Labels clamored to get their artists on this relatively new way of selling merch to the public from the comfort of their living room — via a TV shopping network. They — and their rival, the Home Shopping Network — had a slightly cheesy reputation for selling imitation jewelry and cosmetic packages aimed directly at middle-America. But you wanna sell some records? Get your butt on QVC.

Try as they may, Angel, a major label, couldn't get me on there. But Green Hill, the little engine that could, pulled the right strings.

"Here are our three dressing rooms: Q, V and C. You're in C." It's March 2002, and the host of my segment is giving me the tour of QVC Studio Park, the sprawling headquarters in rural Pennsylvania from which they broadcast. My segment will be shooting live in an hour.

I go to my dressing room and change. I'm doing my pre-show stretching and breathing routine when the host pops his head in the door.

"On in 10! … I'll say a bit about your CD, you'll play a song. I'll come to the side of the piano, ask you about your background, we'll chat for a second, then you play us out on a second song."

An intern then leads me to the piano. Sitting on the bench, I can hear the hosts on a set 20 feet away wrapping up their segment. The nerves are buzzing a bit, but I'm now feeling more under control — just. I take a long, deep breath and smile. I got this.

"We're on in 5… 4… 3… 2…" The director points a finger at my host.

"Boy, do we have a treat for you today!" My host holds up my CD, gives me a brief intro. "I'll tell you more about this incredible album in a minute, but here's Jim Wilson performing the title cut to his CD, *Cape of Good Hope!*"

Boom.

Go … Move your fingers … Stay present … Smile … Feel … LISTEN … Breathe … Focus … Be grateful.

In a flash, the roller coaster is already returning to the platform. The last note of the song is ringing out. The host approaches me.

"That was beautiful, Jim. Just beautiful. Where did you get the inspiration for that incredible piece?"

In yet another flash, our banter is over, I'm half-way through playing the second song when someone yells, *"CLEAR!"*

The host comes over again and slaps me on the back. "Great job! You wanna go see how we fared?" He leads me back to my dressing room where there's a computer monitor. It has a graph that's continuously scrolling slowly left to right. The bottom of the graph is a horizontal timeline broken into minutes and the vertical part of the graph indicates revenue brought in.

"Here's *your* segment." He points to a spot on the graph. "Here was my intro, here's your first song, here's our interview, and here's your second song."

The sales had increased during my first song, dipped a bit during the interview, then took off during my second song and kept going. I'd performed just 12 minutes and sold 2,000 CDs. Damn. Better yet, these are sales that get reported to Soundscan, the company whose sales stats the *Billboard* charts are based on.

Two weeks later, there's my name on the charts once again, next to Enya, Jim Brickman, Yanni, and George Winston. But this time, I'm at #8.

YESSS! Fucking Top Ten! The people at the Studio City newsstand turned to see a crazed but jubilant man pumping his fist in the air. Their startled expressions slowly gave way to smiles. Whatever this guy's celebrating, it must be good.

CHAPTER 27
Jason

Green Hill wasted no time in working this new *Billboard* chart success. My partnership with them was becoming more than I could hope for. They were going all in promoting my albums and finding choice performance opportunities for me.

In the winter of '99, they flew me to Chicago to headline a concert at a trade show. My son Jason, now in his early '20s, was living there and we made plans to hang out most evenings while I was in town. This would be just the third time to connect face-to-face with Jason since he was three. By then, our relationship had evolved into a great friendship – against the odds.

The first "adult meeting" had been just a few years earlier. In the spring of '95, Jason invited me to his high school graduation in Arkansas, where he was living with his mom and stepfather.

As the plane descended into Little Rock, I felt a jumble of excitement, guilt, and anxiety at seeing Jason as a young adult. I'd been so wrapped up in my own myopic world, pursuing self-interests, I'd hardly been a perfect father figure. Even after all these years, the whole fatherhood thing still seemed like an abstract concept to me. Did he feel resentment towards me? I grabbed my bags, hailed a cab and headed to the motel where all the visiting relatives were staying.

"Thanks for coming, Dad!" Jason was happy to see me and gave me a big hug. I wrestled with my emotions, feeling like an outsider as each member of Jason's family welcomed me.

"Hi, I'm the shallow shit who cares far more about his image than owning up to being a father and I don't deserve to be here among you true-blue people," I felt like telling them. I was clinging to my identity as the cool dude from LA, but that held no currency here. I thanked Jason's mom, Jeneanne, and her husband, LeeRoy, for being so gracious; for doing such a great job of raising Jason.

"You hungry?" Jeneanne smiled and motioned to a little buffet they'd laid out for us. I welcomed the distraction and wolfed down some SunChips and a Subway sandwich. After some small talk, we headed for the high school and found our places on the stadium bleachers.

One by one, they announced each graduate's name as they handed them their diploma. When they called Jason's name, our group shouted "Woohooo! That's our boy!" Jason smiled at us and beamed with pride. I felt like I hadn't earned my stripes in this group, but they all treated me like I belonged anyway. After the ceremony, all the parents joined the students on the football field.

"This is my dad!" Jason said as he introduced me to all his friends. The look of pride on his face warmed my heart, but also felt like a sucker punch in the stomach. I was feeling how much I'd been robbing the two of us by having been in denial for so many years.

After he said his goodbyes, Jason and I headed to his favorite Mexican restaurant. We placed our orders. It was time for a long-overdue apology.

"I ... I can't tell you how much I regret not having been there more for you during your formative years." Fighting back the emotion welling in my chest, I took a sip of water. "I'm ... so ... sorry for having been such an absent father." My voice began to break. I looked down at my silverware, trying to get the knife and fork in perfect alignment, while trying to swallow a lump in my throat. "I want you to know how guilty I feel for being so ... self-centered." I swiped my eyes with my shirtsleeve.

"What are you talking about?" Jason was genuinely puzzled, which caught me off guard. "That's crazy talk right there. You never missed calling on my birthday and I've kept all the gifts you sent and letters you've written to me over the years. There's no apology needed. Seriously."

Clearly, we'd been seeing our relationship through different lenses. I should have felt relieved, but his absence of judgment somehow only made me feel shittier. I debated about going into how I was still an irresponsible child who swept under the rug things I didn't want to confront. But it felt like a bullshit excuse, which it was. And maybe that would just invalidate his experience and ruin this moment for him. I got an idea. I straightened up in my seat, took a quick breath and smiled.

"So... how would you like to come visit me in California?"

Jason's face lit up. I was elated by his reaction but felt a sense of yearning for a past we never had. It was becoming clearer that it wasn't Jason who needed to forgive me, it was me.

A couple of months later, as I headed down the 405 to pick him up at LAX, I felt a rush of excitement about this new phase of our relationship. It felt like discovering a secret room in my home. I couldn't wait to learn more about him, to share my world with him. There was a lot of catching up to do, given this would be only the second time to see him as a young adult.

I'd planned the perfect itinerary – we went snorkeling off Catalina Island, checked out the movie star's handprints in front of the Grauman's Chinese Theater in Hollywood, took an epic drive up the California coast to Big Sur with the windows rolled down and the music cranked up. We shared jokes and had late-night discussions about philosophy and politics. I wanted to know what made him tick. I introduced him to my friends, we went to a July 4th fireworks display. He turned me on to artists he was listening to, and we bonded over our shared musical tastes. More and more, I was digging this new role.

But it was a cathartic moment at the Laugh Factory when the last wall of resistance came crashing down. A comedian had just landed a big joke. There in the dimly lit room, as the crowd exploded into laughter, I turned toward Jason. He didn't see me sneaking a glance. Studying the profile of his jawline, it struck me — I was looking at myself. It hit me like an anvil to the solar plexus, shattering my last remnant of doubt. That was my DNA sitting just to my right. It was finally real to me: he is my son; I am his father. I welled with pride.

In no time, our nine-day visit was over and as I watched his plane pull away from the terminal, the tears began to flow. It had been a time filled with joy, but it was tinged with regret about how much we'd missed out on. Still, I was grateful for this new path forward for us.

Years later, over one of our dinners during my Chicago visit, Jason had some big news.

"I can't wait for you to meet her. I've decided I'm going to pop the question." Jason lit up as he told me about his new love, Robin. In just a couple of years, I'd be attending their wedding in Florida. Hardly the future I could have predicted when I got that fateful call from Jason's mom a couple of decades ago.

Nor could I have predicted all those years ago how much more at ease I would become with performing. My Chicago concert felt like a turning point for me. I was slowly learning to make friends with my anxiety and turn it into positive excitement. Performing concerts in venues around the country – from Big Bear, California, Dallas and Little Rock to New Braunfels, Texas, Spokane, and Boise – I was realizing that the more I was willing to be real with audiences, the more I connected with them. My mistakes or word flubs were now welcomed opportunities for a moment of levity.

It reminded me of a story my mom, the Latin teacher once told me. "In the heyday of Rome, merchants would use wax to hide the cracks of their pottery. Pottery that didn't have wax was called *sin – cere,* literally meaning *without wax.*" The essence of this story resonated with me. Being sincere doesn't mean you don't have flaws; it just means you aren't trying to hide them.

CHAPTER 28
Touring Tales

*L*adies *and gentlemen... Please welcome Oscar and Grammy nominee... Stephen Bishop!*

It's the fall of 2004. This is my very first gig accompanying my friend Stephen Bishop. Stephen and I follow closely behind the stagehand whose flashlight illuminates our path backstage to the base of the stairs. My knees are shaky as I walk up the steps to the outdoor stage. In front of us are over a thousand jubilant fans who've come to this community festival that Stephen is headlining. By now, I've performed a few dozen of my own concerts and have gotten to a more relaxed headspace going on stage.

But this feels different. Besides the anxiety of playing music that's a little out of my comfort zone, these are Stephen's devoted fans, and I don't want to let my friend down.

Just a few months before, Stephen asked me if I knew any keyboard players who could back him up on some of his upcoming shows. When I suggested myself, he was surprised, telling me he thought of me more as a solo artist than a sideman.

He was probably right, but I regarded Stephen as one of the great American singer-songwriters and it would be a blast to tour with my buddy. The sophisticated voicings in some of his songs were a little out of my wheelhouse, but I figured the fastest way to learn to swim was to throw myself in the deep end.

Stephen had a lot on the line and needed to see if I was up for the task. He gave me six songs to work up: "On and On," "Separate Lives," "Save It for A Rainy Day," "Send a Little Love My Way," "Red Cab to Manhattan" and "Careless." In a couple of weeks, we met for a tryout. I was beyond relieved when I passed the initial test. I relaxed my shoulders and realized I'd barely taken a proper breath during the whole rehearsal.

I'd been sweating bullets.

But performing these songs in his living room is one thing — how I'd fare in concert in front of a big audience is another thing altogether. Stephen had a gig coming up in La Jolla, California — the perfect opportunity to see if I could handle the demands. He put together a set list of 15 songs. I drilled them relentlessly over the coming weeks. Given my experience with panic attacks, I knew I had to get them bullet-proof.

Looking back on this, I realize now that, as a pianist, my basic wiring is more of a composer who loves to marinate in beautiful chords, to wander in my own secret garden with no time limit. Which is hardly the case with performing live — be it a mall gig, Performing Arts Center concerts, or these possible gigs with Stephen as his sideman. I had to retrain my focus to keeping the train moving at all times. I was creating a new neural pathway — kind of like learning a new language.

As the La Jolla crowd is cheering Stephen's entrance, I take a seat at the keyboard. I go to switch the sound in preparation for the opening song. I haven't accounted for the stage lights blinding me. I can't read the damned display.

Stephen leans towards me and whispers, *"Animal House. One… two… three… four…"* I play the first few chords only to discover the keyboard is on the string preset. Shit. I stop playing, put my hand above my eyes as a shield and get my face a few inches from the digital readout. I finally find the right patch and jump back into the song.

Hardly the inauguration I'd hoped for. I make more than a few mistakes, or "clams" as we call them, but we make it through the set. Stephen gets a huge standing ovation. Granted, the crowd was already standing, but it still counts. We're brought back to the stage for an encore and when we break into the first few chords of Stephen's classic hit, "On and On," they really go nuts.

Over the next 16 years, I'd do hundreds of shows with Stephen in the U.S. and overseas. It was a blast performing all over the world with him: Monoco, Paris, Tokyo, Osaka, and Dublin. Occasionally, we'd add a guitar player, but for most of our gigs, it was just the two of us. All the schlepping could be a hassle but connecting with his fans was an immeasurable reward.

And it turned out to be a great avenue for me to make new fans. Stephen was very supportive of my music and besides inviting me to sell my CDs at the merch table after the shows alongside him, he was kind enough to have me open most of the shows, playing a few of my own songs.

Stephen Bishop's keyboard player, Jim Wilson, is an artist in his own right. Several of his CDs have hit the Billboard Top 20 and he's had two PBS specials. Please welcome... JIM WILSON!

Nothing raises the anxiety stakes more than playing solo piano for a crowd that has come to see an artist other than you. But Stephen's fans were incredibly welcoming and were genuinely appreciative of my music.

Our typical routine was that I'd play a couple of my own songs, then Stephen would come out and we'd do a 45-minute set. Then he'd be brought back for an encore — on special nights, several encores. What joy it was to perform Stephen's incredible songs for his deeply devoted fans. I got to see and feel the power of performing hit songs that everybody knew. After the show, we'd head back to the hotel, order room service and binge-watch episodes of *Forensic Files*.

We played all kinds of concerts in dozens of cities in the U.S., from Boston, New York, and Nashville to Ann Arbor, Pensacola, and Bakersfield. We played at performing arts centers, night clubs, baseball stadiums and on Caribbean cruises. We opened for the likes of Christopher Cross, the Moody Blues, America, Little River Band and Blood Sweat and Tears. Stephen's close friends Art Garfunkel, Mickey Dolenz of the Monkees and Jimmy Webb came to our shows.

But it was playing overseas that gave me a richer appreciation for distinctions between cultures. In Japan, where we toured four separate times, the deeply appreciative crowd would be perfectly quiet throughout the whole song. When we'd finish there would be a couple of seconds of dead silence. Then they'd clap for a few more seconds, then all stop clapping at the same time.

Irish audiences were equally appreciative, but how they displayed it was vastly different.

It's May 2007. Flying somewhere over the Atlantic en route to Dublin,

Bish leans over and says, "I'm just telling you, these people really love music."

I'm like, OK, great. I hadn't quite gotten what he was telling me until the moment we play the first few notes of the first song in our opening set. I can feel this is going to be different. Every culture has its own personality and man, do the Irish love their music.

They start singing along to the choruses of Stephen's lesser-known songs. The libations flow, spirits get freer with each passing song.

Before I know it, it's time to play the last song of the evening. We lay into the first few notes of Stephen's big hit "On and On." The sheer force of a crowd of a thousand Dubliners singing at the top of their lungs — from the very first line of the song to the last — nearly knocks me off my stool. They sing every word with complete abandon, transfixed in pure joy. I'm so choked up with emotion I can barely play.

Looking back, I see how rare these moments were. How magical it was to witness music's ability to unite a crowd of strangers, to elevate them to a state of bliss, to feel its power to transform. Performing with Stephen would lead to many more bucket-list opportunities in the coming years.

―

It's June 11, 2005. Tonight, we'll be performing in front of thousands of people, opening for the Moody Blues at the Greek Theatre in LA. A stagehand leads us onto stage with a flashlight. I look up and see this classic venue from this vantage point. I've been to a dozen concerts here over the years — from Supertramp to Toto to Dan Fogelberg — but I've never properly seen it from the performer's point of view. I feel a rush of excitement as I scan the thousands of people now cheering Stephen's entrance. I've been wrestling with my nerves all day and I'm a bit jittery when I sit at the keyboard.

Then, mid-way through the first song, I look up and in the golden light of the setting sun, I see a beautiful hawk circling above the crowd in the outdoor theater. For just a split second, I'm able to see this scene from the hawk's point of view and how irrelevant my fears are in the big picture. Why not just choose to be here? I settle into the moment and enjoy the music along with the rest of Stephen's appreciative audience. What a trip to open for the Moody Blues in this iconic venue.

—

August 25, 2016. We're in Louisville, opening for Blood Sweat and Tears. A crowd of 7,000 people has streamed into the Kentucky Exposition Center's outdoor baseball stadium. As is our routine, I'll come out, perform a song, then introduce Stephen. But opening for him is a choice he's left to me. It's a massive audience, on the hottest day of the year, and the glare of the setting summer sun in my eyes is brutal.

Panic starts creeping in. People aren't there to hear me, they're there to hear Stephen and Blood Sweat and Tears. There's no M.C., so I'll have to introduce myself. But I know if I cower from a great opportunity, I'll forever beat myself up — an art of self-flagellation I've perfected over decades. Just as it's coming down to the last second for me to decide to perform or bail, I recall the pre-show state of mind of another performer.

Years before, I'd gone with Stephen to hear his dear friend Eric Clapton perform a sold-out show for 20,000 fans at the Staples Center. Stephen and I were ushered backstage just before the show. There in front of his dressing room was Eric, conversing with Sheryl Crow and John Mayer. Eric saw Stephen and hugged him. Introductions were made and Eric chatted casually with the four of us as if we were relaxing by a fire in his living room. After a few minutes, someone tapped Eric on the shoulder and informed him it was showtime. His reaction was as if he'd completely forgotten he was supposed to perform that night.

"Alright then... guess I should be heading to the stage. Lovely to see you!" Oh, to get to that truly carefree headspace about headlining a massive concert.

Now, standing just offstage here in Louisville, I draw a breath and decide to try on Eric's comme ci, comme ça pre-show state of mind for size. I head to the stage, have a seat at my keyboard and lean into my microphone.

"Ladies and Gentlemen... please welcome... *me!*"

The combination of laughter and applause from the audience helps me take a proper breath. I'm hardly Eric Clapton-level of chill, but I'm delivering. I'm surfing on a wave of adrenaline, feeling like I can wipe out at any second, but as long as I keep right on the tip of that wave, I'm OK. It's joy and terror in equal measure.

In a heartbeat, the final note is ringing out and I'm hearing a thunderous round of applause from my biggest audience ever. With a mental assist from Mr. Clapton, the wave has brought me safely back to shore.

When we were traveling, Stephen would often get recognized by fans who'd ask to take a picture with him. I had the same thing happen to me once in Massachusetts.

It's September of 2016. We've just arrived at our hotel and as our driver and the bellhop are unloading our luggage and Stephen's guitar out of the SUV, I notice a guy standing about 10 feet away. He makes eye contact with me. "Are you guys with a band?"

I smile and say, "Nah, we're just the roadies." He smiles, comes a little closer. He leans in and whispers conspiratorially. "You're… You're George Thorogood, aren't you?"

I grin and wink. He nods and winks back as if to say, "I got your back, bro. Mum's the word." As he backs away, I look at Stephen who suppresses a smile.

A minute later he timidly approaches me again. "Sorry man. Would you mind if I got a picture? I'm a huge fan." Oh shit. I really should fess up. But this is too fun.

"Uh… sure … but let's get my friend Stephen in the picture, he plays in my band." The three of us have our picture taken, shake hands and part company. Walking away, I have a mild chuckle with Stephen about this funny case of mistaken identity.

Cut to thirty minutes later. Stephen and I are now getting a bite to eat in the only place open — the sports bar on the second floor. There's that guy again. He's the bartender here. Dammit.

The guy comes over to our table. "Let me treat you to a drink. Whaddya want?"

I smile. "That's very kind of you, but we're good. Thanks anyway." He absolutely insists, so I say, "Just water with no ice will be great." He brings over the water and I thank him, relieved this innocently intended charade is finally behind us.

Stephen and I finish our chicken wings and salads and ask our server for the bill. She turns and points to a couple sitting at the table next to us. "These people have taken care of it." I turn around and see the couple raising a glass to us. "We're *HUGE* fans!"

Shit. shit. shit. The bartender dude has now told several people that the one and only George Thorogood is in their midst.

"Listen, I have to come clean. I sincerely appreciate the gesture but I'm not who you think I am. I'm the keyboard player for my friend here, Stephen Bishop. You know, "On and On?" I was just teasing with you earlier, but it got out of hand. I'm so very sorry I let it get this far!"

If only I'd have actually said that.

Instead, I pause, swallow hard, and coming from my lips I hear the words:

"Thanks so much, man."

Stephen and I stand up to leave. I'm now feeling bad to the bone about this. I finally decide to tell him an innocent joke simply got away from us. I look at the guy and pull out my wallet to reimburse him.

He quickly sticks out his upturned palm and sternly shakes his head. "NO! It's my *honor*. Your music is LEGENDARY!"

I thank them profusely and Stephen and I hightail it out of there.

Yes, I'm a horrible person. But on the other hand, I've given this couple a story they'll be dining out on for years. "Did we ever tell you about the time we bought George Thorogood dinner?" Yeah, only about a dozen times, their friends will say, rolling their eyes.

—

But without a doubt, my fondest memories of touring with Stephen are of performing encores at Billboard Live in Tokyo. We're in the final moments of the night, after the audience has come along on the journey with him. When it all goes right, we're all in a transformed state. We've risen into that timeless, blissful place where worries are miles away. It's life as it should be.

As the crowd is applauding wildly, the staff slowly opens the 30-foot-tall curtains behind the stage. There against the backdrop of a sea of lights twinkling in the Tokyo night skyline, the audience grows silent. Stephen begins playing "Madge" — a stunning ballad that came to him in a dream.

When I remember those magic moments, I see them as if watching them from above, with all of us held in rapturous, suspended animation. The power of art at its finest.

We'd had an awesome London, Glasgow, and Dublin tour lined up in March of 2020 when the COVID pandemic shut down touring, not just for us, but artists around the world. While I've since moved my focus away from traveling and performing, I'm forever thankful for the years I spent cavorting around the globe, performing world-class music for hundreds of thousands of people with my friend.

CHAPTER 29
A Place in My Heart

"Here, try this on." Dan Fogelberg is throwing colorful winter sweaters at me. Just a few days earlier, Green Hill Records had given me the green light to begin production on a Christmas album. And now here I am at Dan's ranch, with Dan going into full support mode. Though I'm here to work on his pianos, he's super excited about seeing my artist career take off and wants to help me however he can.

It's the beginning of 2001, and I need wintry photos for the album artwork. Dan's snow-covered ranch, nestled here in a Colorado forest is the perfect setting. Before I can even form the question, Dan is volunteering to spend the afternoon doing a photoshoot for me. Better yet, his fiancée Jean is a gifted photographer and is enthusiastically supporting the mission. Jean is even more amazing than Dan had described her.

A few months earlier, Dan had come to LA for an ASCAP music awards ceremony — an elegant black-tie affair at the Beverly Wilshire — and asked me to join him. He was staying at the Hotel Bel Air and over dinner, he shared how smart, talented, and beautiful his new love was. ("People mistake her for Bo Derek all the time," he said. He wasn't wrong.) He vividly described the whole tale — from when he first saw and heard her perform in a Santa Fe café, to recently popping the question to her in Italy. It was clear Dan had found the love of his life. I welled up with emotion for my friend. At the same time, his story evoked my own longing for that kind of profound love. But never mind that I wasn't wired like Dan — or like most mature adults for that matter, I was too consumed with my ambitions to make room for something that deep in my life.

Having raided his wardrobe closet of his wool overcoat, turtleneck sweaters and scarves, Dan, Jean, and I now pile into the truck and go scouting around the ranch, finding several stellar locations — by an old wooden barn, by the gate to the ranch, on a bridge overlooking an icy river, by a grove of aspen trees. Jean takes most of the shots, with Dan giving direction: "Smile!" … "Look down, take a breath and look up again." We get a treasure trove of awesome shots.

I haven't even begun the daunting process of choosing which songs I want to tackle. There are thousands of songs in the Christmas canon, and I welcome Dan's input. He brings out a few songbooks of Christmas classics and I spend several hours digging through them, trying them on for size. I only want songs that I can put my own spin on — reimagining and reharmonizing songs to fit the cozy vibe of sitting by a fire on Christmas eve sipping on hot chocolate with a loved one. When I feel like I'm on to something, I call him back into the studio to gauge his reaction.

At Dan's piano, I wade through dozens of candidates, finally landing on "Silent Night," "O Holy Night," "Little Drummer Boy," "O Come, All Ye Faithful," "Greensleeves," and "River" by Joni Mitchell. I would later include several pieces I'd written that lent themselves to a wintery feel. And I had an idea for a song that would become the title cut: "My First Christmas with You." In months to come, I'd write the melody, and the great John Bettis — most famous for all those massive Carpenters hits he co-wrote — would flesh out the lyrics for me. The images in the first verse set up the vibe for the whole record:

Snow is falling down
On cold December ground
I hold you by the window
Nothing makes a sound

It's Christmas night, the firelight
Is in your eyes
You and I know we're making
Sweet memories
My first Christmas with you

TUNED IN: MEMOIRS OF A PIANO MAN

"I'd be happy to sing on the album if you want." Dan is seeing me off, helping me pack up my car. His volunteering to lend his talent to my Christmas record chokes me up. I ask if he has a song in mind. He pauses for a second. "Nah. Just show up at the ranch with tracks."

Holy shit. Dan Fogelberg is trusting me to (a) pick a song that will work for his voice, (b) pick the right key, and (c) do an arrangement that doesn't suck. His willingness to place his hard-earned reputation in my hands feels like someone throwing me the keys to their $200,000 Ferrari and telling me to bring it back — whenever.

It's a few months later, and I've returned to Dan's ranch with backing track tapes on which he can record vocals. We go over the lyrics and select the best verses to use for my arrangement. He asks me to engineer the session and run the tape machine. We set up his vocal mic and get levels. I play the tape a couple of times so he can rehearse to the track. On the third time, he nods at me to start the tape again. I hit play. As the intro is finishing, it occurs to me that Dan looks like he's intending to record one. Shit! Just as he's about to sing, I hit record. Have I made it in time? Should I stop him to make sure we got a clean start? I figure Dan will do a verse then stop and listen to what we've recorded. But he keeps singing all the way to the end.

"That was great! You want to do another one while you're hot?" I'm praying that we'll get a few takes recorded before I have to fess up that I may or may not have started recording in time.

"I know you LA guys like to record a bunch of tracks then comp them together, but I don't work that way. I like to get one good take, top to bottom."

Fuck.

"OK, well that was certainly a great take. Let's listen." I rewind and hit play. Sure enough, I was a nano-second late on punching in and the "G" was missing on the first word. "*...od rest ye merry gentlemen...*" Dan is less than amused. We try punching in just the first line. We listen.

"It doesn't sound the same. We'll have to redo the entire first verse." Shit. I've let my friend down and am now super nervous about making another mistake. Thankfully, we get what we need and have a good laugh about it over dinner. But he never let me live it down. "You have many talents, Jim, but engineering isn't one of them," he'd say with a smile.

As my performing and recording career was gaining momentum, it was not lost on me what a unique, extraordinary blessing I'd been given to be orbiting in the universe of artists like McCartney, Elton, Phil Collins, Carole King, David Crosby, Lionel Richie, and Stephen Bishop. Seeing their creative processes up close and personal — often getting input from them — inspired me to no end. It made me up my game big time.

But it was Dan's support that meant the most to me. His respect and encouragement of my art made me want to make him proud. I'd begun working on a new album and couldn't wait to play it for him. I felt it was my best work yet.

Songs for this new compilation were coming to me effortlessly. I'd be reading a newspaper and wonder what music had been going through my head for the last 15 minutes, only to realize I'd been composing a melody to what would become the song "California." It was an auto-pilot process that dated all the way back to one afternoon when I was nine years old.

I was walking from my Aunt Billie Jo's beauty salon to her home a couple of miles away. I decided to occupy my time by composing my first song. As I was humming it, I began making distinctions in my head about what makes some melodies stronger than others. To this day, I strive to create melodies that adhere to the distinctions I began making on that walk:

The best melodies are unique but still sound familiar. They are familiar, but not predictable. They have an appealing shape to them and are sturdy enough to stand on their own with no accompaniment. They're memorable. They evoke a certain feeling. You get bonus points for "contrary motion" – the melody going one way and the bass line going another. And I knew I liked it when one phrase felt like a question and the next phrase felt like an answer. A quality that I'd later learn in music theory has the fancy name "antecedent / consequence."

When I'm in the throes of making a new album, my mind is working

24/7. Each new melody plays over and over in a loop in the background, being subtly refined in my subconscious music workshop.

With the songs finally composed and all the individual parts recorded, it was now time for my favorite part of the process — mixing. It's a demanding procedure that requires countless hours of intense focus and making hundreds of micro-decisions. Just as I like to say with regard to restoring pianos, the same applies to mixing: when you're 95% done, you're halfway there. The difference between good and great is that extra attention to detail given near the end.

But at the end of that painstaking process is the reward: it's the glorious moment when what began as a melody in my head has finally completed its pilgrimage through the wilderness. It's survived the refinement gauntlet of composition, arrangement, instrumentation, recording and mixing, and now is a tangible thing in the physical world. Claude's passing deeply seared into me just how important that finish line is. Until that exact moment, the song is just an idea floating in your mind. With each finished mix, I'd breathe a sigh of relief and get a deep sense of accomplishment: I'd created one more thing that might outlive me.

—

"Do you think the tambourine could come up one dB?" It was four in the morning on a Saturday in early 2002 and my dear friend and mixing engineer Doug Rider's level of focus and commitment to excellence was putting me to shame. We'd been mixing non-stop for 19 hours straight and I was bleary-eyed.

Two weeks earlier, we'd begun mixing my new album *Sanctuary* in West Hollywood. Doug's client Michael Skloff — composer for the TV show *Friends* — had loaned us his studio. Doug and I would meet there every morning at 9 and work until midnight.

It was a demanding schedule, but I was energized working with some of my best compositions yet, including "Eagle's Flight," "Hunter's Moon," "A Place in My Heart" and "Foolish Me" — a bittersweet song for my girlfriend Shaan who had returned to her homeland of Singapore.

One by one, the songs took beautiful shape, sculpting the 50 to 60 individual tracks into a finished stereo mix. And what amazing overdubs we had to work with. Everyone who took part in the project delivered their A-game: Chris Botti on trumpet, Lili Haydn on violin, Eric Rigler on Irish flute and Uillean pipes, Brad Cole's phenomenal string arrangements, and top players including the Bella Musica string trio, Charlie Morgan, Vinnie Colaiuta, Davey Johnstone, Robbie Buchanan, David Schwartz, Heitor Periera and Chris Standring.

But having all those great individual components means nothing if the mix misses the mark. A great mix can shape all those overdubs into a work of art. A crappy mix can turn them into a muddled mess. Doug constantly encouraged me to 'kill my darlings' in favor of having a simple, pure mix that conveyed the spirit of the song.

Now, it's 4 a.m. and I'm ready to throw in the towel. But I've painted myself into a corner: the mixes must be delivered the following morning to meet the label's scheduled release date. I'm doing jumping jacks, shaking out my hands, splashing cold water on my face. All while Doug remains calm and focused, never yawning once.

Naturally, we've saved the most complicated mix for last: the title track, "Sanctuary." There are many fantastic overdubs to work with — in fact, too many. I'll have to make some hard choices. And I really want to get this mix right. There is something about this composition that feels like it's plugged into a main line for me. The melody draws from deep in my musical DNA — reaching all the way back to the feeling I got when my mom sang "Shenandoah" to me as a child.

And the finished recording of that song contains a section that's among my favorite in my entire body of work. It's when the second verse modulates into the bridge, with the piano guiding the listener through ominous transitional clouds and key changes, then finally drops them off safely into a lovely, open meadow.

Doug and I work on that one section for hours, subtly layering each component, giving each its own special moment: the string trio, Marvin Etzioni's mandolin, the background vocals I sang with my friend Dillon O'Brian, Eric Rigler's emotive Uilleann pipes. It's a tension and release moment that captures a poignant feeling I'm unable to put into words, choking me up every time I hear it. Its interplay between hope and doubt — between joy and heartache — somehow feels emblematic of the artistic well I draw from.

With all the mixes finally complete and uploaded, we stagger out into the blinding afternoon sun. We've worked from 9:00 on a Friday morning to 4:30 Saturday afternoon — over 31 hours straight. Jubilant but exhausted, I somehow manage to make it home and fall into a dead sleep until Sunday afternoon.

The label was thrilled with the record and the critical reception was more than I'd hoped for. But more gratifying to me was that Dan loved it. Higher praise still: he and Jean were getting married and asked me to perform at their wedding. I was elated for them, and it meant the world to me that they valued my music enough to underscore their nuptials.

I started making a list of songs that (a) would be appropriate, and (b) I'd have bullet proof enough to perform solo. My excitement was mixed with a slight sense of panic, knowing I'd be playing solo piano during a very exposed part of the ceremony.

I felt a mixture of disappointment and relief when Dan called me a couple of weeks later with the news that they'd decided to scrap the piano idea. Never mind the rental expenses, the logistics were going to be a nightmare. Still, I was deeply honored that they'd wanted me to be a part of their special life event.

And what a special event it is. It's a beautiful spring day, April of 2002. Dan and Jean's family members and closest friends have flown from around the country to Santa Fe, New Mexico to celebrate their union.

Everything about the ceremony in the chapel is fairy-tale perfect: the stunning image of Jean walking down the aisle in her flowing white dress; the beautiful acoustic guitar music filling the air, played by Elliott Delman, Dan's dear long-time friend from Illinois; the look on Dan's face as his beautiful bride draws nearer. My heart is in my throat. I keep dabbing my eyes with my shirtsleeve.

Later, we all gather for the post-wedding reception in the banquet room of the historic La Fonda Hotel. Someone taps on the microphone a couple of times.

OK! We're gonna pass the mic around for anyone who wants to say something to our newlyweds.

There's a long moment of silence. I feel my mouth go dry and my pulse quicken. I draw a quick breath.

"I'm not one for public speaking," I hear myself say. "In fact, I'm prone to debilitating panic attacks. But this moment is far too important to let that stand in the way. I'm truly overjoyed for Jean and Dan. ... and I'm so sorry... but, which one of you is Dan again? (...*hold for laughter...*) Seriously, I've never seen my friend so happy. From the moment I first heard him describe Jean to me, I knew he'd found the love of his life. In each other, you have found the perfect companion for life's grand adventure. I am grateful beyond measure for the two of you in my life. ... Let's all raise a glass... *to Dan and Jean!*"

At least that's the speech I'll forever wish I'd have given.

Instead, as the question is asked a second time, I sit there in a cold sweat, paralyzed. Goddammit. Finally, David Backstrom, Dan's colorful friend from Hawaii gets up and speaks with ease. Speaking off the top of his head, from the bottom of his heart, he draws big laughs and applause from the crowd.

I would later privately express my joy to Dan and Jean, but I'd always kick myself having let my fears get the better of me on that special occasion.

Over the next several years, I would share quality time with Dan and Jean — at their ranch, over dinner with friends at Dan Tana's after his concert at the Greek Theatre in LA, and I'd even shoot some hoops with Dan in the courtyard of Sunset Sound Recorders in LA.

I lit up whenever I'd see an email from "gopherhead" in my inbox. I savored sending jokes back and forth, exchanging witty repartee, and seeing what hilarious new pseudonym he'd create for signing off each of his emails:

"Notoriously Yours, The Duke of Cunningham"
"Expressions of light and forbearance, Julie (the jeep) Newmar"
"Deliriously, Carlton Fisk"

TUNED IN: MEMOIRS OF A PIANO MAN

"Back to you, Mel, The Scourge of Dordonne"
"Cries and whiskers, Hayden Frothmark"

I did my best to keep up, signing off with my own sobriquets *("Sir Crispin Tickle," "The Honorable Ernest Q. Bogglesnoot,")* but he'd always one-up me, coming back with a brilliant new one each time:

"Fennucci, with two c's. It's Italiano," "Absinthe Lutrell," "Lazlo (the hook) Kovaks," "Eberhardt Faber," "Count Phillipe d'Escargot," "Orloff the Mendicant," "Arnold (The Fez) Stang," or simply, *"Fred Murtz."*

I enjoyed watching his brilliant mind at play and loved making him laugh. ABC Sports had used his song "Beyond the Edge" for a segment they did on downhill ski racing. I emailed him to say how much I enjoyed his song about the famous skier, "Bjorn De Hedge." He said he laughed his ass off at this and it pleased me to no end that he adopted "Bjorn De Hedge" as his new fake name when checking into hotels. Dan felt like the big brother I always wanted and the big brother I wish I could have been for Paul.

―

It's August of 2004. I'm working on a new album, *Beneath the Olympian Skies*, and I'm excited for Dan to hear it. On several occasions, Dan's told me about his and Jean's place in Maine and has invited me to go sailing on his boat, *The Minstrel*. I've dragged my heels on his invitations for too long. Screw it. It's time to finally stop putting off this lovely offer and just go for it — expenses be damned, to hell with any other bullshit "priorities." Sailing off the coast of Maine with my friend and hero — what a perfect opportunity to play him my new record.

Then the news broke.

Singer Songwriter Dan Fogelberg announced ... advanced prostate cancer ... urges male fans to get checked ... requests privacy at this time.

I was devastated. I sent Dan an email saying how shocked I was to hear the news, but assured him, "I believe in you and if there's anyone with the stamina and power of intention to kick this thing in the ass, it's you. Please know if there's ANYthing I can do for you, I'd love to help." I told him I was looking forward to the "celebratory chile rellenos and glass of beer that you, me and Jeanie are going to have at the ranch when you emerge from this in perfect health."

Aside from a few jokes Dan sent in group emails to a handful of his buds, it was pretty much radio silence from him until I heard the news of his passing on December 16, 2007. I immediately called Deb Jelinek, the true-blue fan of Dan's who'd created and maintained a website honoring the legacy of his music.

"He's gone," she said. Those two words broke the dam. We both wept like babies.

Shortly after Dan's cancer announcement, Deb had gone to work gathering thousands of letters of appreciation from his fans across the globe, had them printed and bound into a massive album, then sent the album to Dan. I praised her for her selfless efforts and said how wonderful it was that Dan got to bask in the love of his fans as he was preparing to make his exit.

I then called Dan's dear friend Todd. We cried over the loss of our buddy, discussed how incredibly fortunate we were to have been close friends with such a stellar human being and reminisced about the times we'd shared with him. He filled me in on the previous two years, explaining that once Dan learned how advanced his cancer was, he and Jean cut themselves off from the outside world and split their focus between seeking treatments and finishing their house in Maine.

I told Todd how deeply bummed I was that I couldn't have been there for Dan in the end. Todd said, "Oh but you *were* there in spirit. He truly loved your music and played it all the time. He often bragged about your music to people. He was so proud of you, Jim."

After we hung up, Todd's reassurances made me reflect on what an incredible supporter Dan had been of my evolution as an artist. One conversation in particular stood out from the rest.

I thought back to a trip I'd taken to Dan's ranch. A wonderful five-day visit was coming to an end. I'd packed my luggage in the rental car that was sitting in his driveway. Dan slipped into the passenger seat to say goodbye. He'd told me how elated he was to see my music career taking off.

Over the years, Dan had witnessed every stage of my artistic development, from hearing my production of "Northern Seascape" —

the song I'd written with him, to rejoicing with me when I got the news about my Angel EMI record deal, to teasing me about my mall gigs, to giving me advice about ignoring critics — good or bad. He co-wrote, sang, or played on three of my CDs and often told me how much he loved my music. He encouraged me to "keep creating great art."

In the rental car that afternoon, I told him how terrified I was of performing but how grateful I was for my music to be connecting with people, and to see it reaching a wider audience. Patting me on the elbow, he gave me a pep talk about throwing myself completely into the pursuit of my dreams. He smiled and told me I'd been given a sacred gift. About my anxieties, he told me to not look down, and to just keep my eyes on the horizon. It felt like a big brother giving me words of encouragement.

Often when I hear Dan's music, I'm moved to tears of gratitude for the support he showed me. And it meant the world to me that my music added value to his life. Jean would later tell me that he often played my music when he sailed and that it was among the music being played during his final hours to help him with his transition.

Years later, I would produce *Leader of the Band*, a tribute record to him for Green Hill. I wanted to make Dan proud doing my own spin on my favorite songs of his, including "Same Old Lang Syne," "Dancing Shoes," "Longer," and "Part of the Plan" — the latter being one of my favorite tracks I've ever produced. Dan's and my friend Gerry Beckley, of the band America, played a wonderful acoustic guitar part on that track for me — a true full circle moment, as Gerry had played on Dan's original version 36 years earlier. I ended the album with "Icarus Ascending," which I felt was the perfect send-off to my friend. I did my best to sum up my feelings for Dan in the dedication on the back of my tribute album:

History will shine on Dan Fogelberg as one of the great songwriters of our time, a remarkable storyteller, an American treasure. An authentic artist, Dan crafted honest, passionate songs that are pure reflections of how he lived his life. He left us far too soon, but his phenomenal body of work continues to touch the lives of millions. He was an incredible blessing in my life, and it was an honor to call him a friend. For his brotherly encouragement, his support of my art, and his contributions to my recordings, I am forever grateful. I hope you enjoy listening to this celebration of his spirit as much as I enjoyed making it.

CHAPTER 30
The Genie Grants Me Three Wishes

"**I** want to include a piano and I'd like it to be yours."

Eric Persing had invited me to a private meeting. (Yet another of Claude's enduring gifts was his connecting me to Scott Frankfurt years ago, who raved about me to Eric.) I didn't realize its magnitude at the time, but Eric's offer would prove to have a widespread impact. His company, Spectrasonics, is one of the world's leading music software developers. Their products are essential tools for composers, producers, and performers around the globe.

Their software-based "virtual instruments" can be heard in thousands of hit records, top-selling games, popular TV shows and major motion pictures. Every one of their dozens of products, including "Omnisphere," "Trilian," and "Stylus" has been given a top industry award and garnered rave reviews.

After swearing me to secrecy, he began telling me about a 10-year project his company had been working on. It didn't have a name yet, but it would ultimately be called "Keyscape." Turns out I'd already been tuning some of the instruments to be used in this top-secret library, I just didn't know it. Through "multisampling," he and his team had been working on creating virtual instruments of 36 rare, collector keyboards. It would be the largest such selection in the world.

He wanted the collection to include a piano. Would I be interested in them using my personal Yamaha C7 grand piano? Hell to the yeah! We discussed options for how our working relationship could be beneficial to us both. Neither of us have ever regretted the confidential arrangement we made.

"What if instead of the library including *a* piano, it included *the* piano?" I was starting to really get behind his idea. "There's a cool restoration option I've been doing for artists, and it turns out wonderfully."

I'd been replacing the original hammers with "Renner Blue Point" hammers. They use Weickert felt — a rare, long-fiber virgin wool. I was thinking about doing that to my C7, and here was the perfect opportunity.

We shook hands and I immediately got to work on my piano, installing the new hammers, then diving headlong into the painstaking voicing process.

Voicing — more than any other aspect of piano care — is where craft meets artistry. Through a combination of techniques — deep needling certain areas of the hammer to release compression, filing them, mating them to the strings, sometimes using solutions to add firmness where needed — a good technician can make a piano's tone sing. A less experienced tech can just as easily miss the target, resulting in a dull, dead tone on one extreme, or a clanky, harsh tone on the other. It can be a very fine line.

I was grateful for all my years of experience that had led me to this point. Pulling out every trick I'd garnered over the decades, I spent weeks walking the tightrope, manicuring the voicing to achieve the richest possible tonal palette. The end result was a warm and full, yet clear and focused gorgeous tone.

My piano was moved to Eric's personal studio and he and his team spent close to a year on the project, beginning with auditioning every possible combination of microphones, mic pre-amps and microphone placements, then sampling all 88 notes at dozens of velocities. Eric has a golden reputation for a reason: he has phenomenal ears and sets the bar for perfection impossibly high. What a joy it was to watch him and his team work so meticulously on this project.

The end result was phenomenal. The user buys the software plug-in for their computer, then from a standard MIDI keyboard, they trigger the individual notes of my piano. Having listened to various companies' efforts to produce "piano samples" over a 30-year period, I found them all to be lifeless and missing the mark. To my ears, Keyscape's piano, or "LA Custom C7 Grand Piano" as they dubbed my instrument, is the most natural sounding of them all, with the broadest dynamic range.

After a star-studded event in Hollywood on September 12, 2016, Keyscape became a raging success and went on to become the gold standard in the industry.

The very piano that I'd poured my heart and soul into over the years as I crafted all my compositions — and became my specific sonic signature for all my albums — was now being praised and used by artists around the world, including Jacob Collier, Herbie Hancock, and Chick Corea, to name a few. It blew my mind.

Years later, Eric came to me with the idea for a new addition to the Keyscape collection. A popular sound with composers is a super-muted piano. With an upright, that's an easy enough thing to accomplish — by placing a layer of felt between the strings and the hammers, you get a very dark, muted tone.

But it's not that simple with a grand piano, given the horizontal layout of the strings. I wrestled with the conundrum for several days then flashed on an idea — maybe it's easier to wear sandals than to carpet the whole world. Rather than one piece of large material, what about 88 small ones?

I went to a fabrics store and bought various swathes of felt. After some experimentation, I landed on the right thickness of wool. I meticulously cut 11mm wide strips of felt and covered each individual piano hammer with two strips, attaching them to the wood molding with glue. Viola. The result was a gorgeous, other-worldly tone. The "Double-Felted Grand" sound was met with rave reviews and I'm thankful that our efforts are proving to be of service to composers.

Creating the Keyscape "Double Felt" sound, applying two strips of felt to all 88 hammers. Laborious effort, but such a cool sounding end result!

Not long after Keyscape's debut, I began recording *Remembrance* — an album of the most cinematic pieces I'd composed. "Shadow Falls," "Tangerine Moon," "Diogenes Lantern," "The Girl from Eastland

County" (my tribute to my dear Aunt Billie Jo) ... I wanted each track to sound like a film score, for which the listener could create their own mental movie.

I was in the unique position of being able to record the audio from my piano, as well as using the MIDI output to trigger that very same piano in Keyscape, comparing the two side by side. In many cases, we couldn't tell the difference. I'm extremely proud of that album and to my amazement, in October of 2018, it went to #2 on the *Billboard* charts — not just once, but for two weeks in a row, and was #1 on Amazon and iTunes for multiple weeks. A song from that album, "Tangerine Moon," even received a Hollywood Music in Media Awards nomination in the "Best Dramatic / Crime" music genre. I always knew that the capers and close calls in my teens would pay off one day.

—

It still seems unimaginable that something invisible to the naked eye could bring the entire world to its knees. Yet that's exactly what the COVID-19 virus began doing on March 11, 2020. Hospitals were soon overflowing with victims; people were dying at terrifying rates. People stayed indoors; businesses shut down — some permanently. Panic set in and there were shortages of everything from food to toilet paper. It was chaos like none of us could ever have imagined. The future looked darker with each passing month. To date it has claimed the lives of over six million people worldwide. Unimaginable.

A couple of months into the pandemic, on May 9, I got an email with the subject heading "Howdy Jim." I opened it to find it was from a childhood hero of mine, Arlo Guthrie. As a teen, I was one of millions who bought his *Alice's Restaurant* record, which became a cultural touchstone. I knew he came from Americana royalty: his dad Woody Guthrie wrote Dust-Bowl classics, like "This Land Is Your Land." Woody was a singer of and for the people.

Decades later, Arlo was contacting me out of the blue to tell me he's a big fan of my work. So cool. "Your musical sensibility is quite wonderful — the use of instruments in arrangements etc. You have captured a part of my heart."

Then he threw out a pitch to me:

I woke up this morning (that was good), and I got a crazy idea rolling thru my 2nd cup of coffee. So, I'm just gonna share it with you. There's an old song written by Stephen Foster – "Hard Times Come Again No More." I think your playing and arranging, along with my voice singing it, could be pretty freaking awesome. And could mean something during these times...

I'm just writing to see if you're even interested in the idea. If you are, we could follow up with details... If not, that's okay too. Just checking.

All The Best,

Arlo Guthrie

I jumped on YouTube and started listening to different versions of "Hard Times Come Again No More." And there are a ton of them. The song, written in 1854, has been covered over the decades by everyone from Bob Dylan, James Taylor and Willie Nelson to Jennifer Warnes, Dolly Parton, and Mavis Staples. I got the gist of the song in my head and thought about how I might re-imagine it harmonically, bringing my own version to the table. I went to the piano and started fleshing out ideas. I created my own intro and drawing on Aaron Copeland-influenced Americana chords and voicings, I quickly landed on a basic arrangement I was happy with. I knocked out a rough voice memo.

"You mean something like this?" I sent it to Arlo — along with sincere thanks for his kind words — and immediately got the response, "Exactly like that!"

We spoke the following day and before we jumped into discussing the idea, we talked about our influences.

"Down in my basement," he told me, "my dad had this great collection of '78's — everything from old folk songs to sea shanties to political speeches. I'd spend hours on end listening to everything in the collection." He regaled me with stories about growing up around the corner from James Taylor's family; about family friend Pete Seeger coming around for sing-alongs; and how his dad met his mom, Marjorie Greenblatt, who was a principal dancer with the Martha Graham Company.

The more I talked with Arlo, the more I got that he's the real deal. He has zero artifice. I had to smile to myself — here's yet another artist I'd idolized from my youth that I'm getting the rare opportunity to meet and

TUNED IN: MEMOIRS OF A PIANO MAN

work with. What a rush.

I began to light up with the potential for Arlo's idea. Our reinterpretation of this old classic could be a perfect vehicle for bringing awareness to those hardest hit by the pandemic. I felt like we were taking his father's baton and bringing some light into a dark time.

I immediately got to work. I recorded my piano track and sent it to my arranger Brad Cole in Nashville. Over the next month, some extraordinary artists got behind Arlo's and my vision and volunteered their talents: multi-Grammy winning bass-legend Stanley Clarke, guitar-virtuoso Andy McKee, and long-time friend and incredible drummer Charlie Morgan. Singing-phenom Vanessa Bryan did an amazing gospel choir arrangement and called in her friends Dasha Chadwick and Nic Jackson to fill out the gospel trio. My buddy Dillon O'Brian added additional vocals.

Arlo gave me complete latitude, trusting me 100% as the producer. I held off sending him tracks until they were complete. He told me when he first heard them, he got tears in his eyes. He recorded a wonderful, compelling vocal.

While I was producing the tracks, I was also producing the video, working with my friend, David Beeler. David had the great idea of creating an epilogue verse that would leave the listener with a sense of hope. David, Arlo, and I wrote:

> *"Though faith may be tested, our sorrows will not last*
> *These are hard times and troubles we endure*
> *And it's good to be reminded that this too shall also pass*
> *Oh, hard times come again no more*
> *Oh, better times will come again once more"*

David and I tried over a dozen variations on what theme most effectively served the video. We lit up when we finally landed on an idea that would tie the concept back to Arlo's dad, Woody. The first part of the video features people from the Dust Bowl era dealing with hard times, then the epilogue verse shows current day images of people hardest hit by the pandemic — particularly people of color and folks whose income has just been wiped out.

The first part of the video, which features iconic images by photographer Diane Arbus, is in sepia tone. The video then shifts to color for the modern-day images. There are images in that final section that level me every time I see them: a Black man tearfully hugging a White cop; a closeup of a Black hand shaking a White hand.

"American Folk Music Icon Arlo Guthrie & Acclaimed Pianist Jim Wilson Release a Portrait of the Times with Poignant New Single & Music Video," the press release began. "Legend Arlo Guthrie releases in collaboration with acclaimed solo pianist Jim Wilson a hopeful anthem for a world in crisis with a stunning rendition of the Stephen Collins Foster classic 'Hard Times Come Again No More'. A companion music video coincides with the single release featuring Guthrie performing in quarantine along with Wilson and featured special guests."

The piece went on to quote Arlo: "I grew up in a family that cared about the hardships of others. My father was well known for writing and performing songs to offer hope. 'Hard Times Come Again No More' resonates with me, and I know it did as well with Woody. Though it was first released over a century ago, the message endures with the calamities of today being utterly unjustifiable. We must come together not only as a country, but all across the globe in this dire moment."

Working in conjunction with Arlo's daughter Annie — she on the east coast, I on the west, we were all set to send e-blasts promoting a video premiere on YouTube. Then came her text, "WAIT! It looks like *Rolling Stone* is going to premiere the video!"

Wow. Sure enough, a week later on July 30, 2020, there was the article about our project, with the track and video I produced embedded at the top, featured on the home page of RollingStone.com. I remember singing Dr. Hook's "On the Cover of the *Rolling Stone*" with my friends in high school for a laugh. This was pretty cool. The video immediately got over 100,000 views and phenomenal responses. And better still, it was deeply gratifying to be doing something that might add some measure of solace in a dark time.

A couple of years later, Arlo and I clinked a toast to our musical collaboration during a fun weekend visit to his farm in rural Massachusetts. I told him about my fascination with how one gesture, thought or event can change destiny, and how thankful I was for the moment when he first heard my music, which ultimately led to our collaboration and friendship. He smiled and nodded.

"That's how I regard the day I played the Newport Folk Festival when I was a kid," he told me. "I was an unknown to them, so they put me on in the middle of the day, in the middle of a field, playing to about 70 people. I played 'Alice's Restaurant' and the crowd loved it." He said the promoters saw the enthusiastic reaction and later that afternoon, put him on a stage playing to 300 people or so. "The response was even better that time, so they put me on the mainstage that night in front of thousands of people, with all the other artists joining me on the chorus of 'Alice's Restaurant'. There was a glowing review about me in the paper the next day. That one day changed my life and my recording and touring career took off after that."

Sitting on his porch, watching the sun set on an endless vista of green rolling hills, a smile of gratitude grew on my face as I thought of all my musical blessings over the years: my collaboration with Arlo, having performed around the world with Stephen and on my own, artists around the globe raving about my piano sound in Keyscape, several of my albums topping the Billboard charts, and my music connecting with a widening audience. I'd even had the honor of being flown back to my hometown to address the graduating class upon being inducted into my high school's Hall of Fame.

These were the kinds of wins I'd normally have shared with Mom and Dad. Unfortunately, they had long since left us. In 2005, Dad had passed peacefully in his favorite easy chair at 78; and in 2012, after years of Alzheimer's taking a steady toll, Mom mercifully died of a heart attack at 83. They'd been my biggest champions, my pilot light. How I wished they'd still been around to share these victories with me.[JP1]

Fortunately, years earlier, there was a high watermark that at least my mom had still been around to see — a concert I produced back in 2007 that pushed me beyond my limits and forced me to draw upon every single one of my skills, summoning the courage to confront my biggest demons.

CHAPTER 31
Slaying the Dragon

Before a sold-out audience of 1,300 people at the Globe-News Center for the Performing Arts, pianist Jim Wilson and his band were joined by renowned Irish-flute player, Eric Rigler, LA-based string ensemble Bella Musica and Italian classical pop recording artist Romina Arena.

I wrote that copy six months in advance of the actual concert. In my mind's eye, I could see those words on the back cover of an imagined DVD of the PBS concert special. I printed that paragraph and read it out loud every day, visualizing an auditorium full of people applauding wildly.

I could imagine myself relaxed, fully engaged in the music while performing on a 9-foot concert grand piano with a string trio behind me on the left side of the stage, a three-piece band on the right side, Eric in front of the piano, Romina coming out center stage for a few songs, and an evocative multimedia show projected behind me on a massive screen. The lighting was warm and inviting. I could close my eyes and feel the DVD in my hands.

Now all I had to do was work backwards from those words and make them a reality.

But I had a ton of obstacles to overcome and some scary-ass dragons to slay before this dream could come true.

By this point, I'd headlined 30 or so concerts. But this new goal had all the elements that terrified the holy shit out of me: I'd be performing for my biggest audience yet. I'd be "four-walling" the event — a term in the booking world that means you, not the venue, are running the financial risk. You rent their "four walls," and the rest is up to you. The potential rewards are enticing, but the financial risks are huge.

All the solo concerts I'd done so far began with the encouragement and support of one person: Randy Tupin. Randy had seen me perform

TUNED IN: MEMOIRS OF A PIANO MAN

at the Westgate Mall in Amarillo years earlier and suggested I do a proper concert. As a solo artist, the biggest crowd I'd performed for up to that point was 40 to 50 people. He owned Randy's Music Mart and provided "backline" (musical equipment) for concerts all the time. I was terrified by the idea, but he believed in me and told me he'd do much of the heavy lifting, providing equipment for the concert and coaching me on producing the event. I tried to dodge the subject with him whenever I saw him, but he wouldn't let it go.

Eventually I tapped into his "you got this" point of view and decided to take the leap. I started with four-walling a Christmas concert. In spite of an epic snowstorm on the day of the concert — with weathermen saying, "whatever you do today, DO *NOT* LEAVE YOUR HOUSE! YOU WILL DIE UNTIL YOU ARE DEAD!" — 600 people attended and raved about the concert to friends. We did a couple more shows together, but this GNC concert would be the biggest event I'd undertaken by far.

A major component to my vision was having it be another PBS concert special. KACV had approached me about the first one years ago, but this time it was me taking the initiative. When I contacted them about doing a second one, they were amenable to the idea, but I'd have to do all the heavy lifting: producing the event, coming up with sponsors — basically everything but rolling cameras and editing it into a special. The whole thing was going to be a Herculean task.

So, I used the lesson I learned when I was nine: I'd tackled a seemingly insurmountable task of transforming a storage room filled with boxes and bottles into my first man cave by breaking the project down into bite-sized actions, moving one item at a time. Granted, the man cave makeover was an ant hill compared to the Mt. Everest of the GNC concert and PBS special I envisioned. But the concept was the same. So, I created a to-do list, breaking the project down into small, doable steps:

- Pick a date
- Book the center, pay deposit
- Create budget
- Line up sponsors
- Design look of concert

- Line up musicians
- Line up featured guest artists
- Get charts & CDs to all the musicians
- Book airline flights for LA musicians
- Arrange for lodging and meals for all musicians
- Create & mail flyers to 1,600+ Amarillo area people
- Create & run TV ads
- Do radio interviews
- Arrange for article in newspaper
- Create billboard ad
- Do eblasts targeting 1,600+ Amarillo area people
- Contact Yamaha, arrange for delivery of 9' concert grand
- Produce multimedia videos for 5 new songs
- Print all 16 multimedia videos onto one DV tape
- Arrange for projector, screen, backline
- Practice show 3 hours daily
- Write rough outline of song intros
- Practice with LA band
- Send CDs to venue / line up someone to handle merch table
- Fly into Amarillo early, practice with Amarillo band
- Coordinate production schedule with KACV
- Design and print concert programs
- Create & distribute itinerary
- Tune and voice the piano
- (On day of): Full production rehearsal
- Massage
- *Showtime!*

I didn't have a proper manager at the time, so it was on my shoulders to pull most of this off. Thankfully, Randy oversaw backline and equipment rental for me, and Kris Miller stepped up and handled details that hadn't even been on my radar: arranging for and providing security, insurance, stagehands, technicians, ushers and having EMTs on hand.

I hammered out the budget. The expenses soared to $45,535. I got busy calling potential sponsors. One by one, they came on board in exchange for their names in the program and free publicity in TV and print ads, but mostly because they were supporting my mission. With generous in-kind contributions, I ultimately knocked my total out-of-pocket tab down to $24,354. (Full list of sponsors in Appendix.) This was going to be a big throw of the dice, but even if the worst-case scenario was that I broke even, it would still be a win. I'd come away with a second PBS special, exactly as I'd envisioned it.

I wanted the look to evoke the feel of a magical living room. Texas Furniture came on board, providing Persian rugs and end tables on which we'd place cool-looking lamps. Freeman's Flowers delivered a ton of palm trees, potted plants, gorgeous floral arrangements, and ficus plants adorned with twinkling lights that lined the stage. Colored lights illuminated the chiffon fabric bordering either side of the 25' tall screen behind the piano, onto which my multimedia videos were projected.

Another possible uphill financial battle loomed ahead: I was told that the new $30 million Performing Arts Center had yet to sell out. They'd presented a big gala, a ballet and an opera event and a country artist right after it opened, but it hadn't yet filled to capacity. My event was a few months after the center opened, so I had my work cut out for me to hit my vision of selling it out.

Now, it's 90 days out and one by one, the puzzle pieces are falling into place: My Amarillo buddies Jay Weeks and Scott Nelson are set to play drums and bass respectively. They've lined up Jerry Thompson to play guitar. In LA, I've approached Eric Rigler, the Bella Musica string trio — Kristen Autry, Briana Bandy, and Sharon Rizzo — and my friend Romina Arena, who are all on board.

My Amarillo high school friend, Rick Trafton has a print shop and donates the printing of several thousand flyers. And all those years that I'd performed at Westgate Mall are now paying off: each and every one of the thousands of CDs I'd sold there represented a person with whom I'd shaken hands with, and who was happy to be on our mailing list.

60 days to go: Tickets go on sale. We sell a few hundred out of the gate. I'm working 12- to 14-hour days, booking flights, doing promo, coordinating with KACV. I know this concert and video will be a lasting legacy for me and I'm going to leave no stone unturned.

30 days to go: 656 tickets sold.

15 days to go: 852 tickets sold.

One week to go: 1,152 tickets sold!

Three days before the show, I get the call from Kris. "Congrats buddy! You're the first act to sell out this venue!"

I feel a mix of joy and terror. I now must deliver the goods and give people their money's worth. There's no turning back.

The day before the gig, we all arrive at the venue. It looks stunning. I tune and voice the 9-foot concert grand piano Yamaha has shipped in from Oklahoma. We spend the afternoon ironing out technical kinks, but overall, our first rehearsal goes well. We celebrate over dinner. We knock it on the head early. Tomorrow's a big day.

KACV has set up an interview room and Dale Robinson and my old school friend Buddy Squyres are running the camera shoot, while Ellen Robertson Neal interviews Romina, Eric, and me, discussing each song.

KACV has a great idea for turning our three-camera shoot into a six-camera shoot. They'll position the three cameras on stage to tape close-ups and crane shots for the afternoon run-through of the show, then move the same three cameras further back into the auditorium for the actual concert. They'll later edit the two takes together seamlessly.

It's now 45 minutes to show time. I arrive at the venue and park near the artist's entrance behind the building. I see hundreds of people decked out in their finest attire streaming into the venue for a special night. It's utterly surreal to me that all these people are coming to *my* show. Mind-blowing.

I head inside, walk down the hall towards my dressing room and hear a familiar voice.

"Do you like my shirt?" I turn to see my sister Jenny, who's flown in from Alaska with her husband David just for this event. She's sporting a "Jim Wilson" T-shirt. I'm speechless that she's made such a huge effort to come and support me. I hug her and tell her it means the world to me. My niece Kris and husband Will have driven miles to come support me as well. My heart is in my throat.

It's 15 minutes to showtime. I'm anxious, but I have a better grip this time around. I'm doing some yoga stretches and working on getting into the zone. In his book *Effortless Mastery*, Kenny Werner describes the state that all artists, athletes, and performers strive to get to when it's "*go time*" — all the years of training, piano scales, etc., are behind you and never even enter your mind. There's no effort to your playing. You're present. You're right there enjoying the music along with the audience. I take a moment to see myself in that zone.

There's a knock on my dressing room door. *Five minutes!*

I gather in the hall with the rest of the group. We form a circle. I tell them how grateful I am to share this special night and have the opportunity to make music with them. We say a quick prayer.

One minute to showtime. The band is in place on stage now and I'm waiting in the wings, just behind the curtain. I glance out and see an auditorium full of people — precisely as I'd visualized it so many months ago. I'm slightly nervous, but happy and buzzing with appreciation.

I smile and give a thumbs-up to the stagehand beside me. He nods and, in his headset, says "good to go!" The announcer begins my intro. I do one last internal incantation of my three pre-show reminders: "Breathe…. Focus… Unconditional Gratitude."

I anticipate the two-hour concert ahead. I'm just seconds away from my leap off the high dive and feel a jolt of fight-or-flight adrenaline in my gut. The urge to turn and sprint out the back door is very real. Then I hear a gruff voice in my head. It's my cousin Dudley:

"*Sometimes ya just gotta go for it, Jimmy.*"

They announce my name. I got this. The spotlight follows me as I walk out. I smile and wave to the audience. I stand beside the piano and bow. The auditorium resounds with applause.

For the next two hours, I'm floating out of body, experiencing the event along with the rest of the auditorium. I've finally learned to turn the anxiety into excitement. It feels like the music is connecting us all on a deep level. The show goes flawlessly.

Before I know it, we're playing the final note of the show and all 1,300 people rise to their feet in instantaneous unison. It's the most beautiful sight. I've arrived.

Beaming, the nine of us on stage stand and wave to the audience. We've just been conduits to art's highest function: elevating the listener to a higher state of mind.

Walking off stage, I feel the greatest relief of my life. I feel like Rocky Balboa at the top of the steps, pumping his fists in the air against the Philadelphia skyline. I'd stood up to not just one, but several menacing dragons that have terrorized me since childhood. I'd moved forward in the face of my fears.

The crowd continues cheering for several minutes. We all return to the stage for our curtain call. Shoulder to shoulder, we lock arms, form a line, and take a bow.

After the show, people come up to me with tears in their eyes expressing how deeply moved they are. One of the people who's moved the most? Peter, the bully who'd taunted me on the playground in second grade.

People are especially touched by "To Love and Be Loved" — my tribute to my dad, and his enduring lesson to me about the importance of the immaterial things in life. But the biggest joy is the look of pride on my mom's face. This sense of accomplishment is the biggest prize of the night. With the help of my friends, my dream has come true.

TUNED IN: MEMOIRS OF A PIANO MAN

*A couple of moments from the sold-out GNC concert —
a definite high-water mark for me.*

CHAPTER 32
Dénouement

From the moment I first plucked that guitar string when I was seven years old, my life's direction was set. I was drawn to music like the proverbial moth to the flame. It would ultimately take me on a journey to the far corners of the globe: from the Panhandle of West Texas to Los Angeles, down side streets that led to some of the most influential music-makers on the planet. It would lead me to a dear friend whose untimely death at 37 would force me to re-evaluate my whole life's purpose and throw myself wholeheartedly into creating art that spoke from my truest self.

It would set the stage for me to become a father — a life passage I wasn't ready for at the time but would ultimately become the most extraordinary blessing in my life.

I'm a work in progress. I can still be self-absorbed and judgmental. I'm not a perfect person, but I know that the good in me holds the majority share.

The malcontent in me is still alive and well, but he doesn't command center stage. I'm grateful to him for pushing me to make my music and piano restorations the best they can be. But I know he's always lurking around the corner, ready to convince me that whatever I've achieved, whoever I am, is not enough. I still wrestle with *woulda-shoulda-couldas*, but if I had some bacon, I could have some bacon and eggs, if I had some eggs. Speculating on what-ifs is a bottomless rabbit hole. More and more I'm making the conscious choice to live in a state of gratitude. As Meister Eckhart said, "if the only prayer you ever say in your entire life is thank you, it will be enough."

That insecure kid also still lives inside me, but I've either conquered or called cease-fires with the worst of my demons and signed non-binding peace treaties with the rest. The panic attacks are fewer. I still get intense butterflies, but I've taught them to fly in formation. And I still have leftover wiring that bases my self-worth on what others think of me, but I feel less of a gnawing need to prove myself these days.

All that said, sometimes I'm still nine years old and would give anything just to feel my mom's arms around me, telling me "Everything's gonna be all right."

While I apparently wasn't destined for an old-fashioned Ozzie and Harriet lifestyle, I continue to make progress on the journey from "me" to "we." For the past fifteen years, I've been blessed with a truly wonderful life companion, Virginia, a gifted actress and film producer with whom I share the love of traveling and exploring the great outdoors. We support each other in achieving our dreams and share a laugh about something every day. Our cat, Maxie, reminds us of the importance of playfulness. I'm thankful beyond measure to share the journey with them.

Nor was I destined for a traditional path to fatherhood — but looking back I wouldn't change a thing. My evolution as a parent has been slow but steady over the decades: from my being a teen in denial, to letters and phone calls to my son in his youth, to flying to Arkansas for his high school graduation, to our epic father/son week in California, ultimately to weekly FaceTime sessions and cherished holiday visits to North Carolina where he is an inspector for TSA. I'm beyond grateful that the more I've leaned into my relationship with Jason — who is both my son and best friend — and with his wonderful wife Robin and my four fantastic grandkids Bella, Serena, Jace and Ethan, the more richly rewarding it's become. I'm welcoming this GrandDude chapter with open arms. And my admiration for Jason only continues to grow stronger: he's smart, funny, and even-tempered. He's an amazing, responsible parent, and — unlike his father — isn't tethered to the approval of others. When I grow up, I hope to be just like him.

Recalling the treacherous tightrope of my teens, I'm fortunate I didn't land in prison, or worse, take a fatal fall into the abyss. And thinking back further to the diffident boy playing guitar in his bedroom in West Texas with a vague dream of a life of making music, it would be decades before I would tune in to the purest essence of the music inside me.

The dream I ultimately manifested looks different than my original vision of becoming a famous singer-songwriter — and thank goodness for that. I never had a "hit song," but the music I've created is 100% from my heart. It's all been completely on my own terms, with no label dictating to me. Mine is music that found its way to the surface in an effort to turn poison into medicine — the metamorphosis of deeper emotions into art. That it adds value to the lives of those with whom it resonates is deeply fulfilling to me.

I still have music inside me that I'm excited to share. But I do know that one day, like Claude, I'll get that tap on the shoulder. Time's up, pencils down. Turn in your assignments as is. My final mental highlight reel will certainly include a kaleidoscope of incredible, one-of-a-kind experiences I was gifted with — singing Beatle songs on the same piano bench with Paul McCartney, limo rides with Elton John, a road trip with Carole King, creating music with Dan Fogelberg.

But I know that those memories will pale in comparison to the feeling I get when Jason turns to me for guidance or texts me with a twisted joke. Or the look on my grandchild Serena's face when she first saw the epic waves of the Pacific Ocean crash against the rocks at Cambria. Or hearing the sound of my grandkids Jace's and Ethan's laughter. Or my grand-nephew Aaron presenting me with a hand-drawn Christmas card, or his sister Katelyn lighting up when I taught her a song on piano. Having mattered to them surpasses anything else I might have accomplished in the physical world. St. Exupery's *Little Prince* nailed it: that which is essential is invisible to the eye.

I have no idea what awaits on the other side. And I'm OK with that. But a picture taped to the wall near my desk says it all: it's the beaming face of Stephanie Tyrell — a friend of mine who left us way too soon 20 years ago. The caption is my daily reminder: "Love is all we leave behind."

Dan was right — the calling to create art is indeed a "sacred gift." I'm proud that I've created a body of music that will succeed me and might continue to bring joy to others. But more importantly, if the only thing my life accomplished was that my grandkids or my great-niece and great-nephews might one day read my story and be inspired to go for their dreams in spite of seemingly insurmountable obstacles, that's enough. When they're reaching for the brass ring, I hope they'll hear my voice whispering, *"Take it, it's yours."*

With my "grands" (L-R) Ethan, Jace, Bella and Serena.

Bella looking over (L-R) Serena, Moi, Jason, Ethan, Robin and Jace.

Me dear ol' Mum at the first PBS taping.

Me dear ol' Pop at the first PBS taping.

TUNED IN: MEMOIRS OF A PIANO MAN

Sweet pic of sister Jenny & me – back in the day!

My sweet lil' bro Paul, Dad and I havin' a larf at Dad's farm.

Mom and Dad about to accompany me and band back to LA in Paxton's jet. Best canine photobomb ever.

Dad and Stepmom Andi – in their wedding outfits!

TUNED IN: MEMOIRS OF A PIANO MAN

Claude and me, about to head out for a night on the town.

Dinner with the Genesis lads at their UK studio. (L-R: Phil Collins, Mike Rutherford, Tony Banks, (Unknown).

Backstage with Sir Elton.

Moi with Carole King, after she checked out my MIDI piano. in my North Hollywood apartment.

TUNED IN: MEMOIRS OF A PIANO MAN

Sir Pablo, holding a stained-glass piece my mom made for him.

Fun night on the town with Dan Fogelberg at a Beverly Hills awards ceremony.

Hitting the slopes with my "Amarillo bro" J.D. Souther.

Hangin' with Quincy – a true music legend.

TUNED IN: MEMOIRS OF A PIANO MAN

A cherished note from Quincy.

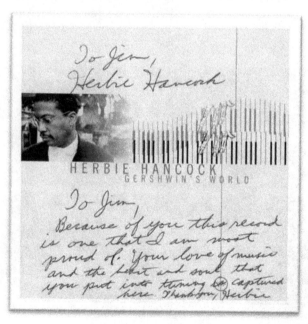

A cherished note from Herbie.

JIM WILSON

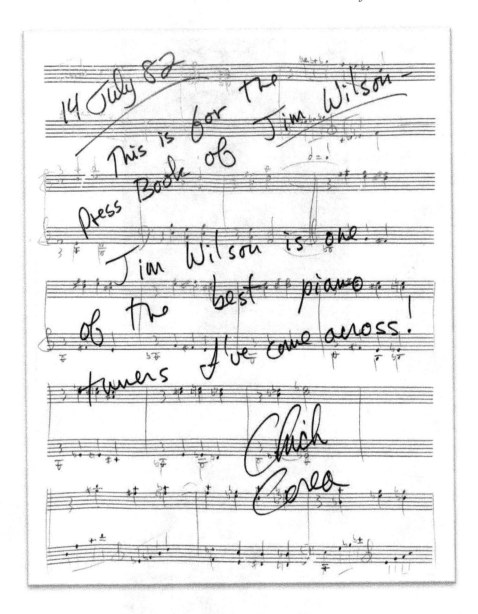

TUNED IN: MEMOIRS OF A PIANO MAN

Me and Arlo Guthrie, in front of the church he sings about in "Alice's Restaurant." It's now "The Guthrie Center" – a non-profit organization helping people in need.

JIM WILSON

*Virginia laughing at me mercilessly,
for which she no doubt had good reason.*

Our ceaseless source of amusement, the Marvelous Ms. Maxie.

Credits

SONG LYRIC CREDITS:
'Shenandoah' – author unknown, (public domain)
'Downtown' – © 1964, Tony Hatch, Universal Music Publishing
'Like a Rolling Stone' – © 1965, Robert Dylan
'Burn On Big River' – © 1972, Randy Newman, Little A Music, Unichappell Music, BMI
'Jim' – © 1941, Caesar Petrillo, Edward Ross, Nelson Shawn (public domain)
'No One Is to Blame' – © 1985, Howard Jones, Howard Jones Music America, BMI
'For A Dancer' – © 1974, Jackson Browne, Swallow Turn Music, ASCAP
'Hey Jude' – © 1968, John Lennon / Paul McCartney, BMI
'You've Got a Friend' – © 1971, Carole King, Colgems EMI Music, ASCAP
Lovers In a Dangerous Time – © 1984, Bruce Cockburn, Rotten Kiddies Music LLC, BMI
'Don't Stand at My Grave' – © 1934, Clare Harner (public domain)
'Our Children's World' – © 2020, Jim Wilson, Willow Bay Music, ASCAP
'My First Christmas with You' – © 2002, Jim Wilson, John Bettis, Willow Bay Music, Big Tractor, ASCAP
'Hard Times Come Again No More' (Epilog Verse) – © 2020, Jim Wilson, Arlo Guthrie, David Beeler

PHOTOGRAPHS:

Cover concept: David Beeler. Cover art: Mike Bundlie. Back cover photo: Andy Keeter. All other photos courtesy of author's personal collection.

SPECIAL THANKS:

Writing an 85,000-word memoir was a years-long, epic undertaking – one that I couldn't have done alone. Everyone who's ever played a role in my life is, in one way or another, an invaluable part of these pages.

I'm eternally grateful to my family and friends for their support over

JIM WILSON

the years: Virginia, Jason & Robin Ihbe, Bella, Serena, Jace and Ethan. Mom and Dad – you gave me roots and wings, and your spirit is alive in this memoir. Andi, Jenny, David, Kris, Will, Henry, Devon, Joel, Aaron, Katelyn, Trevor and Jory. Sincere gratitude to Mary Lee Wegner, Donna Lynn Stillo, Shaan Moledina for the love and support. Thanks so much to all who offered invaluable input in taming this tome: Virginia Schneider, Maggie Paul, Mary Volmer, Hedi Lampert, Anne Helmstadter, David Beeler, Adam Belanoff, Al Secunda, Chris Standring, Tom Lerner, Norm Kachuk, Dan Wilson, Mark Smith, Al Secunda, Bill Jordan, David Chrisman, Tony McShear, Charlie Chiara, Hollye & Troy Dexter, Michael Neill, Loren Gold, Lieschen Bierstedt, Linda Nealon, John Jarvis, Kim Flagg, Aaron Vattano, Jenna Sobelman, Jaz Persing, Julian Williams, Ellen Robertson Green, Loren Gold, Neville Farmer, Magnus Fiennes, Nathan East, Brian Luke Seward, Scott B. Bomar, and Tammy Letherer. Thanks also to Erica Hughes and New Book Authors.

Massive thanks to my mate, Danny Schogger, for being my champion from the get-go, twisting the arms of all the London recording studio owners, making them jump on board the Jim Wilson MIDI piano train. I'm forever grateful for your support and friendship. "I'll phone you from the Departure Lounge at LAX."

Huge thanks to those who lent their name / offered their support to my mission: Adam Belanoff, Alan Bergman, Arlo Guthrie, Barry Manilow, Bill Brandom, Burt Bacharach, Carole Bayer Sager, Chris Standring, Courteney Cox, Dave Koz, David Crosby, David Foster, Denny Tedesco, Diane Warren, Ed Begley, Jr., Eric Persing, Greg Wells, Herb Alpert, Herbie Hancock, J.D. Souther, Jackson Browne, James Newton Howard, Jean Fogelberg, Katey Sagal, Larry Klein, Lili Haydn, Lionel Richie, Lisa Loeb, Loren Gold, Magnus Feinnes, Marc Shaiman, Martin Perlich, Martin Short, Matthew Wilder, Melissa Manchester, Michael Neill, Mike Stoller, Nate East, Neville Farmer, Patrice Rushen, Paul Mirkovich, Peter Collins, Quincy Jones, Ray Romano, Richard Carpenter, Richard Page, Stanley Clarke, Stephen Stills, Steve Kipner, Steve Lukather, Steve Porcaro, Steve Tyrell, Walter Afanasief, and Zac Rae.

Larger than life thanks to Denise Bundlie for the title suggestion.

Thanks as well to Anastasia Savage Ealy, Bob Sharp, Freyda Campbell,

TUNED IN: MEMOIRS OF A PIANO MAN

Chris Earthy, Richard Moakes, Amabelle Bekki Hazlett, Sally Stevens, Ron Kramer, JoAnne & Monte Davis, Jody Perkins, and of course, Toy. Sincere apologies to anyone I might have unwittingly left out.

ARTISTS, MUSICIANS, TECHS & PHOTOGRAPHERS:

Deepest gratitude to all who contributed their talents to my projects: **Artists**: Andy McKee, Arlo Guthrie, Chris Botti, Chris Standring, Dan Fogelberg, Dave Koz, David Sanborn, Everette Harp, Gerry Beckley, J.D. Souther, Lili Haydn, Marilyn Martin, Peter White, Richard Elliot, Rick Braun, Stanley Clarke, and Stephen Bishop. **Musicians**: Alex Acuna, Andy McKee, Angela Scalise, Benjamin Wyatt, Beth Hooker, Brad Cole, Brian Mann, Briana Bandy, Bruce Watson, C.J. Vanston, Casey Stratton, Charlie Morgan, Chuck Tilley, Dasha Chadwick, Davey Johnstone, David Schwartz, Debra Dobkin, Dillon O'Brian, Doug Lacy, Eric Rigler, George Merrill, George Tortorelli, Greg Bissonette, Greg Hilfman, Greg Phillinganes, Heitor Periera, Jay Weeks, Jerrold Launer, Johnny Lee Schell, Jon Gilutin, Jonathan Dane, Jonathan Merrill, Julie Adams, Kristin Autry, Lee Sklar, Lenny Castro, Lisa Lynne Franco, Mark Portmann, Marvin Etzioni, Matt Dame, Matt Rollings, Michael Landau, Micheal Becker, Mitch Forman, Nathan East, Neil Stubenhaus, Nic Jackson, Paul Cartwright, Paul Loredo, Quinn Johnson, Ricardo Silveira, Richie Garcia, Robbie Buchanan, Roger LaRocque, Scott Frankfurt, Scott Nelson, Sharon Rizzo, Steve Porcaro, Steve Salani, Susie Katayama, Tim Pierce, Troy Dexter, Ty Stevens, Vanessa Bryan, and Vinnie Colaiuta. Engineers & Techs: Abe Guthrie, Bernie Becker, Bob Clearmountain, Colin Mitchell, Dale Becker, Daniel McMains, Doug Rider, Gil Morales, Jerrold Launer, Sergio Ruelas, Jr, and Stever Derkle. **Amarillo Musicians:** Steve Dunnagan, Rick Faucett, Randy Palmer, Bob Denton, Jerry Johnstone, Jackie Haney, Charlie Clinton, Frank Romero, Jay Weeks, Scott Nelson, and Jerry Thompson. **Piano Techs**: Norm Neblett, Richard Davenport, Bruce Stevens. Ron Tuttle, Mark Mandell, Frank Muslar; Randy Morton, Rob Morton, Mike Farnell, Charlie Clinton, Danny Richards, Kevin Gallagher. **Photographers & Designers**: Amy Dakos, Andy Keeter, Beth Herzhaft, David Beeler, Davy Knapp, Deyo Glines, Jean Fogelberg, John Williams, Kristen

JIM WILSON

Beahm, Lee Wright, Mick McCarthy, and Mike Bundlie.

CAREER SUPPORT:

Deep gratitude to Emily Simon, Steve Steinberg, David Pringle, Randal Cohen. All at Angel EMI: Bruce Lundvall, Gilbert Hetherwick, Steve Ferrera, Nancy Roof, Andria Tay, Dave Millman. All at Green Hill: Melissa Chambers, Tod Ellsworth, and especially to Greg Howard – I'm so eternally grateful for the invaluable role you played in my life. And to Toy, Bill Jordan, Michael Lehman-Boddicker, Deborah Jelinek, Laurie Williams, Randy Tupin, Bob Flesher, Billy Stull, Norm Petty, Kate McGregor Stewart, the Yamaha Corporation, Dave Weiderman / Guitar Center, Leslie Kogan, Steve Salani, Chuck Monte, and especially my "Mon Ami Eternel," Claude Gaudette.

SPONSORS / CONCERT MUSICIANS:

Sincere thanks to all who helped make my GNC concerts / PBS specials a reality: Ambassador Hotel, Barnes Jewelers, Dr. Richard Bechtol, Randy Burkett / Burkett Family Investments, Ray Cotnoir, Charles Curl, Lillian Doyle, Larry & Donna Cunningham / Eat-Rite Health Foods, The Dick Ford Company, Freeman's Flowers, Vance Hall / H&H Printwear, Kirk Hill / Hill's Sport Shop, Dr. Michael Jenkins, Davy Knapp Photography, Billy Krause / Krause Landscaping, Northwest Texas Healthcare System, Don and Dean Paxton, Randy Tupin / Randy's Music Mart, Steve Spencer, Billie Jo Tevebaugh, Texas Furniture, The Yamaha Corporation. Special thanks to Jay Weeks, Scott Nelson, Jerry Thompson, Eric Rigler, George Tortorelli, Kristin Autry, Briana Bandy, Sharon Rizzo, and Romina Arena. Chris Standring, Deb Dobkin, Quinn Johnson. Also to Joyce Herring, Ellen Robertson Green, Hilda Patterson, Jackie Smith, Buddy Squyres, Dale Robinson and the entire KACV-TV team. Heartfelt thanks also to Kris Miller, Bruce Carter, King Hill, Chip Chandler, Debby Gnepper Murphy, Derek Bradford and Leslie Cunningham.

DISCLAIMERS:

The events in this book are portrayed to the best of my memory. Peter, Greg, Rob, Ken, and Sam are pseudonyms. The GNC concert chapter is an amalgam of two separate GNC concerts.

About the Author

Jim Wilson's life direction was set when he was given a guitar at age 7, then began composing songs at age 9. Soon after moving from West Texas to LA in his early 20's, he gained notoriety as a respected piano technician, catering to the highest echelon of the music industry. Jim helped develop the first MIDI-adapter for acoustic piano in the 80's, which became an instant hit with artists and studios around the world.

Jim also collaborated with Spectrasonics — a leading innovator of world-class, award-winning virtual instrument software plug-ins — on the release of "Keyscape." Keyscape is a virtual instrument that features the largest selection of unique, collector keyboards in the world and features Jim's personal, customized Yamaha C7.

Four of Jim's 10 recordings have hit the *Billboard* Top-20, he's had two PBS specials, and his music has been streamed over 75 million times by fans around the globe. NARAS recently made him a "Lifetime Member" of the Recording Academy. He enjoys scuba diving, skiing, pilot lessons, and shares the love of traveling with his life companion of fifteen years, Virginia, a gifted actress and film producer. *Tuned In* is Jim's first book.

Sign up for the latest updates at:
www.**JimWilsonMusic**.com

Check out Jim's music videos:

Printed in the USA
CPSIA information can be obtained
at www.ICGtesting.com
CBHW031903050324
4990CB00002B/2